FootprintAfrica

# Marrakech
## High Atlas & Essaouira

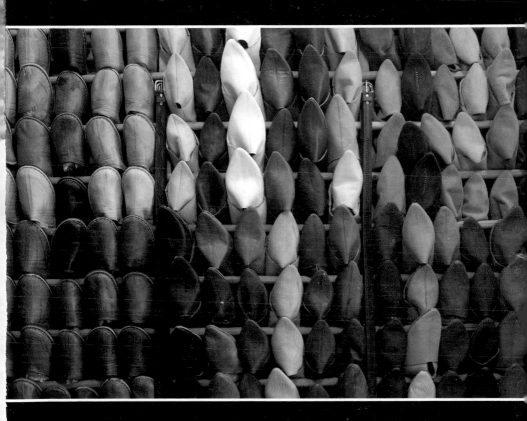

D0774355

**Julius Honnor**

4 About the author
4 Acknowledgements
5 About the book
5 Picture credits
234 Index
240 Credits

# Introducing the region

8 Map: Marrakech,
   High Atlas & Essaouira
9 Introduction
10 At a glance
14 Best of Marrakech,
   High Atlas & Essaouira
18 Month by month
22 Screen & page

# About the region

26 History
34 Art & architecture
40 Marrakech, High Atlas
   & Essaouira today
42 Nature & environment

46 Festivals & events
48 Sleeping
50 Spas, retreats
   & wellbeing
52 Eating & drinking
56 Entertainment
58 Shopping
60 Activities & tours
64 Great days out: Trekking

# Marrakech

69 Introduction
70 Essentials
72 Map: Marrakech
74 Jemaa El Fna &
   the northern medina
76 Great days out:
   A stroll through
   the medina
81 Map: Jemaa El Fna &
   the souks
92 Southern medina
98 Ville nouvelle &
   the gardens
102 Around Marrakech
106 Listings:
106 Sleeping
122 Eating
132 Entertainment
133 Shopping
137 Activities & tours
141 Transport

# Essaouira & coast

145 Introduction
146 Map: Essaouira medina
148 Medina & harbour
152 Beach & coast
156 Sidi Kaouki
158 Oualidia
160 Listings:
160 Sleeping
168 Eating
172 Shopping
173 Activities & tours
174 Transport

# High Atlas

179 Introduction
180 Western High Atlas
184 Great days out:
   Walking in Toubkal
188 Eastern High Atlas
190 Listings:
190 Sleeping
194 Eating
194 Activities & tours
195 Transport

# Gorges & desert

199 Introduction
200 Ouarzazate &
    Aït Benhaddou
204 Dadès Valley & gorges
208 Draâ Valley & desert
210 Great days out:
    Draâ driving
212 Listings:
212 Sleeping
217 Eating
217 Shopping
218 Activities & tours
219 Transport

# Practicalities

222 Getting there
223 Getting around
226 Directory
228 Language
232 Food & cooking glossary

Contents

# About the author

**Julius Honnor** first visited Marrakech in 1990, when he didn't even know what a riad was. He travelled extensively to update Footprint's Morocco guide and went back to take pictures, ride camels and get food poisoning for this guide. He lives in London and has written and photographed many books for Footprint and other travel publishers, on Italy, Britain and Bolivia.

# Acknowledgements

Thanks to everyone who helped with suggestions and support, especially Richard and Daniel Bee, Mouhamed and Sanaa, Michelle at Assakina, Allan and Malika, Emma Joyston-Bechal, Alisdair Luxmoore, Pacha Jahlan, John and Elizabeth Gilbey, Beatrice at Riad Edward, Steven at Kasbah Bab Ourika, Celine and Caroline, Everyone at Casa Lila, Naim Barahat, Philip Brebner, Yasmina at Rocmarra, Sam and Sharon at La Cantina, Dominique at Bouassala, Matt Booth, Jean at Le 16, Heather and Abdel, and Kamal Laftimi. Thanks to Clair for her support and patience and thanks too to everyone who worked on the current and past editions of Footprint Morocco, on which this new guide builds, especially Justin McGuinness and Sarah Thorowgood. Thanks also to Caroline Sylge, author of Footprint's *Body & Soul Escapes*, and Chris Nelson and Demi Taylor, authors of Footprint's *Surfing Europe*, for contributing to this guide.

# About the book

The guide is divided into four sections: Introducing the region; About the region; Around the city/region and Practicalities.

**Introducing the region** comprises: **At a glance** (which explains how the region fits together); **Best of Marrakech, High Atlas & Essaouira** (top 20 highlights); **Month by month** (a guide to pros and cons of visiting at certain times of year); and **Screen & page** (a list of suggested books and films).

**About the region** comprises: **History; Art & architecture; Marrakech, High Atlas & Essaouira today** (which presents different aspects of life in the region today); **Nature & environment; Festivals & events; Sleeping** (an overview of accommodation options); **Eating & drinking** (an overview of the region's cuisine, as well as advice on eating out); **Entertainment** (an overview of the region's cultural credentials, explaining what entertainment is on offer); **Shopping** (the region's specialities and recommendations for the best buys); and **Activities & tours.**

**Around the city/region** is then broken down into four areas, each with its own chapter. Here you'll find all the main sights and at the end of each chapter is a listings section with all the best sleeping, eating & drinking, entertainment, shopping and activities & tours options plus a brief overview of public transport.

# Picture credits

All images courtesy of **Julius Honnor** except the following:

**Tips Images** page 19: Yann Guichaoua; page 211: Guido Alberto Rossi.

**Shutterstock** page 27: Vladimir Wrangel; pages 27, 210: Boris Stroujko; page 31: Dainis Derics; page 32: Philip Lange; page 45: Eric Gevaert; page 60: Philip Lange; page 62: Fernando Jose Vasconcelos Soares; page 64: Andrey Plis; page 90. Ragne Kabanova; page 209: Posztos.

**La Pause** pages 63, 103.

**La Mamounia** Page 114.

**Simple Insomnia** Page 201.

**Nadin Saxer** Page 203.

**Rosino** Page 217.

**Front cover** age fotostock/Superstock.
**Back cover** Prisma/Superstock; Julius Honnor.

Essaouira street.

Marrakech street.

# Contents

8 *Map: Marrakech,*
   *High Atlas & Essaouira*
9 Introduction
10 At a glance
14 Best of Marrakech,
   High Atlas & Essaouira
18 Month by month
22 Screen & page

Introducing the region

# Introduction

**M**arrakech, the so-called Red City, is actually many shades of dusty terracotta, a complex crossroads of a place within reach of cool high Atlas valleys and windsurfing Atlantic beaches. One of the furthest western extremities of the Islamic world, it is a surprisingly open city, its many historical and social influences resulting in an air of tolerance and a sense of possibility.

Out on the coast, whitewashed and wind-whipped Essaouira, designed by a Frenchman, has been home to Roman dyers and Portuguese soldiers and English civil servants. To the south, Berber villages continue their mountain existence much as they have done for centuries, only with satellite dishes on their roofs. And beyond, where the Atlas snows melt into the Saharan heat, the descendents of African warlords and camel traders harvest rose petals around their slowly crumbling kasbahs.

European-influenced, yet so traditional, the high walls of Marrakech's sun-dappled alleys enclose the histories of feudal medieval mountain clans and French colonialists as well as extraordinarily crafted and lofty Islamic architecture. No guidebook can tell you about the mass of life around every medina corner, the candlelit fountains behind every heavy wooden door or the soaring mountains and secret valleys around every bend in the road. And the impossibility of knowing it all just adds to the seduction of trying.

# At a glance

A whistle-stop tour of Marrakech,
High Atlas & Essaouira

Marrakech, Morocco's tourist capital, has most of the country's attractions in concentrated form, its markets, music and performers almost omnipresent accompaniments to its palaces, museums and gardens. The city's alleyways, tanneries and souks could keep explorers busy for months but can also create sensory overload; a side-trip out into the extraordinary landscapes of Marrakech's surroundings provides a counter-balance of relative calm.

Out on the coast, Essaouira's narrow winding streets have an air of whitewashed seaside relaxation, its beach offers camel rides and kite- and wind-surfers enjoy its winds. Up and down the coast, Oualidia and Sidi Kaouki offer quieter beach bumming.

South of Marrakech, the towering High Atlas peaks offer a rarefied environment that is ideal for both walking and gawping, or even skiing. For further adventures, beyond the mountains are steep gorges and roads that snake south towards the camels and dunes of the desert.

## Marrakech

A heaving mass of dust, noise and colour, the old centre of Marrakech is for many the enduring image of the country. The apparent chaos hides many cool, calm courtyards of luxurious riads, islands of relaxed and pampered sanctuary.

The elegant 12th-century Koutoubia Mosque towers above Jemaa El Fna, a misshapen 'square' famed for its seething mass of entertainments and

Souk Sebbaghine, the dyers market, Marrakech.

Above: Medersa Ben Youssef, Marrakech.
Below: Sunset from roof terrace of Le Tanjia restaurant.

open-air restaurants. Around them stretches the medina, a maze of narrow streets and minarets.

North of Jemaa El Fna are the souks, or markets, thronged with colourful carpets, pottery drums and carved wooden chests. Beyond is the Sidi Ben Youssef Mosque, the city's main mosque after the Koutoubia. Also here is the ancient Almoravid structure of the Koubba, the Medersa Ben Youssef, and the Museum of Marrakech. On the eastern side of the medina are the smelly but colourful tanneries at Bab Debbagh. South of Jemaa El Fna, down Riad Zitoun el Kedime, is an area of palaces, the Saadian Tombs and an ethnographic museum, the Maison Tiskiwin.

Around the edges of the medina are various lush gardens, including the artistically colourful Jardin Majorelle, the Menara, with a large square pool set in a vast olive grove, and the Agdal, an olive grove.

The ville nouvelle, Marrakech's new town, is about as stark a contrast to the medina as it's

possible to imagine. Guéliz, the centre, is well dressed and organized, with European cuisine in its smart restaurants and Western clothes in its chain shops. There are bars and cafés, modern hotels and contemporary art galleries.

# Introducing the region

## Essaouira

The medina streets of the Atlantic port are Essaouira's top attraction. Wave-worn and whitewashed, the town retains a fishing fleet and has plenty of seaside character despite its increasing gentrification. Ramparts, the oldest of which are Portuguese-built, protect against the waves; a walk along them is a good way to appreciate the town. They also make a good spot from which to watch the sun set over the sea. Seagulls wheel above the fishing boats in the port, from where the day's catch is taken to be sold in the central market. Nearby are plenty more shopping opportunities in streetside stalls and shops. Fishy menus dominate the town's restaurants, some of which are excellent.

Sea breezes keep Essaouira fairly steadily warm year round and turn the beach into a wind- and kite-surfing playground. Camels are led up and down looking for riders, while the sky is filled with coloured sails.

The riad revolution has affected Essaouira too: it may not be as saturated as Marrakech but there are plenty of stylish places to lay your head after a hard day on the beach.

## The High Atlas

Rising out of the haze to the south of Marrakech, North Africa's highest mountains offer the scope for skiing in winter and walking and cooling off the rest of the year.

The Ourika Valley is rich in walking opportunities and the Toubkal National Park centres on Jbel Toubkal, the highest peak and destination for many treks. Oukaïmeden is the

Top: Sunset from the sea walls, Skala de la Ville, Essaouira.
Above: Cliffs just south of Oualidia.
Right: Path from Imlil to Aremd.

Above: Grasslands on the Plateau du Kik to the west of Asni.
Below: Todra Gorge.

High Atlas ski resort and Setti Fatma makes a fine day-trip destination, with waterfalls, spring blossom and riverside cafés.

Two main routes from Marrakech cross the mountains: the first, heading to Ouarzazate, crosses the Tizi-n-Tichka pass near the Glaoui citadel of Telouet. To the west, en route to Taroudant, the Tizi-n-Test is equally spectacular and the route passes the ancient, semi-ruined mosque of Tin Mal, one of two in the country that can be visited by non-Muslims.

Further east, the Vallée des Aït Bougmez is a good base for walks into the vastness of the Irhil Mgoun, the second highest summit of the High Atlas range. Nearby are the Cascades d'Ouzoud, Morocco's biggest waterfalls.

### Gorges and desert

Beyond the mountains Morocco slowly peters out into the Sahara. This is a dry area of valleys and rivers disappearing into the arid landscape, punctured every now and again by the surprising greenery of oases. Ouarzazate is the biggest town, a wannabe Moroccan Hollywood. More interesting is Aït Benhaddou, a crumbling real life film set of a kasbah, and Skoura, an oasis and palmery. Further south, Zagora and M'Hamid are bases for camel treks into the dunes.

To the east, the Dadès and Todra gorges are dramatic slices cut into the mountains and filled with palms and red-rock villages.

# Best of Marrakech, High Atlas & Essaouira

Top 20 things to see and do

**❶ Medersa Ben Youssef**
Marrakech's most beautiful building is a fine example of Islamic architecture. The ex-holy school was built by the Saadians in the 16th century and once held up to 900 students. In the heart of the medina, it is a calm and noble space, beautifully proportioned and with exquisitely detailed stucco plaster carving and *zellij* tiling. Page 84.

**❷ Tombeaux Saadiens**
Hidden from prying eyes for centuries, the 66 intricately decorated tombs here date from the 16th century but were only discovered by westerners in the early 20th century. Finely wrought stucco, *zellij* tiling and 12 Carrara marble columns embellish the central room. Outside, stray cats and tour groups wander among the notably less grand graves of children and servants. Page 97.

**❸ Tin Mal**
High in the hills near the pass of Tizi-n-Test, this huge mosque has been partially restored to something approaching the glory of the 12th century: a time

3. Tin Mal.

5. Teapots for sale in the Marrakech souks.

4. Essaouira's fish market.

## ❺ Shopping in the Marrakech souks
The city's souks are for many the defining image of Morocco – a tightly packed labyrinth of alleyways, heaving with colour, sound and retail opportunities. The purchasing part of the experience is optional, though few manage to resist for too long. Be prepared to haggle and to laugh off the sales patter of eager slipper sellers. Page 82.

## ❻ Lalla Takerkoust
A favourite getaway from the city heat for Marrakchis, the lake is actually a reservoir created by the Barrage Lalla Takerkoust hydroelectric dam. The expanse of blue surrounded by the dusty pink foothills of the High Atlas may be a little unreal but it's a peaceful spot, the countryside is beautiful and it offers some of the best natural swimming around. Page 103.

when this remote spot was the power base of the mighty Almohad Empire. The mosque itself is one of only two in Morocco that non-Muslims can enter and it's a stunning design – one that the Koutoubia in Marrakech was subsequently based on. Page 181.

## ❹ Essaouira's fish market
The port fish stalls have been greatly spruced up in recent years, and though these still offer good value food, for a really fishy experience the town's central fish market tops them. Select your fish from the market and then take it to the covered benches at the back, where for a small fee it will be cooked for you. Page 170.

## ❼ Toubkal National Park
For serious walking, many head to the peak of Jebel Toubkal, the highest in Northern Africa, and the national park that surrounds it. At a height of 4167 m, the panoramic views from the top are striking, and, except in winter, the route is a relatively easy one. There's also plenty to be seen further down and there are five other peaks over 3800 m. Page 184.

### ❽ Spring blossom in the Ourika valley

These days cherries are the predominant fruit crop in the Ourika Valley, and a journey in spring up to Setti Fatma goes through a wonderful film set of blossom. Once you're there it's an attractive place for a walk up to some waterfalls, or enjoy a tagine at a café by the mountain stream. Page 186.

### ❾ Oualidia's lagoon

Touted by some as a new Essaouira, Oualidia is in fact a very different place, with some excellent seafood restaurants but almost nothing in the way of antique atmosphere. What it does have, however, is a strikingly beautiful lagoon, into which rolling Atlantic waves break through gaps in a natural sea wall, making it a calm and unusually safe place for kids. Page 158.

9. Oualidia's lagoon.

11. Tanneries.

### ❿ Sand dunes near M'Hamid

In many ways a camel trek into the sub-Saharan sand dunes is a tourist trap, with little connection to the realities of desert life. On the other hand, spending the night under the bright stars of the dark desert sky and watching the sun rise over the majestic dunes is an experience hard to beat. Page 211.

### ⓫ Tanneries

The bowels of Marrakech's leather industry, the city's tanneries are a smelly, colourful place where animal skins are conditioned and dyed before being carted away to become bags and shoes. A series of pits filled with noxious mixes of lime, dye and pigeon dung are worked by half naked men and for a small payment visitors can wander around with a sprig of mint clamped to the nostrils for olfactory protection. Page 88.

### ⓬ Skiing at Oukaïmeden

Given a good winter, High Atlas skiing can be a surprisingly satisfying experience. The slopes are not long, or especially challenging, but they are seldom crowded and the prices are much cheaper than in Europe. Page 186.

### ⓭ Early morning ballooning

Once you've got over the shock of the early start, a balloon ride over the dusty pink countryside around Marrakech is a stunning start to the day. It's hard to imagine a better way to see the sun rise. Page 137.

### ⓮ Hammam

Smarter hotels and riads in Marrakech often have their own hammam, where you can get a massage and sweat your troubles away. For the full Moroccan slapping, scraping and rubbing experience, however, head to the local medina bath house. Page 138.

### ⓯ A night in a Marrakech riad

If you possibly can you should aim to spend at least a night in one of the city's old courtyard-garden houses, where the quality of the welcome often matches that of the finely crafted carved plaster.

**15. A night in a Marrkech riad.**

**19. Jardin Majorelle.**

**18. Jemaa El Fna.**

Essaouira is catching up in the riad stakes too, with some luxurious rooms in handsome places overlooking the Atlantic. Page 106.

**⑯ Surfing at Sidi Kauki**
While the kite-surfers cross strings in the crowded Essaouira surf, just down the coast at Sidi Kaouki is a huge expanse of beach where life moves at a more spaced-out pace. Page 154.

**⑰ Mosqueé de la Koutoubia**
Marrakech's dominant landmark is not open to non-Muslims but anyone can wander around the Koutoubia gardens and watch the last rays of the evening sun catch the minaret through the palm trees. Page 79.

**⑱ Jemaa El Fna**
A smoky, noisy melange of Moroccan society, Jemaa El Fna is by turns a marketplace, a city square, and a street theatre stage. Snake charmers, acrobats, story tellers and food sellers with a fine line in mock cockney patter create a heady if chaotic mix. Page 75.

**⑲ Jardin Majorelle**
Owned by the late Yves St Laurent, the Majorelle gardens are Marrakech's most rewarding, a striking mix of water, leaves, flowers and the piercing eponymous Marjorelle blue. Page 99.

**⑳ Palais de la Bahia**
The absence of furniture and possessions only emphasizes the beauty of the painted ceilings and the light streaming across the peaceful patios of the 19th-century palace of Bou Ahmed. Page 93.

# Month by month

A year in Marrakech, High Atlas & Essaouira

Morocco is a good destination all year round, although January and February can be cold and wet in the mountains and July and August unbearably hot in Marrakech and in the desert. The coast has remarkably little seasonal variation, with days rarely far away from 20°C.

Spring is a good time to visit, especially after a wet winter, when the usually dry landscape bursts into flower and the air has not yet developed its summer haze. Autumn is similarly agreeable. Spring is the best time of year for rafting, and for visiting the Cascades d'Ouzoud, when snow-melt contributes to the water levels in the rivers. Spring and autumn are also good times of year for walking in the mountains.

Visiting during Ramadan, the Islamic month of fasting, can be hard work. The dates change every year: in 2010 and 2011 Ramadan begins in August, in 2012 and 2013 in July and in 2014 and 2015 in June.

## January

Snow in the mountains gets the skiing season into full swing, though it can also close the High Atlas passes. Rain can sometimes turn Marrakech's medina streets into muddy tracks, though average rainfall for the month is only 25 mm – similar to a northern European summer month. Daytime temperatures are often very pleasant, on average hitting 18°C, with seven hours of sunshine, though nights can be cold, and open fires in riads are often used.

## February

Spring comes early to the south, with the Dadès and Todra gorges blooming from late February onwards. Essaouira is pleasant, as always, with temperatures around 19°C and good swell for surfers. Already in Marrakech the daytime temperatures hit 20°C, though nights still dip to around 6°C. Snow can continue to fall in the mountains, though in many years the ski slopes are made icy by the growing strength of the sun.

## March

Daytime temperatures climb in Marrakech to 23°C, though March is also the wettest month, with an average monthly rainfall of 33 mm. In the valleys of the High Atlas the trees come into blossom, and in the desert the stronger sun means the days are warmer still. Higher up, however, fresh snowfalls are still common.

Oukaïmeden in the High Atlas is Morocco's skiing centre.

### April

In Marrakech, spring is one of the most pleasant times of year: temperatures climb to around 26°C and the sun shines for around nine hours a day.

### May

The first hot days in the city are often in May, when the temperatures usually hit 30°C for the first time. On an average day the mercury hits 29°C. In the mountains the snow has mostly melted, though the peaks usually remain white-topped, and nights remain cold.

### June

The winds in Essaouira are often stronger at this time of year, making it ideal for wind- and kite surfers, though the lack of swell is less good for boarders and sunbathers are often battered by blown sand. South of the High Atlas, days can become unbearably hot from June through to September and much of the tourist infrastructure closes down. In Marrakech the average maximum temperature is 33°C but nights are seldom unbearably hot, falling to around 17°C.

### July

Occasional thunderstorms in the mountains boil up out of the hot, humid air and can cause flash flooding. In the city, however, rain in July is very rare. Marrakech's record high temperature of 49°C was recorded in July, though mostly days peak at around 38°C. Humidity, however, is low. Essaouira is usually 15°C or so cooler, with a strong onshore breeze.

## August

Another very hot month in Marrakech, the weather in August changes very little from July. Out on the coast, the contrast between the cool sea and the warm land means that fog sometimes lingers over Essaouira.

## September

Although often still hot, the worst of the oppressive summer heat usually ebbs away in September: days reach around 33°C.

## October

A very pleasant month in Marrakech, with temperatures of around 28°C by day, 14°C by night. Rain is not unheard of but most days have eight hours of sunshine. In the hills and mountains the weather can begin to feel decidedly autumnal, with frosts at night.

## November

The first snows of the winter fall in the High Atlas. Days in Marrakech are mostly still warm, with temperatures rising to 23°C, though nights are noticeably cooler, at around 9°C.

## December

The second consecutive month with around 30 mm of rain in Marrakech, temperatures finish off the year at around 19°C by day, 6°C by night. Out on the coast days are similar, with warmer nights: around 12-14°C. Snow falls in the mountains and nights are also cold in the desert.

**Head to the Menara Gardens in Marrakech to cool down in the summer heat.**

# Screen & page

Marrakech, High Atlas & Essouaira in film & literature

The international films made in Morocco vastly outnumber those made about Morocco.

### *Hideous Kinky*
### Giles MacKinnon, 1998

A 1998 adaptation of Esther Freud's novel, starring Kate Winslet, about a mother and her two daughters who leave 1960s London for a life on the hippy trail. It has some great scenery, filmed on location south of the Atlas Mountains.

### *Babel*
### Alejandro González-Iñárritv, 2007

Critically acclaimed when it was released, and starring Cate Blanchett and Brad Pitt, a modern story of cross-cultural fear and misunderstanding.

The main thread of interweaving stories is a coach trip through Morocco where an American woman is shot by Moroccan kids playing with a gun. It's a well-constructed film, but in the end more about America than Morocco.

### *Casablanca*
### Michael Curtiz, 1942

The most famous of all films with a Moroccan connection was not filmed in Morocco at all, but it has enough great lines to make up for that.

The high walls of Marrakech feature in the film *Hideous Kinky*.

Aït Benhaddou has appeared as a Biblical backdrop in several Hollywood films.

### The Voices of Marrakech
### Elias Canetti, 1967

Thin and readable but also wry and sharply observed, the Nobel Prize winner's travel observations have gathered little dust in the 40 years since the book was first published.

### The Tenth Gift
### Jane Johnson, 2008

A meticulously researched romantic tale of white slavery that follows the story of a Cornish girl kidnapped by Moroccan pirates, Johnson's tale entwines a modern storyline with a historical counterpart to exciting effect.

### A Year in Marrakesh
### Peter Mayne, 1953

This is the account of an Englishman who, in the 1950s, moved to the city to write a novel. Though the novel itself did not survive, his travel journals have become something of a minor classic. He tells of life on the Moroccan streets as both an insider and an outsider, becoming at once part of the world he inhabits and yet keeping a critical distance.

### The Caliph's House
### Tahir Shah, 2006

If, as happens to many visitors to Morocco, you become intrigued by the idea of buying and renovating a house, this amusing account may do enough to put you off.

Shah paints a colourful and affectionate picture of the characters and the frustrations involved in doing up an old building on the edge of the Casablancan slums.

### Valley of the Casbahs:
### A Journey Across the Moroccan Sahara
### Jeffrey Tayler, 2003

Jeffrey Tayler journeys by camel through the Drâa Valley and gives an evocative account of the southern Moroccan landscape, Kasbahs, gazelles, unexploded mines and secret sex with Moroccan women.

# Contents

26 History
34 Art & architecture
40 Marrakech, High Atlas
   & Essaouira today
42 Nature & environment
46 Festivals & events
48 Sleeping
50 Spas, retreats & wellbeing
52 Eating & drinking
56 Entertainment
58 Shopping
60 Activities & tours
64 Great days out: Trekking

Festival Gnaoua et Musiques
du Monde, Essaouira.

**About the region**

# History

Morocco was for centuries 'the Land of the Farthest West', *El Maghreb el Aqsa*, to the Arabs, the westernmost country in the Muslim world. Despite being the closest Arab land to Europe, Morocco was the last to come under European domination. Moroccans are highly aware of the particularities of their location, and see their history as having given them a civilization combining the virtues of the Arabs, Berbers, Andalucíans, Jews and Christians who converted to Islam.

Marrakech and Essaouira in particular, on important trading routes, embody these cosmopolitan influences.

The distant pre-Islamic past, marked by the Phoenicians and Romans, is much less documented than more recent times of the Islamic dynasties – at their most brilliant during a period roughly equivalent to the European Middle Ages. From the 16th century onwards the rulers of Morocco were constantly fighting back the expansionist Iberian states, and then later France. The last areas under colonial rule, the former Spanish Sahara, were retaken in the 1970s. The 20th century also saw the formation of the modern Moroccan state.

## Pre-Islamic history

Human settlement in Morocco goes back millennia. Rock carvings in the High Atlas and Sahara and objects in stone, copper and bronze have survived from early times. Nomadic pastoralism is thought to have existed from around 4000 BC.

The enterprising Phoenicians traded along North Africa's coast and archaeological excavations at Essaouira have shown that the town started life as a Phoenician settlement. Daring Carthaginian seafarers also undertook journeys far to the south, along the West African coast. Lost in the mists of ancient times is the history of the Imazighen, the Berber peoples of inland Morocco, referred to by the Romans as the Maures – hence the Latin name 'Mauritania' for the kingdom which seems to have taken shape in the fourth century BC over part of what is now Morocco.

The last Mauritanian king, Ptolomey, grandson of Antony and Cleopatra, was put to death by the Roman emperor Caligula and the client kingdom was transformed into a Roman colony. Roman administration and Latin culture were grafted onto Punic and Berber peoples. A major Berber revolt, led by Tacfarinas, took seven years to suppress. Such tensions were probably generated as Roman centurions retired from military life to farm wheat and olives on lands once grazed by the nomads' flocks. Roman towns in the area had all the trappings of urban life, and flourished until the third century. A Roman settlement in or around contemporary Essaouira extracted sought-after purple dye from shellfish living on the islands just off the coast.

## Arrival of Islam

The third to eighth centuries are a hazy time in northwest Africa's history. As the Roman Empire collapsed and fell it was a time of frequent rebellions and protests. Politically and economically unstable, there was a marked lack of social or religious cohesion.

The conquest by the Muslim Arabs in the eighth century was the key event in shaping Morocco's history. Islam, the religion of the Prophet Mohamed, was born in the oases of Arabia in the seventh century. It gave the warring Arab tribes and oasis communities, formerly pagan, Jewish and maybe Christian, the necessary cohesion to push back the Byzantine and Sassanian Empires, exhausted by years of warfare. The first Arab conquerors of North Africa founded Kairouan, in present day Tunisia, in AD 670, and pushed on as far as the Atlantic.

In eighth-century North Africa, Islam was welcomed by the slaves – who freed themselves by becoming Muslims – and by Christian heretics, who saw the new religion as simpler and more tolerant than Byzantine Christianity. In 711, therefore, it was an Islamized Amazigh army which crossed the Straits of Gibraltar under Tarik Ibn Ziyed, conquering the larger part of the Iberian peninsula. Along with North Africa, the southern regions of the peninsula, referred to as Al Andalus (whence Andalucía), formed a unified socio-cultural area until the 15th century.

**Above: Berber man in the Sahara Desert.**
**Below: Roman mosaic in Volubilis.**

Islam, which vaunts a spirit of brotherhood within a vast community of believers, and condemns petty clan interests and local loyalties, was to prove an effective base for new states based on dynastic rule, with central governments drawing their legitimacy from their respect for the precepts of the Quran and the Hadith, the codified practice of the Prophet Mohamed.

From the moment that Islam arrived, Morocco's history thus became that of the rise and fall of dynasties, often ruling areas far wider than that of the contemporary nation state. These dynasties were the Idrissids (ninth century), the Almoravids (11th century), the Almohads (12th-13th centuries), the Merinids (13th-15th centuries), the Wattasids (15th-16th centuries), the Saadians (16th century), and finally the Alaouites, rulers of Morocco from the 17th century to the present.

At the same time, the Sahara and the Atlas were becoming more economically important, with development in the ninth and 10th centuries of the trans-Saharan caravan trade, notably in gold. There were routes leading up into what is now Tunisia and Libya, and other, longer routes across the western regions of the Sahara. The shorter, western route finished in the Draâ Valley and the southern slopes of the Atlas.

## Almoravid origins

The Saharan gold trade in the 11th century came to be dominated by a nomad Berber group based in fortified religious settlements (*ribats*), hence their name, *el murabitoun*, which transposes as Almoravid, the name of the dynasty in English. Based in the northern Sahara, they founded their capital at Marrakech in 1062, later expending their empire to include much of Spain and present-day Algeria.

Marrakech was founded by Youssef Ibn Tachfine, the Almoravid leader, as a base from which to control the High Atlas mountains. A kasbah, Dar al Hajar, was built close to the site of the Koutoubia Mosque. Under Youssef Ben Tachfine, Marrakech became the region's first major urban settlement. Within the walls were mosques, palaces and extensive orchards and market gardens, made possible by an elaborate water transfer and irrigation system. The population was probably a mixture of haratine or blacks from the Oued Draâ, Imazighen from the Souss Valley and the nearby Atlas, and Amazigh Jews. The city attracted leading medieval thinkers from outside Marrakech.

In the 12th century, the Almoravids were overthrown by the Almohads: *el muwahhidoun* or unitarians, whose power base lay in the Berber tribal groupings of the High Atlas. United by their common religious cause, the Almohads took Sijilmassa, the gold port, far to the east, and their empire expanded to include the whole of present day Morocco, Algeria and Tunisia along with Andalucía.

Marrakech was taken by the Almohads in 1147, who almost totally destroyed and then rebuilt the city, making it the capital of their extensive empire. Trade grew with southern European merchant cities, and Arabic took root as the main language. Under the Almohad Sultan Abd el Moumen, the Koutoubia Mosque was built on the site of Almoravid buildings, with the minaret added by Ya'qub al Mansur. Under the latter, Marrakech gained palaces, gardens and irrigation works, and again became a centre for musicians, writers and academics, though on his death it declined and fell into disarray.

## Merinid neglect

The Beni Merini, rulers of Morocco from the mid-13th to mid-15th centuries, were not champions of any particular religious doctrine. Nomads from the Figuig region, they appear in Moroccan history in the late 12th century and grow in influence during the early 13th century.

While the Merinids added several medersas to Marrakech, Fès received much more of their attention, and was preferred as the capital.

Saadian Tombs, Marrakech.

In the 15th century a European threat emerged, and Ceuta was occupied by the Portuguese in 1415. When the Merinids proved ineffective in fighting back the Europeans, alternative local leaderships appeared, suitable symbols around which unity could be built due to cherifian descent. The Saadians exemplified this trend.

## Saadian revival

In 1492, Granada, the last Muslim stronghold in Andalucía, fell to Ferdinand and Isabella and Columbus sailed for America. The era of European imperialism had begun, and the Maghreb was first in the firing line as the Catholic monarchs continued the Reconquista into Africa. The two Iberian powers occupied strong-points along the Atlantic and Mediterranean coasts (the Spanish garrison towns of Ceuta and Melilla date from this time). However, under Iberian powers, resources were soon taken up with the commercially more important development of far-flung empires in the Indies and Americas. And the Arabo-Berber peoples of North Africa (and the terrain) put up solid resistance.

The Saadians sprang from the Souss region around Taroudant, and under Ahmed el Mansour (1578-1603) destroyed an invading Portuguese army, re-established (for a short while) the gold trade, developed sugar cane plantations in the Souss and re-founded Marrakech.

Marrakech was revitalized by the Saadians from 1524 with the rebuilding of the Ben Youssef Mosque, and the construction by Ahmed al Mansour Ad Dahbi of the El Badi Palace and the Saadian Tombs. Marrakech also became an important trading post, due to its location between the Sahara and the Atlantic.

## Alaouite Marrakech

The Alaouites took control of Marrakech in 1668 and the first sovereigns, Moulay Rachid (1666-72) and Moulay Ismaïl (1672-1727), a tireless builder,

tried to restore order. Anxious not to align themselves with either Marrakech or Fès, however, they moved their capital to Meknes. In the early 18th century the city suffered from this relocation, with many of the major buildings, notably the El Badi Palace, stripped to glorify the new capital. The destructive effects of this period were compounded by the civil strife following Moulay Ismaïl's death. However, under Alaouite Sultan Moulay Hassan I, from 1873, and his son, the city's prestige was re-established. A number of the city's fine palaces such as the Bahia Palace, date from this time.

## Colonialism

The European peace of 1815 established conditions favourable to colonialism, and France, anxious to re-establish lost prestige, looked towards North Africa. Algiers was taken in 1830, and French colonial expansion continued throughout the 19th century, with a settler population of largely Mediterranean origin putting down roots. European farming grew, thanks to the redistribution of land confiscated after revolts and modern land registration. New European-style cities were constructed.

Because of the development of French Algeria, Morocco increasingly found itself isolated from the rest of the Islamic world – and subject to severe pressure from the European powers who were steadily growing in confidence. France attacked Morocco for providing shelter to the Algerian leader, the Emir Abdelkader, defeating the Moroccan army at the Battle of Isly in 1844. Great Britain forced Morocco to sign a preferential trade treaty in 1856, while in 1860 a Spanish expeditionary force took the key northern city of Tetouan. Sultan Aberrahman was forced to accept unfavourable peace terms, with customs coming under foreign control by way of an indemnity, and an ill-defined Saharan territory was ceded to Spain.

In 1906, the Conference of Algeciras brought 12 nations together to discuss the Moroccan debt. France and Spain emerged as key contenders for occupation. In 1907, following the killing of some Europeans during unrest, France occupied Casablanca. A new sultan, Moulay Hafidh (great-uncle of the present king), was proclaimed the same year. In 1911, with Fès surrounded by insurgent tribes, he called in Algerian-based French forces to end the state of siege. The last act came in 1912, when the Treaty of Fès, signed by France and Moulay Hafidh for Morocco, established the French Protectorate. A subsequent Franco-Spanish treaty split the country into a northern zone, under Spanish control, a vast central area under French rule, and a southern zone, also assigned to Spain.

## Early 20th century: Glaoui rule

The French took control of Marrakech and its region in 1912, crushing an insurrection by a claimant to the Sultanate. Their policy in the vast and rugged southern territories was to govern through local rulers, rather as the British worked with the rajahs of India. Until independence Marrakech was thus the nerve-centre of southern Morocco, ruled practically as a personal fiefdom by the Glaoui family from the central High Atlas.

With French support, Pacha T'hami el Glaoui extended his control over all areas of the south. His autonomy from central authority was considerable, his cruelty notorious. And of course, there were great advantages in this system, in the form of profits from the new French-developed mines. Exploitation of Morocco's natural wealth turned out to be a capitalist venture, rather than a settler one.

In the 1920s, Marrakech saw the development of a fine ville nouvelle, Guéliz, all wide avenues of jacarandas and simple, elegant bungalow houses. On acquiring a railway line terminus, Marrakech reaffirmed its status as capital of the south. It was at this time, when travel for pleasure was still the preserve of the privileged of Europe, that Marrakech began to acquire its reputation as a retreat for the wealthy.

## Nationalism

A focal point for nationalist resentment was the so-called Berber *dahir* (decree) of 1933, basically an attempt to replace Muslim law with Berber customary law in the main Berber-speaking regions. French colonial ethnography, which had provided the reasoning behind this project, had made a fundamental miscalculation: Morocco could not be divided into Berbers versus Arabs.

The educated urban bourgeoisie demanded a reform programme in 1934 and, with the Second World War, the international situation shifted to favour independence. The urban elite formed the Istiqlal (Independence) Party in 1944 – with the goodwill of Sultan Mohamed V.

Tension grew in the early 1950s; under the Pacha of Marrakech, contingents of tribal

Above: Jardin Majorelle in ville nouvelle, Marrakech.
Opposite page: Palais de la Bahia, Marrakech.

horsemen converged on Rabat to demand the deposition of the sultan. In 1953 the resident-general, in violation of the protectorate treaty, deposed Mohamed V and replaced him with a harmless relative. The royal family found themselves in exile in Madagascar, which gave the nationalist movement yet another point of leverage. The sultan's return from exile was a key nationalist demand.

The situation elsewhere in the French Empire ensured a fast settlement of the Moroccan question. France had been defeated in Indochina in 1954, and there was a major uprising in Algeria. Extra problems in protectorates like Morocco had to be avoided. The La Celle-St Cloud agreements of November 1955 ensured a triumphal return from exile for the royal family, and independence was achieved in March 1956, with Spain renouncing its protectorate over northern Morocco at the same time.

The Istiqlal Party had fostered political consciousness in the Moroccan middle classes, and a confrontation between a colonial regime and the people had developed into a conflict between colonial rulers and the Muslim ruler. The sultanate under foreign protection became an independent kingdom.

## Independence

After independence, the national pact was increasingly criticized by the urban elite, who thought to push the monarchy aside – rather as had happened in Egypt, Tunisia and Iraq – and rule the country under a one-party system supported by the educated middle classes. The Istiqlal and socialist parties jockeyed for leadership; a revolt in the Rif was put down. The monarchy proved to be durable, however.

After the death of his father, Mohamed V, in 1961, the new king, Hassan II, turned out to be an able political player. An alliance with conservative rural leaders ensured the success of the constitutional referendum of December 1962. After the Casablanca

**National flag of Morocco.**

riots of 1965, the army was called in to guarantee order. The Left lost its leader, Mehdi Ben Barka, assassinated in Paris in November 1965. As of July 1965, Hassan II was to rule without parliament.

## The 1970s & 1980s

Such a centralized system was fraught with risk, as was realized following two attempts on the king's life. So the king sought to rebuild a political system which would end the monarchy's relative isolation on the political scene – and leave considerable room for manoeuvre.

The 'Moroccanization' of the remaining firms still (mainly) in French hands, launched in 1973, was part of the strategy, winning the support of the middle classes. A number of key players emerged to second the king on the political scene. The early 1990s saw the king actively working to bring the opposition into government. Finally, in November 1997, elections were managed to produce a parliament with an opposition majority, led by the USFP (Union socialiste des forces populaires).

## The 1990s

In steering things to bring the opposition into government, it is clear that Hassan II was trying to leave Morocco in good running order for his son. By the late 1980s, the palace was clearly aware that the political elite born of the independence struggle was running out of steam, and that the opposition's criticism of the inequalities in living standards had very good grounds. World Bank 'remedies', strenuously applied in the 1980s and early 1990s, have only helped to impoverish a large section of the population.

Drought and poor harvests accelerated the rural exodus, rendering the split between poor and wealthy all the more visible in the cities. The first opposition government of 1998 thus had a very clear remit to 'do something' – and quickly – for the poorest in Moroccan society. Underlying

the opposition's coming to power, however, was a very real fear that a large part of the poor population might be tempted by radical Islam.

## July 1999: a new reign

The equation changed on the death of Hassan II on 23 July 1999. His eldest son, crown prince Sidi Mohamed, came to the throne as Mohamed VI. The battle against social inequality soon figured at the top of the royal agenda. And for the first time in decades, areas of the country never visited by the reigning monarch received a royal visit. In early 2001, the International Federation of Human Rights held its annual conference in Casablanca.

## Islamist attacks

On 16 May 2003, tragedy struck. The country was dumbstruck by suicide bomb attacks in the centre of Casablanca. Targets included a Jewish social club and a downtown hotel. Over 40 people were killed, all Moroccans, and many were injured. The bombers were members of the Salafiya-Jihadiya purist Islamist movement. Several hundred arrests in Islamist circles swiftly followed. For Moroccans, the bombings were truly shocking: unprovoked urban slaughter of this kind could only happen elsewhere – notably in neighbouring Algeria.

## Issues & pressures

The Islamists, now clearly a part of the political equation, are not the only source of pressure on a system which needs to create decent income levels for all Moroccan citizens. Other issues include the future of the Saharan provinces, and relations with the European Union, the North African states and international lenders. Businesses, farmers, a vocal, liberal-minded middle class, unemployed graduates, the Amazigh communities and shanty town dwellers all have their agenda.

# Art & architecture

## Buildings of Islam

In 682, the Arab general Okba Ibn Nafi and his army crossed the Maghreb, bringing with them a new religion, Islam. This religion was to engender new architectural forms, shaped by the requirements of prayer and the Muslim urban lifestyle. The key building of Islam, the mosque, evolved from its humble beginnings as a sort of enclosure with an adjoining low platform from which the call to prayer could be made. Mosques became spectacular buildings demonstrating the power of ruling dynasties, centring on colonnaded prayer halls and vast courtyards. Originally inspired by the church towers of Syria, elegant minarets gave beauty to the skylines of the great Muslim cities. Mosques cannot generally be visited in Morocco by non-Muslim visitors, with some notable exceptions, including the restored Almohad mosque at Tin Mal in the High Atlas.

## Minarets

As an essential feature of the mosque, the minaret probably developed in the late seventh century. Islam had adopted a call to prayer or *idhan* rather than bells to summon the faithful. Moroccan minarets are generally a simple square tower, with a small 'lantern' feature on the top, from which the muezzin makes the call to prayer. Older minarets tend to have blind horseshoe arches and a small dome on the topmost 'lantern' room. On top of the dome is an ornamental feature resembling three metal spheres on a pole, topped by a crescent. This is the *jammour*, and tourist guides have a number of entertaining explanations for this, for example that the spheres represent the basic ingredients of bread (flour, water and salt).

The great Almohad mosques – including the Koutoubia in Marrakech – are characterized by an interlinked lozenge pattern, executed in stone on their façades. One school of art history sees the proportions, arcades and decorative motifs of these buildings as setting a stylistic trend which was reproduced and eventually transformed in European Gothic architecture.

## Layout and decoration

Mosques tend to have large covered prayer halls, comprising a series of narrow transepts, created by lines of arches supporting pitched roofs, generally covered with green tiles. There will be a main 'aisle' leading towards the *mihrab* (prayer niche), which indicates the direction of Mecca, and for prayer. The main nave in the traditional Moroccan mosque does not, however, have the same dimensions as the main nave of a Christian cathedral. Islam also does not favour representation of the human form, hence the use of highly elaborate geometric decorative motifs executed in ceramic *zellij* (mosaic), and on wood and plaster. There is no religious pictorial art. The same geometric motifs can be found in domestic architecture too. A mosque will also have an open courtyard, sometimes with a decorative fountain.

## Schools of religious science

Non-Muslim visitors can get a very good idea of Muslim sacred architecture by visiting one of the medersas, the colleges which were an essential part of the Moroccan Muslim education system from medieval times onward. One of the largest is the Medersa Ben Youssef in Marrakech (see page 84), a 14th-century foundation entirely rebuilt in the 16th century. Like all medersas, it is essentially a hollowed-out cube, the blockiness of the architecture being relieved by mesmerizingly decorative detail on every flat surface: ceramic mosaic, and densely carved stucco and cedarwood.

Below: Koutoubia Mosque. Opposite page: Medersa Ben Youssef.

## About the region

inland there are hot summer winds from the south. The city therefore has to provide protection from this climate, and networks of narrow streets are the ideal solution. Streets could be narrow as there was no wheeled transport, there being plenty of pack animals for carrying goods around. And narrow streets also ensured that precious building land within the city walls was not wasted.

For housing the Muslim family, the courtyard house was the ideal solution. This is an architectural model which goes back to Mesopotamia, Greece and Rome. For Islamic family life, with its insistence on gender separation in the public domain, the courtyard house provides a high level of family privacy. In densely built-up cities, the roof terraces also provided a place for women to perform household tasks – and to share news and gossip. The biggest houses would have several patios, the main one having arcades on two levels. Thus extended families could be accommodated in dwellings with large open areas. Old Moroccan courtyard homes were generally not easily visited, until the riad revolution saw countless houses restored and altered to function as upmarket restaurants and riads.

In Marrakech you can also discover a superb concentration of Moroccan craftwork in a lovingly restored patrician house, the Maison Tiskiwin (see page 93) as well as in the literary café and art gallery of Dar Cherifa (see pages 87 and 127).

### Medinas

Visitors to Morocco quickly have to learn to navigate through the narrow streets of the medina or old towns. In much 19th-century European writing, the medinas of the Maghreb – and of the Arab world in general – were seen as chaotic places, which, although harbouring exotically clothed populations, were also home to disease and ignorance. The medina was taken as a metaphor for the backwardness of the indigenous population. In fact, the tangled streets of the average Moroccan medina are no more disorganized than many a European medieval town.

The medinas of Morocco do, however, obey a logic, satisfying architectural requirements arising from climatic and religious factors. The climate is hot in summer, but often very cold in winter. In the coastal towns, damp ocean mists roll in, while

### Earthen architectures

The courtyard home, or riad, is the most characteristic building in Marrakech and Essaouira, discreet and anonymous to all but a neighbourhood's inhabitants from the outside, spectacularly decorated in its patrician form on the inside. There are other, more rustic, building traditions in use, however, the best known being the kasbahs of the areas south of the High Atlas, the valleys of the Dadès and the Draâ. Much of this traditional building in the south is in compacted earth and gravel.

## Kasbahs

The word kasbah probably derives from the Turkish *kasabe*, meaning small town. In contemporary North Africa, it is generally used to refer to the fortified strong point in a city.

Morocco has numerous kasbahs scattered across its territory, many erected by energetic 17th-century builder-ruler Moulay Ismaïl. In the southern reaches of Morocco, the term kasbah is used to denote often vast fortified villages, with spectacular tower houses often several storeys high. Good examples can be found near Ouarzazate, at Aït Benhaddou (see page 201) and up in the High Atlas at Telouet (see page 187), where a vast crumbling kasbah testifies to the power of T'hami el Glaoui, ruler of Marrakech in the early part of the 20th century. There are a fair number of Glaoui kasbahs scattered across the southern valleys, and they tend to have decorative features of more urban inspiration than the kasbahs of the old Berber communities. There are good examples at Tamnougalt, south of Agdz in the Draâ Valley, and in the Skoura oasis in the Dadès Valley.

Spectacular though they often are, the kasbahs are under threat. This form of earth building is vulnerable to the weather, and despite its excellent qualities in terms of temperature regulation, it needs maintenance. Reinforced concrete building, perceived as 'modern', is now popular. However, in the southern regions, there is a new wave of mock kasbah architecture. The crenellations, window slits and tapering towers of the ancient earthen buildings can be found on official buildings, hotels and electricity sub-stations. The tourist industry may yet fuel some sort of return to traditional – and more ecological – building types. Kasbahs are being recycled as hotels at Skoura, Tineghir and Nekob.

Below: Aït Benhaddou kasbah. Opposite page: Street in southern medina, Marrakech.

## About the region

### Fortified ports

On the coasts of Morocco is another form of defensive architecture, the military port of early modern European inspiration. During the 15th century, both the Atlantic and the Mediterranean coastlines were targets for the expanding Iberian powers. In the early 16th century, Portugal was still at the height of its glory as an imperial power, and elaborate fortifications were erected at Mogador (today's Essaouira), equipped with monumental gateways, cannons, watchtowers and round bastions.

### Modern cities

The contemporary Moroccan city is very much an early 20th-century achievement, the work of two far-sighted people, Hubert Lyautey and urban planner Henri Prost.

France's first Resident General in Morocco had been much impressed by Prost's plans for the redesign of Antwerp in Belgium and was willing to give such schemes a chance in the new French protectorate. Prost's Antwerp plan included features that seemed particularly adaptable to the Moroccan context. Old walls were not demolished and re-used as development land, but were kept as part of a buffer zone between old and new.

The new areas had large open spaces planted with regular rows of trees, while a system of avenues within the city enhanced existing monumental buildings and linked into a system of highways leading in and out of the city. The crucial point on which Prost focused was the preservation of the aesthetic face of the city, without totally cutting it off from new forms of transport and infrastructure. Prost, like Lyautey, was all for technological innovation. However, this position was balanced with a strong dose of social conservatism: existing hierarchies were to be kept. In Morocco, 'respect for difference' was the justification for the strict zoning between old and new quarters, rich and poor.

**Art**

### Contemporary painting

Morocco has proved a considerable bed of painting talent, perhaps surprisingly for a country that had no tradition of representing human and animal form. Easel painting soon took root after the arrival of the French protectorate, and European artists settled in Morocco, among them Jacques Majorelle, best known for his scenes of the High

Atlas, Edouard Edy-Legrand and Marianne Bertuchi. In the 1940s, self-taught Moroccan painters emerged, sometimes directly imitating European styles – others, such as Moulay Ahmed Drissi, illustrating the rich heritage of oral literature.

After independence in 1956, a generation of Moroccan painters came to the fore, working in varied registers – abstract, naïve, calligraphic. Naïve painting has an important place in the Moroccan art scene. The Galerie Damgaard in Essaouira (see page 151) has enabled many local artists to exhibit and live on their work, and an Essaouira school of painting has emerged, filled with movement and joyful figures. Leading figures include Abdallah el Atrach and Rashid Amerhouch. Of Morocco's self-taught naïve painters, the best known is Chaïbia, creator of raw and colourful scenes of daily life.

**Galerie Rê, Marrakech.**

# Marrakech, High Atlas & Essaouira today

Marrakech is Morocco's fourth largest city. The population is around 1½ million, nearer two million if you include the suburbs. Its people are a mix of Arab and Amazigh; many are recent migrants from surrounding rural regions and further south. For centuries an important regional market place, Marrakech now has a booming service economy and there is still a wide range of handicraft production and small-scale industry, particularly in the medina.

Increasingly, tourism is seen as the mainstay of the city's economy. Marrakech is one of the major tourist attractions of Morocco and many of the city's large number of unemployed or under-employed supplement their incomes by casual work with tourists.

Divisions within the Moroccan population, however, are obvious as you move from the Marrakech medina into the ville nouvelle, and from a largely poor, and poorly educated, population, to a much wealthier upper middle class.

**Above: Jemaa El Fna is now mostly closed to traffic.**
**Opposite page: Donkey-driven cart on a Marrakech street.**

## High walls, bolted gates

In recent decades Marrakech has grown enormously, its population swelled by civil servants and armed forces personnel. Migrants are attracted by the city's reputation as 'city of the poor', where even the least qualified can find work of some kind. For many rural people, the urban struggle is hard, and as the Tachelhit pun puts it, Marrakech is ma-ra-kish, 'the place where they'll eat you if they can'.

New neighbourhoods and villa developments are springing up all around the city. The most upmarket area is on the Circuit de la Palmeraie. Little by little, the original farmers are being bought out, and desirable homes with lawns and pools behind high walls are taking over from vegetable plots under the palm trees. East of the medina is the vast Amelkis development, a gated community complete with golf course and the discrete Amenjana resort. Here the money and privilege are accommodated in an area equal to one third of the crowded medina.

Morocco has ambitious plans to increase the numbers of tourists visiting the country, but it's not clear that the new mega-hotels going up outside Marrakech will ever be full, or, perhaps more worryingly, that it would be a good thing for the city if they were.

## Sardine tourism

The beginning of the 21st century saw Marrakech in an upbeat mood. The Brigade Touristique, set up to reduce the hassling of tourists, has been reasonably successful.

The on-going problem is how to deal with the influx of visitors. Certain monuments have reached saturation point: the exquisite Saadian tombs, for example, are home to a semi-permanent people jam. And while being packed with people is an important part of the attraction of Jemaa El Fna, there is the danger that the magic of the place will eventually be diluted by the massive numbers of visitors. The square is now closed to traffic for some of the time, but the roads around the edge of the medina are hellishly busy.

## Surviving gentrification?

Marrakech continues to draw the visitors in and to maintain its hold on the Western imagination. The setting is undeniably exotic, eccentricities are tolerated, and (rather less honourably) domestic help is cheap.

Features in international decoration magazines fuel the demand for property and major monuments are being restored. One-time resident the late Yves St Laurent even dubbed Marrakech 'the Venice of Morocco'. Still, for the moment at least, the Red City retains a sense of rawness despite the creeping gentrification, and remains the closest Orient one can find within a few hours' flight of the grey north European winter.

**For the moment at least, the Red City retains a sense of rawness despite the creeping gentrification, and remains the closest Orient one can find within a few hours flight of the grey north European winter.**

# Nature & environment

## Wildlife & vegetation

Regional variations in climate, vegetation and relief have given Morocco a diverse and interesting flora and fauna. Although the country is too densely settled to have many large mammals, birdwatchers will find much to twitch about, and the spring flowers can be wonderful.

## Arid lands

Semi-desert scrub is widespread, and gives a green hue to wide expanses after the spring rains. In regions even less likely to receive precipitation, vivid desert flowers appear at infrequent intervals. On the steppes, clumps of alfalfa grass help to stabilize the fragile soils and sage bushes appear here too, an ungainly plant but able to withstand the wind, the cold and the drought. The soft pink flowering tamarisks hold back the sand, while handsome oleanders flower white and red in the *oueds*. Though attractive, the leaves are highly poisonous to animals.

## Forests

Morocco's woodlands are both natural and human-made. On the northern, better watered slopes of the High Atlas, thick trunked junipers and bushy thuya are the main trees, surviving best when too far from human habitation to be cut for fire wood. Walnuts and poplar are the trees of the valleys, while Aleppo pine survives in protected areas. In February, in the valleys south of the Atlas, the wild almond, which ought to be the national tree, produces its own breathtaking version of 'snow'.

## Arganeraies, the rarest woodland

Central Atlantic Morocco, from Essaouira down to Sidi Ifni, is home to rare argan groves, until recently the most threatened of Morocco's trees.

A survivor of a remote time when the region had a tropical climate, the argan tree requires a unique climatic cocktail of aridity tempered by ocean mists to survive. Looking for all the world like a wild and woolly version of the olive, the argan trees grow over some 650,000 ha, some of which is human-planted in groves.

Goats climb into the trees to graze. Most importantly, the oil produced from the soft white heart of the argan 'almond', now internationally recognized for its therapeutic value, is one of the costliest nut oils on the market. And in the production process, no part of the fruit is wasted: the flesh can be fed to pack animals while the hard shell can be used to fuel a fire.

Recognizing the argan's importance, UNESCO has declared the Essaouira-Agadir region a specially protected biosphere. In the same zone

Jardin Majorelle, Marrakech.

grow the caroubier, the red juniper and the Barbary thuya, whose large underground roots are much used in the Essaouira craft and carpentry industry.

## Oases

The date palm is the miracle tree of the arid desert expanses of southern Morocco. Wherever there is a good supply of water, oases have sprung up. Although the oasis was originally a wholly natural environment, given the pressure on the scarce resources of the desert, it has been 'domesticated' for centuries now. Black haratine populations and Berbers kept cultivation going under the protection of nomad tribes. The special *khettara* underground 'canals' were created to bring melt water from the foothills to the oases.

Under the protective canopy of the date palms, the ideal oasis has different layers of cultivation, including the pomegranate and crops like wheat, barley, oats and coriander. Today, the palm trees in many Moroccan oases suffer from the bayoud fungus. Increasingly, the production of food for local consumption is abandoned and the cultivators focus solely on date production. Oases can also be rewarding areas for birdwatchers.

## Birdlife

Home to 460 species, Morocco has the greatest diversity of birdlife north of the Sahara. The untrained eye will spot bright coloured bee-eaters and blue rollers, storks nesting on ramparts and minarets, pink flamingos and the striped hoopoes. Many a riad garden has a resident pair of dowdy bulbuls, 'oasis nightingales'. The trill of a moknine (goldfinch) can be heard coming out of shops in the souk. Of the raptors, lesser kestrels and owls are often taken for use in obscure magic preparations.

Top destinations for birdwatchers include coastal marsh and lagoon sites such as Oualidia and Essaouira.

## Reptiles

Morocco's reptilian fauna is among the richest in the Mediterranean region. While Europe has 60 species of reptile, Morocco has over 90. You will, however, see few lizards and even fewer snakes as many are nocturnal and most shun areas inhabited by humankind. In tiny shops in the souks, sad chameleons may be seen clambering in tiny cages – or dried on skewers, ready for pounding into powder to complete a special incense.

## Mammals

Morocco's mammals include genets, jackals, striped hyena, wild cats, fennecs, gerbils and jerboas, as well as the famed Barbary apes of the Middle Atlas. The endangered Dorcas gazelle can be found in desert regions. With their nocturnal habits, most of these animals are sufficiently elusive to evade casual visitors. You will, however, see a selection of animal pelts and horns at apothecaries' stalls in the medinas.

The most easily observed of all the large mammals are the Barbary apes, which are to be found at the Cascades d'Ouzoud near Demnate, east of Marrakech. The Barbary ape can live for as long as 20 years. It forages on the ground for food (leaves, roots, small insects), and has been known to enjoy the yoghurt, bread, occasional Flag beer and other titbits thoughtfully contributed by passing picknickers.

Another observable mammal is the *anzid* or *sibsib*, known as the Barbary squirrel in English.

## Insects

Insects are much more easily observed than large mammals. As pesticides are far beyond the means of most farmers, there are beautiful butterflies and a multitude of moths, both in evidence when the spring flowers are in bloom. There are flies both large and small, bees, wasps and mosquitoes; these

Barbary apes can be seen around the Cascades d'Ouzoud.

are not elusive and can at times be too attentive. Scorpions are to be found in arid areas. If camping, make sure you check your boots in the morning.

## Wildlife under threat

Most Moroccan mammals manage to evade all but the keenest visitor. Some animals are not elusive enough, however, and you will see shops offering stuffed varans, tortoises – both live and converted into banjo-like instruments – snakeskin bags, and the furs of fennecs, genets and wild cats. (Leopard and lion skins are likely to have been brought up from Mali.)

With modern medicine out of people's reach due to poor education and cost, traditional lotions, potions and spells find a ready market, putting heavy pressure on the population of crows, owls, chameleons and other lizards.

Snakes suffer even more. For the entertainments of Jemaa El Fna, the Egyptian cobra is much favoured, as is the puff adder. In some cases, their mouths are sewn up to ensure no one gets a nasty bite. The ecological consequence of snake collection from the wild is a rapid growth in the rodent population, the snakes' natural snack.

Saddest of all are the Barbary macaques. For the first few years of their lives as tools of the tourist trade, they are amusing and seem to enjoy life with their keepers. But on reaching early adulthood, they want to assume a position in the troop, turning aggressive and potentially dangerous in their bid to win top place in the hierarchy. Happily, however, there are signs that Morocco is waking up to the fact that its wild species and their denizens can be maintained hand-in-hand with the development of sustainable forms of tourism.

# Festivals & events

The region has a number of local festivities, often focusing around a local saint or harvest time of a particular product and fairly recent in origin. There are also the more religious festivals, the timing of which relates to the lunar Islamic year, as well as a new generation of music and film festivals.

## April

**Les Alizés** (Essaouira)
*alizesfestival.com.*
A four-day classical music festival featuring artists from all over the world, Les Alizés includes some free concerts held in the squares of Essaouira.

## May

**Rose Festival** (El Kelaâ des Mgouna, Dadès Valley)
Three days of celebration of the year's crop of tons of rose petals, gathered from over 4000 km of rose hedges in the valley of the roses. A Rose Queen is elected and there are processions, music, dance and rose garlands.

## June

**Festival Gnaoua et Musiques du Monde**
*festival-gnaoua.net.*
The pretty streets of Essaouira sway to the sounds of gnaoua, the so-called Moroccan blues, a melding of sub-Saharan, Arabic and Berber styles, and traditionally the music of black Moroccan slaves. Acrobatic dance accompanies the music and tens of thousands of visitors flood the town. The festival is often a place of exciting musical experimentation, as the age-old spiritual traditions of the music are combined with international jazz, reggae, blues and hip-hop influences.

Right and opposite page: Festival Gnaoua et Musiques du Monde, Essaouira.

### Festival National des Arts Populaires
*marrakechfestival.com.*
A bringing together of music and dance troops from all over Morocco to perform in the wide open space of the ruins of the Badi palace for a week. The festival is kicked off by a parade of hundreds of artists from the Place la Liberté to Jemaa El Fna. Some international acts also appear and there are smaller performances around the city.

### August

### Moussem of Settl Fatma (Ourika Valley)
The holy Koubba, or shrine, of Setti Fatma is the centrepiece of this four-day religious celebration. The Koubba is closed to non-Muslims, but processions take place around the village and a carnival atmosphere pervades the valley.

### Ramadan
One of the holy months in the Islamic calendar, the date for its start changes from year to year in the western calendar. In 2010 and 2011 it starts in August; in 2012 and 2013 in July and in 2014 and 2015 in June. During Ramadan, Muslims must fast during daylight hours. The first day after Ramadan, Eid ul-Fitr, is spent celebrating.

### August/September

### Moussem des Fiançailles (Allamghou)
More than 2500 m up in the Atlas, isolated Imilchil's wedding festival in August/September is a chance, at the end of summer, for thousands of locals to dress up in their jewellery and finest clothes and find a partner. Music, dancing, sheep and cows accompany the party.

### December

### Festival International du Film de Marrakech
*festivalmarrakech.info.*
A celebration of the best of Moroccan and International film, Marrakech's film festival in December, chaired by Morocco's Prince Moulay Rachid, awards the Golden Star to the best film of the past year, and provides a chance to see the best of North African arthouse cinema.

# Sleeping

## The riad experience

A relatively recent form of accommodation in Marrakech, the riad (*maison d'hôte* or guesthouse) gives you the experience of staying in a fine private house, generally small places in the medina. Prices are high for Morocco, but you get service, style and luxury in bucketloads. The often painstakingly restored houses are managed either directly by their owners or via an agency which deals with everything from reservations to maintenance. There are hundreds of riads in the city – perhaps as many as 500, though estimates vary wildly.

Guests are met either at the airport or the edge of the medina and the price includes cleaning. Prices vary enormously, and some are extremely luxurious. Reactions to this type of accommodation are generally very positive. The riads have created a lot of work for locals (and pushed property prices up), so many feel they have a stake in the guesthouse system. With regard to tipping, err on the generous side.

Most riads are available to rent in their entirety, making a great base for a group or family holiday. Staff are usually included and food and entertainment (acrobats, musicians, dancers) can often be arranged.

When booking a stay in a riad in winter, check for details of heating. All riads should provide breakfast, included as part of the price, and most will also cook an evening meal on request, though advance warning is usually required. Cooler, darker ground floor rooms are preferable in summer, lighter, warmer first floor rooms in winter. Note too that in winter it can rain heavily in Marrakech, turning dusty streets in the old town to less charming muddy tracks. In Essaouira, riads can often suffer from damp. Ground floor rooms in riads near the sea are worse affected.

What riads consider to be high season varies but always includes Christmas and Easter holidays. Rates often fall substantially outside these times. Riads usually quote their fees in euros and usually accept credit cards.

In the Atlas, and in the south, the best kasbah hotels, some in genuinely old *pisé*-walled buildings, have more in common with riads than the expensive hotels whose traditional clientele they are poaching.

## Expensive hotels

Top hotels, at least in the towns and cities, are generally run by international groups. Upmarket hotels can either be vast and brash, revamped and nouveau riche, or solid but tasteful and even discreet with a touch of old-fashioned elegance. Generally they struggle to match the quality of service offered by riads, however.

Villa de l'Ô, Essaouira.

## Mid-range hotels

More expensive one-star type hotels may or may not have en suite bathrooms; breakfast (coffee, bread and jam, a croissant, orange juice) should be available, possibly at the café on the ground floor, for around 20dh. Next up are the two and three star-ish places in Marrakech, either in the ville nouvelle, or in a cluster just southeast of Jemaa El Fna. Rooms will generally have high ceilings, breakfast will be included and there will be en suite bathrooms. Light sleepers need to watch out for noisy, street-facing rooms. In Essaouira there are some decent mid-range options in the poorer Mellah area of town.

## Cheap hotels

At the budget end of the market are simple hotels, especially in the High Atlas. There may be a washbasin, sometimes a bidet. Loos and showers will usually be shared and you may have to pay for a hot shower. The worst of this sort of accommodation will be little better than a concrete cell, stifling in summer. The best is often quite pleasant outside summer, with helpful staff and lots of clean, bright tiling. Rooms often open on to a central courtyard, limiting privacy and meaning you have to leave your room closed when out. Hot water, especially in the mountains, can be a problem. Both Marrakech and Essaouira have excellent hostels.

# Spas, retreats & wellbeing

**A**way from the hectic hubbub of the Marrakech souks, escape for some supple high-altitude bending on Berber yoga mats, sweaty spa pummelling or peaceful meditation among the spring blossom of the Atlas foothills. Retreats in the region make the most of some stunning settings, from hilltop kasbahs to the wide open expanses of Atlantic beaches.

**Above: Kasbah Toubkal.**
**Opposite page: Kasbah Bab Ourika.**

## In:Spa
*T(+44) (0)845-458 0723, inspa-retreats.com.*
In:spa runs regular, week-long luxury wellbeing retreats led by a hand-picked team of experts including a nutritionist, yoga teacher, two personal trainers and a private chef. The weeks take place either on the dry plains near Marrakech at **Jnane Tamsna** (jnanetamsna.com) or in the Atlas foothills at **Kasbah Bab Ourika** (babourika.com). Expect walks in the northern valleys of the Atlas Mountains as well as a full programme of yoga, massage, personal training, nutrition consultations and tasty but healthy food.

## Kasbah du Toubkal
*T(+44) (0)1883-744392, kasbahdutoubkal.com.*
About 1½ hours' drive from Marrakech into the Atlas Mountains, the Kasbah du Toubkal has a rough-and-ready hammam where rubber tyres are used as water buckets and there's an ice-cold plunge pool. Perched above the village of **Imlil** and only accessible by donkey track, this Berber hospitality centre ploughs its profits back into the local community and has won a string of awards for sustainable and responsible tourism. You won't be blown away by the erratic service or the mediocre food but it's a perfect base for well-

guided treks and the views over the mountains are staggering. A room in the tower gives you easy access to its small rooftop – ideal for doing your own yoga or meditating in private.

### Kasbah Itran
*T(+44) (0)7764-963138, janecraggs.co.uk.*
Yoga teacher Jane Craggs runs holidays to Kasbah Itran (kasbahitran.com), on the outskirts of **El Kelaa M'gouna**, south of the Atlas Mountains. It's an eco-project run by a Berber family who have created a very relaxed, easygoing atmosphere where nothing is too much trouble. Twice-daily yoga classes are held on the terrace overlooking the mountains and the Mgoun Delta, sometimes watched by curious children. Three vegetarian meals are served each day and, after dinner, the chef Mohamed usually leads a session of traditional Berber music. There's also the opportunity to take guided treks through mountain villages and the desert.

### Yoga and sound
*T(+44) (0)20-8450 2723, yogaandsound.com.*
Inspirational healer and teacher Judith Seelig runs annual four-night yoga and sound retreats at the sumptuous Riad Ifoulki (riadifoulki.com) in **Marrakech**. Designed to accommodate beginners as well as experienced practitioners, her sessions will give you a very deep and slow introduction to hatha yoga with sound. Riad Ifoulki is run like a private home rather than a hotel, so retains an intimate, friendly atmosphere. The yoga takes place among orange trees and fountains sprinkled with rose petals in one of the riad's five beautifully tiled courtyards. There are two sessions a day, with optional evening meditation before a rooftop candlelit dinner.

### Trance
*yogamarrakech.wordpress.com.*
Opening in 2010, **Marrakech**'s first healing retreat centre will offer nine guest rooms, retreat courses, detox programmes, dance and meditation lessons, as well as power flow yoga with visiting teachers and lessons from the founder and owner, New

Zealand-born Aisha, who specializes in Ashtanga yoga. The centre will have a spa and pool and the healthy food will be supplemented by nutrition consulting.

### Yoga travel
*T(+44) (0)870-350 3545, yogatravel.co.uk.*
If you want to enjoy the coast as well as **Marrakech**, Yoga Travel runs two eight-day yoga holidays a year, which include two nights on the beach at **Sidi Kaouki** and two at **Essaouira**. 'On Hendrix's Trail' offers twice-daily yoga. In Marrakech you stay in the Moroccan-owned 18th-century Riad Omar (riadomar.com), Sidi Kaouki is a vast, empty Atlantic beach, where you stay in a hotel overlooking olive groves and grazing goats; you then move on to Essaouira, staying at the Riad Al Médina (riadalmedina. com). Yoga is taught by expert kundalini teacher Julie Cuddihy (anaharta. com), and you'll be guided by Will Cottrell.

# Eating & drinking

The Moroccans consider their traditional cooking to be on a par with Indian, Chinese and French cuisine.

The climate and soils of Morocco mean that magnificent vegetables can be produced all year round, thanks to irrigation. Although there is industrial chicken production, in many smaller restaurants the chicken you eat is as likely to have been reared by a smallholder. Beef and lamb come straight from the local farms.

In addition to the basic products, Moroccan cooking gets its characteristic flavours from a range of spices and minor ingredients. Saffron (*zaâfrane*), though expensive, is widely used, turmeric (*kurkum*) is also much in evidence. Other widely used condiments include a mixed all spice, referred to as *ra's el hanout* (head of the shop), cumin (*kamoun*), black pepper, oregano and rosemary (*yazir*).

Prominent greens in use include broad-leaved parsley (*ma'dnous*), coriander (*kuzbur*) and, in some variations of couscous, a sort of celery called *klefs*. Preserved lemons (modestly called *bouserra*, or navels, despite their breast-like shape) can be found in fish and chicken tajines. Bay leaves (*warqa Sidna Moussa*, or the leaf of our lord Moses) are also commonly employed. Almonds, much used in pâtisserie, are used in tajines too, while powdered cinnamon (Arabic *karfa*, *cannelle* in French) provides the finishing touch for pastilla. In pâtisserie, orange-flower water and rose water (*ma ouarda*) are essential to achieve a refined taste. See also the food and drink glossary, page 232.

Marrakech gets up early – and goes to bed early, too – so people tend to sit down to dine around about 2000. Across the country, the big meal of the week is Friday lunch, a time for people to gather in their families. The main meal of the day tends to be lunch, although this varies according to work and lifestyle. Locals will tend to favour restaurants with French or southern European cuisine, while Moroccan riad restaurants are patronized almost exclusively by tourists.

Colourful salad served at After 5, Essaouira.

## Starters

*Harira* is a basic Moroccan soup; ingredients vary but include chick peas, lentils, veg and a little meat. It is often eaten accompanied by hard-boiled eggs. *Bissara* is a pea soup, a cheap and filling winter breakfast. *Briouat* are tiny envelopes of filo pastry, akin to the Indian samosa, with a variety of savoury fillings. They also come with an almond filling for dessert.

## Snacks

Cheaper restaurants serve kebabs (aka *brochettes*), with tiny pieces of beef, lamb and fat. Also popular is *kefta*, mince-meat brochettes, served in sandwiches with chips, mustard and *harissa* (chilli pepper spicy sauce). Tiny bowls of finely chopped tomato and onion are another popular accompaniment. On Jemaa El Fna, strong stomachs may want to snack on the local *babouche* (snails).

## Main dishes

*Seksou* (couscous) is the great North African speciality. Granules of semolina are steamed over a pot filled with a rich meat and vegetable stew. Unlike Tunisian couscous, which tends to be flavoured with a tomato sauce, Moroccan couscous is pale yellow. In some families, couscous is the big Friday lunch, an approximate equivalent of old-fashioned English Sunday lunch.

Tagines are stews, the basic Moroccan dish. It is actually the term for the two-part terracotta dish (base and conical lid) in which meat or fish are cooked with a variety of vegetables: essentially, carrots, potato, onion and turnip. Tajine is everywhere in Morocco. Simmered in front of you on a *brasero* at a roadside café, it is always good and safe to eat. Out trekking and in the South, it is the staple of life. For tajines, there are four main sauce preparations: *m'qalli*, a yellow sauce created using olive oil, ginger and saffron; *m'hammer*, a red sauce which includes butter, paprika (*felfla hlwa*) and cumin; *qudra*, another yellow sauce, slightly

Harira soup.

lighter than *m'qalli*, made using butter, onions, pepper and saffron, and finally *m'chermel*, made using ingredients from the other sauces. Variations on these base sauces are obtained using a range of ingredients, including parsley and coriander, garlic and lemon juice, *boussera*, eggs, sugar, honey and cinnamon (*karfa*).

In the better restaurants, look out for *djaj bil-hamid* (chicken with preserved lemons and olives), sweet and sour *tajine barkouk* (lamb with plums), *djaj qudra* (chicken with almonds and caramelized onion) and *tajine maqfoul*. Another traditional dish is *tajine kefta*, fried minced meat balls cooked with eggs and chopped parsley. In eateries next to food markets, delicacies such as *ra's embekhar* (steamed sheep's head) and *kourayn* (animal feet) are a popular feed.

## About the region

All over Morocco, lamb is much appreciated, and connoisseurs reckon they can tell what the sheep has been eating (rosemary, mountain pasture, straw, or mixed rubbish at the rubbish tip). Lamb is cheaper in drought years when farmers have to reduce their flocks, expensive when the grazing is good, and is often best eaten at roadside restaurants where the lorry drivers pull in for a feed.

### Desserts

A limited selection of desserts are served in Moroccan restaurants. In the palace restaurants, there will be a choice between *orange à la cannelle* (slices of orange with cinnamon) or some sort of marzipan pâtisserie like *cornes de gazelle* or *ghrayeb*, rather like round shortcake. *El jaouhar*, also onomatopoeically known as *tchak-tchouka*, is served as a pile of crunchy, fried filo pastry discs topped with a sweet custard sauce with almonds. Also on offer you may find *m'hencha*, coils of almond paste wrapped in filo pastry, served crisp from the oven and sprinkled with icing sugar and cinnamon, and *bechkito*, little crackly biscuits.

In local laiteries, try a glass of yoghurt. Oranges (*limoun*) and mandarins (*tchina*) are cheap, as are prickly pears, sold off barrows. In winter in the mountains, look out for kids selling tiny red arbutus berries (*sasnou*) carefully packaged in little wicker cones. Fresh hazelnuts are known as *tigerguist*.

### Dishes for Ramadan

At sunset the fast is broken with a rich and savoury *harira* (see above), *beghrira* (little honeycombed pancakes served with melted butter and honey) and *shebbakia* (lace-work pastry basted in oil and covered in honey). Distinctive too are the sticky pastry whorls with sesame seeds on top.

### Restaurants

Full blown restaurants are generally found only in larger towns. In Marrakech there are several riad restaurants set in old, often beautifully restored private homes. Food here can be very expensive and there is often a fixed-price, multiple-course menu.

### Eating out cheaply

If you're on a tight budget, try the ubiquitous food stalls and open-air restaurants serving various types of soup, normally the standard broth (*harira*), snacks and grilled meat. The best place for the adventurous open-air eater is Jemaa El Fna in Marrakech. Another good place is the fish market in the centre of Essaouira. There is a greater risk of food poisoning at street eateries, so go for food that is cooked as you wait, or that is on the boil. Avoid reheated fish.

### Vegetarian food

Moroccan food is not terribly interesting for vegetarians, and in many places vegetarian cuisine means taking the meat of the top off the couscous or tajine. There are some excellent salads, however. Be prepared to eat lots of processed cheese and omelettes.

## Drinks

### Tea

All over Morocco the main drink apart from water is mint tea (*thé à la menthe/attay*) – a cheap, refreshing drink which is made with green tea, fresh mint and

Tea glasses for sale in the souks of Marrakech.

## Tip...

Ask for sugar on the side of your mint tea if you want to go home with a full set of teeth.

masses of white sugar. The latter two ingredients predominate in the taste. If you want a reduced sugar tea, ask for *attaymsous* or *bila sukar/sans sucre*).

In cafés, tea is served in mini metal teapots. In homes it is poured from high above the glass to generate a frothy head. Generally, tradition has it that you drink three glasses. To avoid burning your fingers, hold the glass with thumb under the base and index finger on rim. In some homes, various other herbs are added to make a more interesting brew, including *flayou* (peppermint), *louiza* (verbena) and even *sheeba* (absinthe).

## Coffee

Coffee is commonly drunk black and strong (*kahwa kahla/un exprès*). For a weak milky coffee, ask for a *café au lait/kahwa halib*. A stronger milky coffee is called a *café cassé/kahwa mherza*.

## Other soft drinks

All the usual soft drinks are available in Morocco. If you want still mineral water (*eau plate*) ask for Sidi Harazem, Sidi Ali or Ciel. The main brands of fizzy mineral water (*eau pétillante*), are Oulmès and Bonacqua. The better cafés and local *laiteries* (milk-product shops) do milkshakes and smoothies, combinations of avocado, banana, apple and orange, made to measure. Ask for a jus d'avocat or a *jus de banane*, for example.

## Wines & spirits

For a Muslim country, Morocco is fairly relaxed about alcohol. In riads and the top hotels, imported spirits are available, although at a price. The main locally made lager is Flag.

Morocco produces wine, the main growing areas being Guerrouane and Meknès. Reds tend to prevail. Celliers de Meknès (CdM) and Sincomar are the main producers. At the top of the scale are Médaillon and Beau Vallon. Another reliable red is Domaine de Sahari, Aït Yazem, a pleasant claret, best drunk chilled in summer. The whites include Coquillages and Sémillant, probably the best. At the very bottom of the scale is rough and ready Rabbi Jacob.

The colourful Guéliz market in Marrakech is full of high-quality produce.

Coffee is usually served black and strong.

# Entertainment

Marrakech's best entertainment stage is Jemaa El Fna, where you can take a café seat and see jugglers, acrobats, gnaoua musicians, snake charmers and story tellers. These shows are hard to match in the city's cinemas and theatres.

## Bars & clubs

Rules restrict the sale of alcohol inside the medina to smart restaurants and riads, which means that neither central Marrakech nor Essaouira has much in the way of a bar scene. In the ville nouvelle things are a little different, with a mix of old-style bars such as the **Chesterfield** (see page 132) and the megaclub **Pacha** (see page 133), which claims to be the largest in Africa. For something a bit more Moroccan, try **Theatro** (see page 133).

If you do want a drink in the medina, the terraces of **Café Arabe** (see page 132) or **Kosybar** (see page 132) are as good as any. **Le Comptoir Darna** (see page 133) and **Le Tanjia** (see page 128) both have regular belly dancers – not really a Moroccan tradition, but fun nonetheless. You might also try the **Grand Casino de la Mamounia** (see page 133). In Essaouira, **Café Taros** (see page 171) is the nearest thing to a nightlife scene.

Above: Festival Gnaoua et Musiques du Monde, Essaouira. **Opposite page: Kosybay, Marrakech.**

Above: Festival Gnaoua et Musiques du Monde, Essaouira. Opposite page: Kosybay, Marrakech.

### Cinema

In Marrakech, the **Colisée**, Blvd Mohamed Zerktouni, and the **Regent**, Av Mohamed V, show films in French, as does the **Institut Français**, Route de la Targa, Guéliz, ifm.ma.

### Gay & lesbian

Homosexuality is officially illegal but generally tolerated, and Marrakech is a popular gay travel destination. That doesn't mean that there's anything really resembling a gay scene, however, with most activity restricted to pick-ups in Jemaa El Fna, on Av Mohamed V and in **Café les Négociants** (see page 131).

### Music

Music is the most ubiquitous entertainment in and around Marrakech. Most smart restaurants,

and quite a few simple ones, will have a band strumming away in the corner, possibly playing grika, improvised percussive Berber music.

Gnaoua music, with origins in sub-Saharan Africa, is hypnotic dance music related to ritual and trance. Its players are considered to have special powers to cure scorpion stings and gnaoua music is used to drive out evil. The themes of the music are often related to its historic origins in slavery. Gnaoua has gained an international following and big name stars such as Robert Plant have collaborated with gnaoua musicians. The annual **Festival Gnaoua et Musiques du Monde** in Essaouira (see page 46) is the biggest music event around.

Apart from restaurants and the gnaoua festival, however, there are few opportunities to hear live music in the region.

# Shopping

Marrakech is a shopping wonderland, with an extraordinary wealth of crafts, clothes and miracle cures for sale in myriad colours, shapes and sizes. Shopping here is also a sensory and very human experience a world away from anodyne European shopping. There's an enormous choice of leather bags and shoes, carpets and blankets, clothes, pottery and jewellery, and, in Essaouira, of polished thuya wood boxes and games. Earthenware tagines (the glazed ones are ornamental) and argan oil-based cosmetics are other possible purchases. Usually these items are handmade, often in workshops at the back of the shops where they are sold.

## Carpets & weavings

Moroccan carpets and pottery are made by women, jewellery and metal utensils by men. The signs and symbols used to decorate these items are generally geometric, arranged in simple, repetitive combinations, combining lines, dots and dashes, lozenges and squares. The isolation of rural communities meant that the peoples of different areas could develop very individual styles of craftwork. Sometimes these decorative forms are linked to the tribal marks tattooed on women's faces and arms.

Made from thick wool, the carpets of the Middle Atlas, used both as mattresses and blankets, may have striking red and deep brown backgrounds. Carpets from the Haouz Plain (the Marrakech region) also have strong orange-red backgrounds.

A few carpet-buying places offer fixed prices without the touristy spiel – riad owners are often good for advice on carpet-buying as they usually have good sources themselves.

Approximate prices are: Rabat, Glaoui or Ouzguita knotted carpets, 1000dh-2000dh sq m; Chichaoua red knotted or Middle Atlas white carpets, around 750dh sq m.

Be prepared to haggle for rugs and carpets.

## Jewellery

Jewellery in southern Berber communities is always silver; necklaces include silver tubes and spheres, along with tozra, oversized orange copal beads. *Serdal*, silk headbands hung with silver coins and coral beads, and *khalkhul* ankle bracelets are also worn. Simple enamel *cloisoné* work is another feature of southern jewellery. Urban jewellery, on the other hand, is often in gold, set with precious stones, and very finely worked. Gilded and engraved jewellery is also popular. Much of the jewellery produced for the local market, as seen in the jewellery souks in Marrakech and Essaouira, is overly showy for Western tastes. Silver jewellery generally costs around 5dh per gram, gold around 100dh per gram.

Browse the souks in Marrakech's medina for earrings and other jewellery.

## Haggling

Part of the fun of shopping in the medina is the haggling that comes with every purchase. To buy in the souks you will have to engage in the theatre and the mindgames of the haggle. In order to come out of the process happy, there are some things to bear in mind.

Don't get too hung up on the idea of 'a good price'. The best price is the one you are happy to pay. Have one in mind before you start and don't go above it. Be prepared to walk away if the price is too high – whatever you're buying, there will almost certainly be another stall around the corner selling the same thing.

Be friendly and polite but firm and don't suggest a price you would be prepared to pay for anything you're not sure you want. Once you start talking numbers you are in negotiation and you may find it hard to extricate yourself.

The price you are first quoted might be twice as much as the seller is prepared to accept, but there is absolutely no firm rule about this. A decent starting point from the buyer's point of view is to take about a half to a third off the amount you'd be prepared to pay and start by offering that.

As a very rough guide, and depending on quality, size, etc, expect to pay these sort of prices: *babouches* 50-150dh; leather bag 200-400dh; teapot 50-200dh (more for silver); spices 30-60dh/kg; pouffe 150-450; blanket 300-600dh.

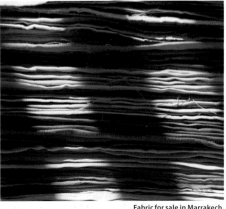

Fabric for sale in Marrakech.

# Activities & tours

### Ballooning

Drifting over the Haouz plain with the Atlas Mountains rising out of the red earth is a great way to get a sense of the importance of the Red City to the surrounding area. **Ciel d'Afrique** (see page 137) organize hot-air balloon flights, leaving Marrakech around 0600 for a flight over the Jebilet, the hills north of Marrakech. A flight shared with other people will cost €205.

### Birdwatching

Home to 460 species, Morocco has the greatest diversity of birdlife north of the Sahara. There are coastal marsh and lagoon sites, and top destinations for birdwatchers include Oualidia and Essaouira. The reserve at Tidzi, south of Essaouira, is home to Morocco's rarest resident bird, the bald ibis, and Eleonora's falcon migrates from Madagascar to the Iles Purpuraires, just off the coast from Essaouira.

UK operators **Nature Trek**, T(+44) (0)1962-733051, naturetrek.co.uk, and **Sunbird Tours**, T(+44) (0)1767-262522, sunbirdtours.co.uk, offer several birdwatching holidays to Morocco.

### Camel trekking

Camel trekking saw a real growth in popularity in the 1990s with beasts being brought up from Mali to satisfy the growing demand. Apart from the quick camel ride into the dunes, popular at Zagora and M'Hamid, there are two options: the *méharée* and the *randonnée chamelière*. The *méharée* actually involves you riding the camel, the *randonnée chamelière* (camel hike) means you walk alongside the camels, which are essentially used as pack animals.

Camel trekking is popular around Zagora.

Obviously, in the former option, you can cover a lot more ground, riding for four to five hours a day. A good organizer will lay on everything apart from sleeping bags, although blankets are generally available.

The best time of year for treks in the south is October to April, although sandstorms are a possibility between November and February.

A six-night camel hike out of Zagora would enable you to see a combination of dunes and plains, palm groves and villages, taking you from Zagora down to the dunes of Chigaga, with an average of five hours walking a day. Most general agencies (see Walking, page 63) will organize camel treks as well as short rides into the dunes combined with a night under canvas.

Camels can also be ridden along the beach at Essaouira and Sidi Kaouki, or through the Marrakech palmery (see page 105). Budding cameleers can take lessons at **La Maison du Chameau**, near Essaouira (see page 166).

### Cooking

Three cookery schools in the region are recommended: **Maison Arabe** (see page 140) and **Souk Cuisine** (see page 140) in Marrakech and **L'Atelier Madada** (see page 173) in Essaouira.

It's often possible to get cookery lessons at riads – these may be relatively structured, or they may amount to little more than helping out in the kitchen. The **Earth Café Farm** (see page 104) teaches visitors how to make traditional Moroccan bread.

### Golf

Golf is a fast-growing sport in Morocco, though that doesn't mean you'll find many Moroccans playing it. Marrakech has three courses: the long-established **Royal Golf Club** (see page 140), the neighbouring **Amelkis** (Ancienne Route de Ouarzazate, Km 12, T0524-404414), which has less of the colonial atmosphere but is a better course,

and the brand new **Assoufid** (Rue du Temple Résidence Oumnia A1-4, T0524-339800, assoufid. com), an international calibre course. Essaouira also has a brand new course, **Golf de Mogador** (see page 173).

Learn about traditional Moroccan cuisine at a cookery school.

## About the region

### Horse riding

The horse is the object of a veritable cult in Morocco. Fantasias – spectacular ceremonies where large numbers of traditionally dressed horsemen charge down a parade ground to discharge their muskets a few metres away from tentfuls of banqueting guests – are a great occasion to see Moroccan riding skills. The late King Hassan II assembled one of the world's finest collections of rare black thoroughbred Arab horses and wealthy Moroccans are often keen for their offspring to learn to ride. Many towns have riding clubs and national show-jumping events are programmed on TV.

Equitours, ridingtours.com, organize week-long trips across the Atlas and the desert.

Try also: Le Roseraie at Ouirgane (see page 190) in the Atlas foothills; Cavaliers d'Essaouira, 14 km inland from Essaouira, T0665-074889 (mobile) who do rides by the hour and short treks in beautiful rolling countryside through argan and olive groves and thuya plantations; and Les Cavaliers de l'Atlas outside Marrakech (see page 140).

### Mountain biking

Areas popular with mountain bikers include the Dadès Gorge and Toundoute, north of Skoura. Clay washed onto the tracks by rain dries out to form a good surface for bikes. Most towns have bike hire companies.

Unique Trails, uniquetrails.com, and Wildcat Adventures, wildcatbike-tours.co.uk, are UK-based operators running cycling trips to Morocco.

### Rafting

Splash Rafting Morocco (see page 140) organize winter and spring trips in the Ourika Valley, Moulay Ibrahim Gorge and the Tizi-n-Test Gorge.

### Skiing

Oukaïmeden (2600 m, see page 186), an hour's drive up in the High Atlas south of the Red City, is Morocco's premier ski resort. A good winter in 2009

Below: Morocco has some excellent areas for rafting. Opposite page: Horse riding at La Pause outside Marrakech (see page 103).

and some new investment has improved Morocco's reputation as a ski destination. You can't depend on good snow for an Alpine-style skiing holiday, but there is a certain cachet to being able to say you've skied in Africa. It tends to be busy only on snowy weekends: keen locals rush down from Casablanca or Rabat as soon as good conditions are announced. The summit above the plateau is Jbel Oukaïmeden (3270 m). There are several lifts and pistes ranging from black to green.

The **Refuge of the Club Alpin Français** in Oukaïmeden, T0524-319036, hires out ski gear and should be able to advise on skiing conditions.

### Surfing

Winter is the surfing season in Essaouira. From April to October, the wind is up and the windsurfers are out in force. If you don't have your own gear, you can rent. Surf gear gets intensive use so ages quickly. Check carefully when you rent. There are a couple of surf places, of which the best is **Océan Vagabond** right on the main beach (see page 171). Sidi Kaouki also has a good scene, with a surf club and miles of empty beach (see page 154).

### Walking

The High Atlas are the obvious place for trekkers, with many descending on Toubkal National Park wanting to reach the peak of North Africa's highest mountain, Jbel Toubkal (see page 185). Shorter routes lower down are equally satisfying, however, with good day walks from Setti Fatma (see page 186) or Imlil (see page 183). See also page 64.

The beautiful high valley of Aït Bougmez (see page 189) is a more remote Atlas walking option, and the southern gorges (see page 199) also offer good opportunities.

Kasbah Bab Ourika (see page 192) offers guided walks through the Berber villages in the valley below and there are good walks along the coast from Sidi Kaouki (see page 156).

**Atlas Sahara Trek**, 6 bis Rue Houdhoud, Quartier Majorelle, T0524-313901, atlassahara-trek.com. One of the best trekking agencies in Marrakech, with 20 years' experience.

**Mountain Safari Tours**, 64 Lot Laksour Route de Casa, Guéliz, T0524-308777, mountainsafaritours.com. A specialist travel agency with 20 years of experience.

**Mountain Voyage**, Immeuble El Batoul, 2nd Floor, 5 Av Mohamed V, Guéliz, T0524-421996, mountain-voyage.com. Organized and recommended tour operator with English-speaking staff running treks in the Toubkal area.

# Trekking

There are great opportunities for hiking in Morocco. The most popular area is the Toubkal National Park in the High Atlas (see page 184). However, as roads improve and inveterate trekkers return for further holidays, new areas are becoming popular. To organize your trip, you can either book through a specialist trekking operator from home or hope to find a guide available when you arrive. Guides are plentiful in trailhead settlements such as Imlil or Setti Fatma.

## Where

The Toubkal High Atlas is best from late April to October, with various loops up into the mountains. You will probably want to climb North Africa's highest peak, Jbel Toubkal (4167 m); the only problem is that the mountain has become almost too popular.

South of Azilal, the beautiful Vallée des Aït Bougmez is also becoming popular. For weekend trekkers, there are gentle walks along the flat valley bottom but the Aït Bougmez also makes a good departure point for tougher treks, including the north-south crossing of the west-central High Atlas to Bou Thraghar, near Boumalne and El Kelaâ des Mgouna. On this route, you have the chance to climb the region's second highest peak, Irhil Mgoun (4071 m).

## When

In the heat of summer, keep to the high valleys which are cooler and where water can be obtained. The views are not generally as good in the High Atlas at the height of summer because of the haze.

## Where to stay

Camping or bivouacking is fine in summer but in autumn indoor accommodation is necessary, in refuges, shepherds' huts or local homes. Note that classified guest rooms in rural areas now have the GTAM (Grande Traversée des Atlas Marocains) label of approval.

## Maps

Specialist maps and guides are useful and can be obtained at the Hotel Ali in Marrakech (see page 117).

## Trekking Independently

The use of mules or donkeys to carry the heavy packs is common. If you are setting up a trek yourself, note that a good mule can carry up to 100 kg (approximately three rucksacks). A mule with a muleteer costs around 120dh per day, a good guide should be paid 250dh per day, a cook around 150dh. When buying food for the trek with your guide, you will have to buy enough for the muleteers, too. Generally, trekkers will consume about 100dh worth of food and soft drinks a day. If you do a linear trek rather than a loop, you will generally have to pay for the mule days it takes to get the pack animals back to their home village.

A good trip leader will ensure you make an early start, to enjoy walking in the cool mornings.

Vehicle pistes look alluring to walk on but are in fact hard on the feet. Keep to the softer edges or go for footpaths when possible. Gorges are not the easiest places to walk in, so your local guide should know of the higher routes, if there is one that is safe. Pay particular attention if your route involves scree – you don't want to leave the mountains on a mule because of a sprained ankle.

In order to fully appreciate the beauty of the Atlas, trekkers need to ensure that the walking is as comfortable as possible, and this includes finding ways to deal with dehydration and fatigue. As on any hill trek, a steady, regular pace should be maintained. If you are not used to walking at altitude, try to avoid high routes in the early stages of your trip. Ensure you pause if a dizzy feeling sets in.

In villages that see a lot of tourists, the kids will be on the lookout, ever ready to scrounge a dirham or a 'bonbon'. They can, however, be useful in showing you the way through to the footpath on the other side of the settlement.

# Contents

69 Introduction
70 Essentials
72 *Map: Marrakech*
74 Jemaa El Fna &
   the northern medina
76 Great days out:
   A stroll through the medina
81 *Map: Jemaa El Fna & the souks*
92 Southern medina
98 Ville nouvelle & the gardens
102 Around Marrakech
106 Listings:
106 Sleeping
122 Eating
132 Entertainment
133 Shopping
137 Activities & tours
141 Transport

Marrakech

Dried flower heads for sale in a Berber
pharmacy opposite the Museum of Marrakech.

# Introduction

## What to see in...

**... one day**
Begin with the focal point of the medina, and indeed of the whole city: **Jemaa El Fna**, a chaotic open space filled with street entertainers and food sellers. North of here, lose yourself in the **souks**, a maze of alleys and stalls where you could shop for hours. A cluster of sights is buried just north of the souks: the stunning **Medersa Ben Youssef**, the Almoravid **Qoubba**, and the **Museum of Marrakech**.

C ome to Marrakech for its elusive magic and exotic mystery, and you will probably leave with more prosaic, yet intimate, human memories: kids playing with a punctured football in a dusty backstreet, a tanner up to his armpits in a putrid vat of dye, a blind woman selling bunches of fresh mint.

At the centre of the city is a wonderful juxtaposition of high religion and earthy populism: the elegant 12th-century Koutoubia Mosque and Jemaa El Fna, a square famed for its seething mass of entertainments, its energetically retold oral histories and its hectic open-air restaurants. Around them stretches the medina, a place of narrow streets, minarets and the beautiful hidden courtyards of flat-roofed riad houses. And the souks, overflowing with brightly coloured leather slippers and battered old teapots, with caged chameleons and the orange woollen expanses of Chichaoua carpets.

The Medersa Ben Youssef is as fine a piece of soul-lifting architecture as you will see anywhere, there is more finely wrought carved and tiled exuberance in the Saadian Tombs, and the Jardin Majorelle is a glorious celebration of colour and light. But Marrakech's sights are overwhelmed by the volume of the city's bluster. The romance of its reputation is real enough, but it is also a viscerally lived-in place, a seething mass of humanity and inhumanity, of wonderful sounds and startling colours and memorably unpleasant smells.

**... a weekend or more**
Choose between two palaces, **Dar Si Said** and **Palais La Bahia**, south of Jemaa El Fna, down Riad Zitoun el Kedim. In the afternoon, explore three large gardens outside the impressive city walls, notably the sleek blue **Jardin Majorelle**. Busy **Guéliz** has cafés, galleries and smart boutiques. End the day with dinner in a restaurant in this area, which has some of the city's best.

Outside the medersa.

# Essentials

**❷ Getting around**

**By foot** In the medina, walking is a necessity – try to stick to the right to ease the flow of donkeys, carts, couriers and other pedestrians.

**Taxis** Petit taxis (little beige Fiats) are useful for trips to and from the ville nouvelle. Nominally metered, overcharging is rife. Your chances of finding an honest driver are better if you hail one away from the obvious tourist spots. From the medina to Guéliz should be about 10dh; prices rise by 50% after 2000 and you may find yourself sharing with other passengers. For trips out of the city, grands taxi (usually old Mercedes, also beige) are useful. If you want one for a group of people or for a whole day, you'll find one off Jemaa El Fna – agree a price first. For a seat in a fixed-price, fixed-route grands taxi, departure points vary (see page 141), though Bab Doukala and Bab er Robb are the most useful, for journeys to the west and south. If you're staying in a riad, ask about drivers – most have one whose services you can rent for the day.

**❷ Bus station** The main *gare routière* is at Bab Doukala, just outside the city walls, from where buses leave to most destinations. Suprabus buses leave from near the train station.

**❷ Train station** The train station is at the top of Av Mohamed VI.

**❷ ATMs** There are several on the southern side of Jemaa El Fna and down Rue Bab Agnaou. In the souks they're few and far between, though there is one on Place Rahba Kedima, and another on Rue Dar El Bacha.

**❷ Post office** The main Poste Medina is on the southern side of Jemaa El Fna.

**❷ Pharmacy** Every area has its own pharmacy, marked with a green cross or crescent. If closed, a sign should direct you to the nearest open alternative.

**❷ Hospital** 24-hr **Polyclinique du Sud** (Rue Yougoslavie, Guéliz, T0524-447999) is private but used by most expats. Ring a doctor direct rather than their switchboard; **Dr Samir**, T066-1243227, is recommended.

**❷ Tourist information office** Office du Tourisme, Place Abd el Moumen Ben Ali, Guéliz, T0524-448889, Mon-Fri 0900-1200 and 1500-1830. Free maps but little else.

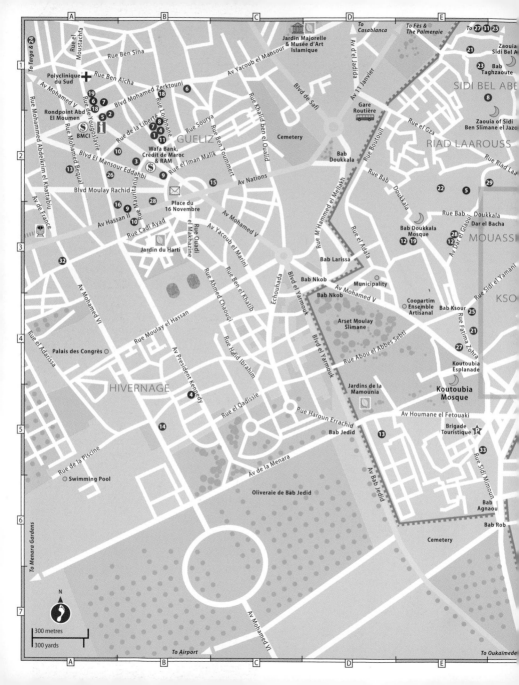

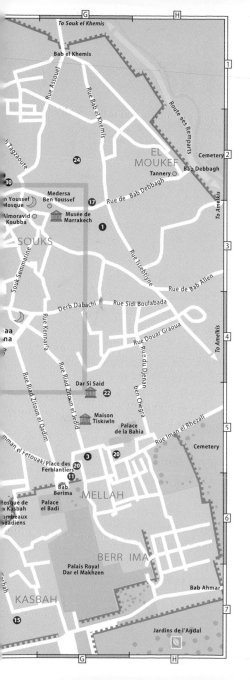

# Marrakech listings

**❶ Sleeping**

1 Dar Hanane G3
2 Dar Najma F2
3 Dar One G5
4 Dar Rhizlane B5
5 Dar Rocmarra E2
6 Djwane A1
7 Hotel des Voyageurs A1
8 Hotel du Pacha B2
9 Hotel Farouk B3
10 Hotel Fashion B3
11 Hotel Toulousain B2
12 La Maison Arabe E3
13 La Mamounia D5
14 La Sultana F6
15 Les Jardins de la Medina F7
16 Les Jardins Mandaline F2
17 Marianis F2
18 Moroccan House Hotel B1
19 Riad 72 E3
20 Riad Assakina G5
21 Riad Charaï E1
22 Riad Chergui E2
23 Riad Edward E1
24 Riad Elizabeth G2
25 Riad El Fenn E4
26 Riad el Ouarda F1
27 Riad Porte Royale E1
28 Riad Sara E3
29 Riad Tizwa E2
30 Riad Tlaatawai-sitteen F2
31 Riad Zamzam E1
32 Ryad Mogador Opera A3
33 Villa des Orangers E5

**❶ Eating & drinking**

1 Adamo B2
2 Al Fassia A2
3 Bar L'Escale B2
4 Café du Livre B2
5 Café Les Négociants A2
6 Casanova B1
7 Catanzaro B2
8 Dar Zellij F1
9 Grand Café de la Poste B2
10 Kechmara A2
11 Kosybar G5
12 Kousina E3
13 La Trattoria A2
14 Le 6 B5
15 Le 16 C2
16 Le Chat qui Rit A3
17 Le Foundouk G3
18 Le Jacaranda A1
19 Le Lounge A1
20 Le Tanjia G5
21 Le Tobsil E4
22 Mamatilee G5
23 Nid'Cigogne F6
24 Pizzeria Niagara A1
25 Riad des Mers F1
26 Rôtisserie de la Paix A2
27 Venezia Ice F4
28 Yellow Sub B3

# Jemaa El Fna & the northern medina

Heaving with Moroccan humanity, Jemaa El Fna, the sprawling square at Marrakech's core, is the city's most popular sight and, together with the neighbouring Koutoubia mosque, its most easily located landmark. The Jardins de la Koutoubia, the mosque's gardens, make a good viewing area for the minaret. North of the square are the souks, a huge labyrinth of narrow streets packed tightly with markets. Thread your way up Souk Semmarine and its continuations to reach a cluster of the city's most important Islamic monuments: the city's oldest structure, the Almoravid Qoubba, and its most beautiful, the Medersa Ben Youssef. Also here are two more fine examples of Moroccan architecture: the Museum of Marrakech and the arts foundation of Dar Belarj. Many visitors to the Marrakech medina concentrate on this central zone, but there is plenty of interest in the quieter, more residential streets further north and east. Out east towards the gate of Bab Debbagh are the pungent and colourful tanneries, while to the north the Zaouïa of Sidi Bel Abbes commemorates the holiest of Marrakech's seven saints. Further west, Avenue Mohamed V leads past the Cyber Parc Moulay Hassan, a green space with internet access just inside the city walls, to the Ville Nouvelle. The 16 km of city walls, originally Almoravid, are themselves an impressive sight.

## Jemaa El Fna

Map: Jemaa El Fna & the Souks, p81.

Special enough to be given UNESCO recognition, the central square of Jemaa El Fna is both the city's greatest pull for tourists and a social area for Moroccans. Despite its fame, popularity and snake charmers, it remains an essentially Moroccan space, big and vibrant enough to absorb its visitors without bowing to them. It's also useful for navigation around a city that is remarkably easy to get lost in, a place that visitors return to again and again.

The atmosphere of 'La Place' changes through the day. Open to limited traffic during daylight hours, you can wander between sellers of orange juice, herbs and spices, clothes, shoes, alarm clocks and radios. There are snake charmers and monkey tamers, watersellers and wildly grinning gnaoua musicians with giant metal castanets, all too ready to pose for photographs, for which they proceed to charge a small fortune.

Sheltering from the sun under their umbrellas, fortune tellers and public scribes await their clients. As dusk falls it takes on an increasingly carnival atmosphere, with acrobats and musicians vying with story-tellers for the attention of the crowds. Many tourists retreat to the rooftop cafés (see page 127) to watch the spectacle.

Watching the setting up of the food stalls in the early evening is another piece of theatre, as is walking between them and braving the food, be it sheep's heads, snails, fried fish or lentil soup. People have been known to fall ill after eating in the square, though in general hygiene is fairly good (see page 125).

Jemaa El Fna means 'assembly of the dead', and, though there is disagreement over the origins of the name, it may refer to the traditional display of the heads of criminals, executed here until the 19th century. In 1956, the government attempted to close down the square by converting it into a corn market and car park, but soon reverted it to its traditional role. In the late 1980s, the bus station was moved

Jemaa El Fna.

# A *stroll* through the medina

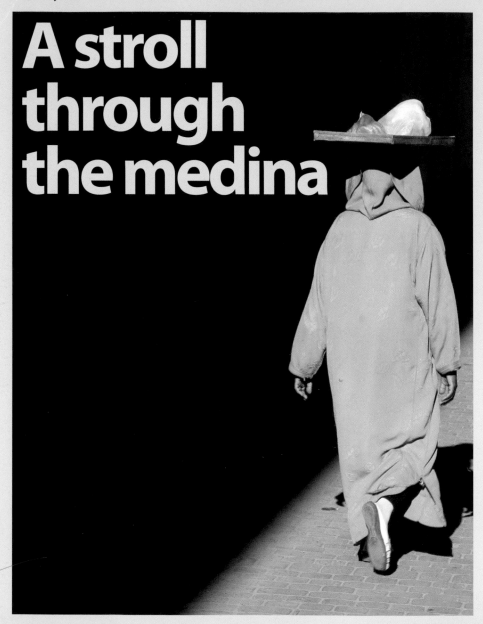

**T**he highlights of the city are less its museums and historic sites than the streets and souks of its medina, and you should allow plenty of time for wandering, stopping for mint tea, and, almost inevitably, getting lost.

Jemaa El Fna makes a good place to start with a fresh orange juice. The long straight Rue Riad Zitoun el Jedid, to the southeast of the square, is an easily navigated introduction to the medina. Keeping the tall minaret of the Koutoubia Mosque behind you, head for the narrower northeastern arm of the square and turn right at the Marrakchi restaurant along Rue des Banques. Bear right at the end onto Rue Riad Zitoun el Jedid. Off to the left of this street is the riad museum of Dar Si Said (see page 93) and the fascinating Maison Tiskiwin (see page 93). At the end of the street, also on the left, is the beautiful Palais de la Bahia (see page 93).

Turn right at the end of Rue Riad Zitoun el Jedid and almost immediately you'll have the jewellery market straight in front of you – look for the finely carved Grand Bijouterie sign above the entrance. Opposite is the small and much earlier Mellah souk, with stalls selling everything from spices to footballs. Following the road around to the left will bring you to the Place des Ferblantiers, a traditional place for metalworkers – you can see them at work around the edge of the square making lanterns. On the corner of the square, Kosybar (see page 128) is a good place for a drink or a bite to eat.

Near here are two more sights you could make a detour to: the ornate Tombeaux Saadiens (see page 97) and the barren spaces of the ruined Palais El Badi (see page 95). Also here is the marché couvert, good for a taste of how the locals shop for fruit, veg and live chickens.

From Place des Ferblantiers, head northwest to find the end of Rue Riad Zitoun El Kedim. The parallel twin of Rue Riad Zitoun el Jedid, this is another long straight route with plenty of small shops along the way, heading back to Jemaa El Fna.

To the north of the square, the souks are a tightly packed network of markets on narrow streets, many protected from the sun by rush matting overhead. Enter the souks by the medicine men on the square, opposite the Marrakchi, bending round to the right and crossing a junction to head north along Rue Semarine. Shopping in the souks can be overwhelming and disorientating, but this is a sort of souk high street – the straightest, widest route through.

On the right, about half way along is Rahba Lakdima, a pretty square with a good café (see page 126). Continuing north along Rue Semarine will eventually bring you (with a little left-right necessary at the end) blinking out into the sunshine just south of another cluster of Marrakech's sights, the Medersa Ben Youssef (see page 84), Musée de Marrakech (see page 85), and the Qoubba Ba'Adyin (see page 86).

Retracing your steps into the souks, take a sharp right at the main junction just before Rahba Lakdima. This is Souk Staila. Taking the first left off here will bring you past the Souk Sebbaghine, with freshly dyed wool hanging out to dry, to the Mouassine fountain and mosque. Keep the mosque on your left and turn down Rue Mouassine, which will take you to Place Bab Fteuh. Keep straight on across here to reach Jemaa El Fnaa again, where you can grab a drink on one of the café terraces overlooking the square as it comes to life at sundown.

## Tip…

Ask before taking photographs of people. Often a gesture is enough. In Jemaa El Fna the musicians and water sellers make their money from having their photo taken – don't be fooled by friendly insistences that it's free.

out to Bab Doukkala. In 1994, the square was fully tarmacked for the GATT meeting. The food stands were reorganized, and the orange juice sellers issued with smart red fezzes and white gloves.

Jemaa El Fna's storytellers have long been a part of its magic and they can still be seen working their magic on crowds of locals today. Even for non-Arabic speakers these are worth a look, as much for the rapt reactions of the crowd as for the skills of the storytellers. Thanks to campaigning by a team led by Spanish writer and Marrakech resident Juan Goytisolo, Jemaa El Fna received UNESCO recognition for its place in humankind's oral heritage. Sheltering from the sun under their umbrellas, fortune tellers and public scribes await their clients.

More recent attractions include the *nakkachat*, women with syringes full of henna, ready to pipe a design onto your hands. 'Hook the ring over the coke bottle' is popular, and golf putters have recently appeared. You may find an astrologist-soothsayer tracing out his diagram of the future on the tarmac with a scrubby piece of chalk. A modern variation on the traditional *halka* or storyteller's circle touches harsh social reality: local people listen to a true tale told by the relatives of a victim of poverty or injustice. And should you need an aphrodisiac, there are stalls with tea urns selling cinnamon and ginseng tea and little dishes of black, powdery *slilou*, a spicy sweet paste.

Pickpockets are occasionally a problem on Jemaa El Fna. Have plenty of change handy for entertainments and orange juice. The hassling of tourists by false guides which marred visiting Jemaa El Fna in the 1980s and 1990s is largely a thing of the past: the plain clothes Brigade Touristique is watching, and the penalties are severe. You will, however, experience plenty of enthusiastic encouragement to buy orange juice, or to have a snake draped around your neck.

## Tip...

There are two types of henna used in henna 'tattoos' – brown and black. The former is natural and safe; the latter lasts longer but can cause nasty reactions. Henna painters in Jemaa El Fna can be overly insistent; your riad will probably recommend someone better and cheaper.

Above: Food for sale in Jemaa El Fna.
Opposite page: Koutoubia mosque.

## Mosquée de la Koutoubia

**Closed to non-Muslims. Map: Marrakech, E4, p72.**

The 67-m high **minaret** of the Koutoubia Mosque is the city's tallest building and dominates the whole of Marrakech. Built in pale pink stone and lit up at night, it is visible from afar, and provided the focal point for urban planner Henri Prost when he laid out the modern neighbourhood of Guéliz. Legend says that as this structure once overlooked the harem, only a blind muezzin was allowed to climb it to call the faithful to prayer. The name Koutoubia derives from the Arabic *kutub* (books) and means the 'Booksellers' Mosque', reflecting the fact that the trade of selling manuscripts was conducted in a souk close to the mosque.

Unusually, the Koutoubia is a **double mosque**, both parts dating from the reign of the second Almohad ruler, Abd El-Mumin (1130-1163). The ruins of the first Koutoubia, now behind railings, were first excavated in the late 1940s. The bases of the prayer hall's columns and the cisterns under the courtyard are clearly visible. The ground plan of the second Koutoubia, still standing, is the same as that of the ruined one, with 17 naves. The Almohad mosque at Tin Mal (see page 181), open to visits by non-Muslims, has a similar plan.

The site of the mosque is itself historic, originally being occupied by a late 11th-century kasbah, the Almoravid **Dar al-Hajar**.

The Almohads destroyed much of the previous Almoravid city, and in 1147 built their first huge mosque. Unfortunately, the orientation of the new Almohad mosque was not quite right – the focus point in a mosque is the direction of Mecca, indicated by the *mihrab* or prayer niche, and this one missed its target. The solution was to build a second mosque – the present Koutoubia.

The two mosques existed for some time side by side, the first probably functioning as an annexe. Given Almohad religious fervour, the congregations were large. Today, bricked-up spaces on the

**Tip...**

Ask for directions in shops rather than accepting offers in the street from people who will then charge you for their help.

northwest wall of the Koutoubia Mosque indicate the doors which connected them. However, the double complex was excessively big and the older structure fell into disrepair and eventual ruin. The excavations of 1948 revealed a *maqsura*, or screen, in front of the *mihrab*, which could be wound up through the floor to protect the Sultan, and a *minbar*, or pulpit, which was moved into position on wooden rollers. Two cisterns in the centre may have been from a previous Almoravid structure. On the eastern flank of this mosque was an arcade of which a niche and the remnants of one arch remain.

The existing Koutoubia Mosque was built by Abd el-Mumin in 1162, soon after the building of the first mosque. The minaret is 12½ m wide and 67½ m to the tip of the cupola on the lantern, and is the mosque's principal feature, architecturally admired alongside later Almohad structures, the Hassan Tower in Rabat and the Giralda in Seville. A great feat of engineering in its day, it had a huge influence over subsequent building in Morocco. Holding 20,000 worshippers, the mosque's interior is made up of 17 horseshoe-arched aisles.

The minaret is composed of six rooms, one on top of the other. The cupola on top of the minaret is a symmetrical, square structure topped by a ribbed dome and three golden orbs. These are alleged to have been made from the melted down jewellery of Yaqoub al Mansour's wife, in penance for having eaten three grapes during Ramadan. The proportions of the minaret match the Almohad architectural principle of being five times as tall as it is wide. The cupola has two windows on each side, above which is a stone panel in the *darj w ktaf*, 'step-and-shoulder' motif. The main tower has a band of coloured tiles at the top.

The Koutoubia, a vast structure for 12th-century North Africa, had to be a mosque equal to the lofty ambitions of the western caliphate. It is held to be the high point of Almohad construction, a cathedral-mosque of classic simplicity. It is here that the innovations of Hispano-Moorish art – stalactite cupolas, painted wooden ceilings, sight-lines through horseshoe arches – reach their peak. The elaborate *minbar* (preacher's chair), set

# Jemaa El Fna & the souks listings

**❶ Sleeping**
1 Dar Tamkast *10-12 Derb Sidi Bou Amar, Zaouiat Lahdar*
2 Equity Point Hostel *80 Derb el Hammam, Mouassine*
3 Hotel Ali *Rue Moulay Ismail*
4 Hotel Assia *32 Rue de la Recette*
5 Hotel Belleville *4 194 Riad Zitoun el Kedime*
6 Hotel Essaouira *3 Derb Sidi Bouloukate*
7 Hotel Gallia *30 Rue de la Recette*
8 Hotel Ichbilia *1 Rue Bani Marine*
9 Hotel Jnane Mogador *116 Riad Zitoun el Kedime*
10 Hotel La Gazelle *13 Rue Bani Marine*
11 Hotel Medina *1 Derb Sidi Bouloukate*
12 Hotel Sherazade *3 Derb Djama*
13 Jardins de la Koutoubia *26 Rue de la Koutoubia*
14 Maison MK *14 Derb Sebaai, Quartier Ksour*
15 Riad el Cadi *86/87 Derb Moulay Abdelkader,Dabachi*
16 Riad El Zohar *56 Derb El Hammam, Mouassine*
17 Riad Enija *9 Derb Mesfioui, Rahba Lakdima*
18 Riad Magellan *62 Derb El Hammam, Mouassine*
19 Riad Yima *52 Derb Aarjane, Rahba Lakdima*
20 Riad Zolah *114-116 Derb El Hammam*
21 Sindi Sud *109 Derb Sidi Bouloukate*

**❶ Eating & drinking**
1 Bougainvillea *33 Rue el Mouassine*
2 Café de France *Jemaa El Fna*
3 Café des Épices *75 Rahba Lakdima*
4 Café Glacier *Jemaa El Fna*
5 Café-Restaurant Argana *Jemaa El Fna*
6 Chez Bahía *Rue Riad Zitoun el Jedid*
7 Chez Chegrouni *46 Jemaa El Fna*
8 Dar Cherifa *8 Derb Charfa Lakbir, Mouassine*
9 Dar Moha *81 Rue Dar el Bacha*
10 Dejeuner a Marrakech *2/4 Place Douar Graoua*
11 Earth Café *2 Derb Zawak, Riad Zitoun Kedime*
12 Jemaa El Fna Foodstalls
13 Ksar Essaoussan *3 Rue des Ksour, Derb El Messoudyenne*
14 Les Premices *Jemaa El Fna*
15 Les Princes *32 Rue Bab Agnaou*
16 Les Terrasses de l'Alhambra *Jemaa El Fna*
17 Marra Book Café *53 Derb Kabada*
18 Snack Toubkal *Jemaa El Fna*
19 Terrasse des Épices *15 Souk Cherifa*
20 Venezia Ice *opposite Koutoubia mosque*
21 Villa Flore *4 Derb Azzouz*

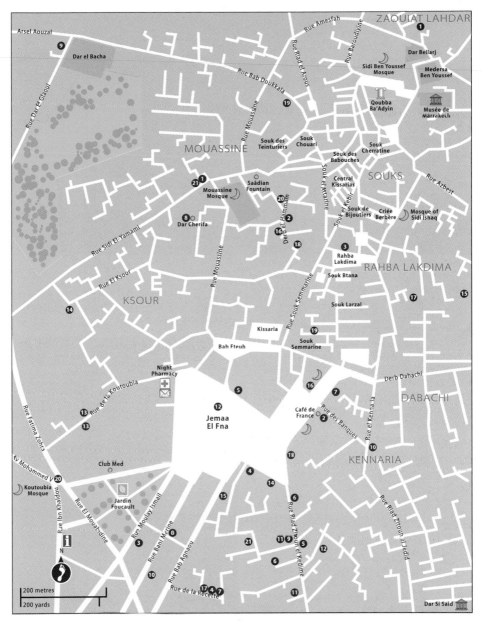

ZAOUIAT LAHDAR

Arset Aouzal

Dar el Bacha

Rue Dar El Ghoui

Rue Bab Doukkala

Rue Amesfah

Rue Riad el Arous

Rue Baroudyine

Dar Bellarj

Sidi Ben Youssef
Mosque

Medersa
Ben Youssef

Qoubba
Ba'Adyin

Musée de
Marrakech

Rue Mouassine

MOUASSINE

Souk des
Teinturiers

Souk
Chouari

Souk
Cherratine

Souk des
Babouches

SOUKS

Rue Azbest

Saâdian
Fountain

Mouassine
Mosque

Central
Kissarias

Souk el Kebir

Souk de
Bijoutiers

Criée
Berbère

Mosque of
Sidi Ishaq

Dar Cherifa

Derb el Hammam

Rue Sidi El Yamami

Rahba
Lakdima

RAHBA LAKDIMA

Rue El Ksour

Rue Mouassine

Souk Btana

KSOUR

Souk Larzal

Rue Souk Semmarine

Kissaria

Souk
Semmarine

Bab Fteuh

Derb Dahachi

Night
Pharmacy

DABACHI

Rue de la Koutoubia

Jemaa
El Fna

Café de
France

Rue des Banques

Rue el Kennaria

Rue Fatima Zohra

KENNARIA

Club Med

Av Mohammed V

Koutoubia
Mosque

Jardin
Foucault

Rue El Mouahidine

Rue Moulay Ismail

Rue Bani Marine

Rue Riad Zitoun el Kedime

Rue Riad Zitoun el Jedid

Rue Ibn Khaldoun

N

Rue Bab Agnaou

200 metres

200 yards

Rue de la Recette

Dar Si Said

against this apparent simplicity, is all decoration and variety – and very much in keeping with the elaborate taste of Ummayad Spain. The original *minbar*, recently restored, can be viewed at the Badi Palace (see page 95). Both prayer hall and chair were to be a source of inspiration for later generations of builders and decorators.

To the west of the mosque, the floral **Jardins de la Koutoubia** are open to all and are a pretty spot from which to view the mosque.

## Souks

Map: Jemaa El Fna & the Souks, p81.

Marrakech's huge network of colourful street markets, or souks, lies to the north of Jemaa El Fna. With flickering slivers of sunshine filtering down through the slatted sunshades and donkeys and motorbikes pushing through the massed ranks of shoppers and sellers, a day perusing the treasures in the city's bazaar is one of the great Moroccan pleasures.

Nominally the souks are separated into distinct areas, each specializing in certain goods; in reality this isn't clearly observed: leather goods, for example, can be found just about everywhere. However, some areas do retain their original function.

## Tip...

Stalls in the souks tend to close down around midday on Friday for prayers.

Top: Souks. Above: Babouches for sale in the souks.

Bab Fteuh is an open space just to the north of Jemaa El Fna, usually filled with men resting in their handcarts, waiting for business. The central route through the souks is Rue Semarine; useful for orientation, it runs fairly straight north-south from the eastern end of Bab Fteuh up to the Medersa Ben Youssef. At the western end of Bab Fteuh, Rue Mouassine is another useful route, skirting the western edge of the souks. Finally, on the eastern side, Rue Rahba Kedima, starting near the Mosquee Quessabine arm of Jemaa El Fna, is another possible route north to the medersa.

Souk Semmarine is a busy place, originally the textiles market, and although there are a number of large, expensive tourist shops, there are still some cloth sellers. To the left is a covered *kissaria* selling clothes. The first turning on the right leads past **Souk Larzal**, a wool market, and **Souk Btana**, a sheepskin market, to the attractive open space of **Rahba Kedima**, the old corn market, also known as the Place des Epices. There's a good café overlooking the square (see page 126) and stalls selling a range of hats, traditional cures and cosmetics, spices and cheap jewellery. Around the edge are some good carpet shops and other places piled high with cages containing chameleons and other assorted reptiles. Walk back onto the main souk past the bank machine in the corner of the square. Here the souk forks into **Souk Stailia** on the left and **Souk el Kebir** on the right.

To the right of Souk el Kebir is the **Criée Berbère**, where carpets and *jallabahs* are sold. This was where slaves – men, women and children – mainly from the Sahara, were auctioned until the French occupation in 1912. Further on is the **Souk des Bijoutiers**, with jewellery. To the left (west) of Souk el Kebir is a network of small alleys, the *kissarias*, selling various goods. Immediately north of the *kissarias* is the **Souk Cherratine**, with leather goods; a good place to bargain for camelskin bags, purses and belts.

To the west of the *kissarias* is the colourful **Souk Smata** (you'll also reach it by taking the left-hand Souk Stailia at the fork by Rahba Kedima), centre of Marrakech's *babouches* industry. The ubiquitous leather slippers are the souks' iconic product and this is probably the best place to buy them, if you can face the task of choosing a colour and style from the enormous selection on offer. Parallel to Souk Smata to the north is Souk el Attarine, the spice and perfume souk. Heading west along Souk el Attarine brings you to one of the souks' great sights, the **Souk des Teinturiers**, or dyers' market, where wool recently dyed is draped over the walkways to dry.

Continuing past the skeins of wool brings you out of the souks at the Saadian **Fontaine Mouassine**, one of the medina's most beautiful fountains, and the 16th-century **Mosquée Mouassine**. This important mosque gives its name to this part of the medina.

North of the Souk el Attarine is the carpenters' **Souk Chouari**, one of many specialist areas in the tight northern souks that include ironworkers in Souk Haddadine, musical instruments in Souk Kimakhine and lanterns in Souk Jdid. This area of the souks, furthest from Jemaa El Fna, is one of the best places to see craftsmen at work behind their stalls.

Before leaping into impulse purchases in the souks, it may be a good idea to get an idea of prices in shops in Guéliz, or in the Ensemble Artisanal on Mohamed V. Many people, however, get overly obsessed about getting a bargain; ultimately, the good price is the one you are happy to pay.

## Fondouks

Map: Jemaa El Fna & the Souks, p81.

Around the northern souks are many old *fondouks*. Originally these were inns, with bedrooms on the upper floors, and often stalls set up on the ground floor where passing tradesmen could sell their wares. Handsome old buildings, some have been restored and now house craft workshops. There are several around the junction of Rue Dar El Bacha and Rue Mouassine (including the Fondouk Kharbouch and Fondouk Almisane) and several more on Rue de Souk des Fassis, to the east of the medersa, where you'll also find Le Foundouk restaurant (see page 123). Visitors are usually free to look in.

## Around the city

### Medersa Ben Youssef

Daily 0900-1830. 40dh, 60dh with the Museum
and Qoubba.
Map: Jemaa El Fna & the Souks, p81.

The city's most beautiful and most important
Islamic monument, the 16th-century Medersa Ben
Youssef is one of the few Islamic buildings open
to the general public. Restored by the Fondation
Ben Jelloun it is now Marrakech's architectural
highlight. Cool, calm corridors, beautiful arches,
*zellij* tiles and the light reflecting in the central
pool make it a breathtaking place to visit.

Functioning as a boarding school for students
of the religious sciences and law, and attached to
the mosque of the same name, in its current
incarnation it was founded in 1564-65 by the
Saadian Sultan Moulay Abdellah on the site of a
previous 14th-century Merinid medersa. Though
the name translates as 'school', it is likely that most
lectures were carried out at the adjoining mosque.

Centred around a square courtyard containing a
rectangular pool and with arcades on two sides, it is
influenced by Moorish Andalucían architecture and

Above and top: Medersa Ben Youssef. Opposite page: Musée de Marrakech.

At the far end is the prayer hall covered with an eight-sided wooden dome. Beneath the dome plaster open-work windows illuminate the tilework. In the *qibla* wall is a five-sided *mihrab* indicating the direction of prayer. The stalactite ceiling of the *mihrab* and the carved stucco walls with pine cone motif are particularly impressive. The inscription here, dedicated to the Sultan, translates as: "I was constructed as a place of learning and prayer by the Prince of the Faithful, the descendant of the seal of the prophets, Abdellah, the most glorious of all Caliphs. Pray for him, all who enter here, so that his greatest hopes may be realized." The massive marble columns are carved out of Italian Carrara marble.

On the way out of the medersa, a visit to the toilets on the right of the vestibule reveals another elaborate stalactite design on the ceiling.

### Musée de Marrakech

*Place Ben Youssef, T0524-441893, museedemarrakech.ma.*
Daily 0900-1830. 40dh, 60dh with the medersa and Qoubba. Map: Jemaa El Fna & the Souks, p81.

In Dar M'nebhi, the early 20th-century palace of a former Moroccan minister of war, the setting of Marrakech's museum is more spectacular than its contents. After the entrance courtyard, a narrow corridor takes you into the exhibition areas proper. The simple whitewashed walls of the domestic wing shelter temporary exhibitions of contemporary art. Large pieces here are often striking, though quality varies. The main courtyard is protected by a plexi-glass roof that bathes the place in a strangely yellow light. Under this hangs a brass chandelier the size of a small spaceship, and there are plenty of nooks and comfortable seats in which to rest. A handful of photos of old Morocco have an air of abandonment, with cracked glass and skewed mounts cut from crumpled corrugated card. Rooms behind the main courtyard display Koran manuscripts, coins, ceramics and textiles. The Fes pottery is most impressive, dating from the 18th to the 20th century. Semi-abstracted fruit and flower motifs are mixed with geometric patterns in

# Marrakech for kids

There's plenty to entertain children in Marrakech, from the Jemaa El Fna snake charmers to acrobats that will come somersaulting your way the moment you sit outside at a restaurant. But there's little that's specifically designed for kids.

A day out at a pool outside the city (Oasiria is especially good for kids, see page 104) is a good bet, and a trip to the mountains provides some needed space. Ice creams at **Venezia Ice** (see page 128) near Jemaa El Fna and fresh orange juice are good for flagging limbs in the heat.

A horse-drawn *calèche* tour of the city walls is a good way to see something without the scrum of street level and there are camels that can ridden through the palm groves (see page 101).

**Families Worldwide** (T+44(0)845-051 4567, familiesworldwide.co.uk) specialize in organizing family trips to the Atlas and the Desert.

# Tip…

"Mister, mister, this way is closed" is a common cry of children in the Marrakech medina. It's usually untrue and a precursor to taking you a long way around and charging you for the privilege.

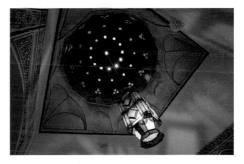

yellows and greens. The elaborate wooden façades in the rooms on the left show Portuguese influence. A small passageway to the left of the main reception room takes you through to the restored hammam. In front of the museum in the courtyard is a good café and a bookshop.

Above and right: Qoubba Ba'Adyin. Opposite page: Dar Cherifa.

## Qoubba Ba'Adyin

*Place Ben Youssef.*
Daily 0900-1830, 40dh, 60dh with the Museum
and medersa. There is a rather bureaucratic
enforcement of the order in which you see the
three Islamic monuments and the Qoubba
should be the last of the three.
Map: Jemaa El Fna & the Souks, p81.

Protected by wrought-iron railings, the 11th-
century Almoravid Qoubba (Qoubba Ba'Adyin) is
the only complete Almoravid building surviving in
Morocco. The Qoubba dates from the reign of Ali
bin Youssef (1107-1143), and perhaps formed part
of the toilet and ablutions facilities of the mosque
that at the time existed nearby. At first glance it is
a simple building, with a dome surmounting a
square stone and brick structure. However, the
dome has a design of interlocking arches, plus a
star and chevron motif on top. The arches leading

into the Qoubba are different on each side. Climb down the stairs to view the ceiling of the dome, and you will begin to appreciate the architectural significance of the building, with its range of Almoravid motifs, including the pine cone and acanthus. Around the corniche is a dedicatory inscription in cursive script. Set into the floor is a small, almost square, basin. Finely proportioned, the building has many elements that became the standards of subsequent eras.

Standing with the Almoravid Qoubba behind you, the minaret of the large 12th-century Ben Youssef Mosque, rebuilt in the 19th century, is clearly visible.

### Dar Bellarj

*9 Toulalat Zaouiat Lahdar, T0524-444555.*
0900-1800, free.
Map: Jemaa El Fna & the Souks, p81.

Turning right out of the medersa, a brass sign indicates the entrance of Dar Bellarj, 'the House of Storks', on your left. The 1930s building, around a beautiful large, bright and open courtyard, was restored by Swiss artists. Previously there was a fondouk on the site, housing a hospital for birds. Today, the building, austerely but simply refurbished, houses a cultural foundation and is used as a gallery space for well-meaning but rather dull contemporary arts and displays. There are places to sit and contemplate and coffee and tea is also for sale.

### Dar Cherifa

*8 Derb Charfa Lakbir Mouassine, off Rue Mouassine, T0524-426463, marrakech-riads.net.*
Daily 0900-1900.
Map: Jemaa El Fna & the Souks, p81.

A magically beautiful and peaceful place, Dar Cherifa is both a literary café (see page 127) and a fantastic contemporary art space. Wind down narrow alleyways off Rue Mouassine and knock on the door to be let in. Exhibitions of mostly local contemporary art are held downstairs and the café extends onto the roof terrace. The riad, one of the city's oldest,

dates back to Saadian times, and has been wonderfully restored by Abdelatif Ben Abdellah, one of the key figures behind the rejuvenation of the medina. The soaring courtyard is one of the finest examples of Islamic architecture in Marrakech.

### Sidi Bel Abbes

Map: Marrakech, F1, p72.

North of the Medersa Ben Youssef are quiet residential neighbourhoods where you will see few tourists. Built on an area of former orchards and market gardens, it is a more recent area of the medina, incorporated in the 18th century. Beyond the open square of **Bab Taghzaoute** is the **Zaouïa of Sidi Bel Abbes**. Usually considered the most important of the seven saints of Marrakech, and sometimes the patron saint of the city itself, Bel Abbes was born in Ceuta in 1130. He championed the cause of the blind in Marrakech and was patronized by Sultan Yaqoub al Mansour. You are free to wander through the religious complex, though non-Muslims are barred from the mausoleum. It's a striking place, with bright squares and shady alleyways. A series of arches is filled with potted plants and blind people chatting and waiting to receive food and alms. Nearby is the **Zaouïa of Sidi Ben Slimane el Jazouli**, a 14th-century sufi.

## Around the city

### Tanneries near Bab Debbagh

Map: Marrkech, H2, p72.

The tanneries near Bab Debbagh ('Tanners' Gate') are one of the most interesting (if smelly) sites in Marrakech. Wandering towards the tanners' area, you will almost certainly be approached by someone who will offer to show you the tanneries – it's possible to see them without a guide, but easier with. Agree a price first and beware of excessive demands. You will be given a rather ineffective sprig of mint to hold to your nostrils to mask the stink and led through a small door into an area of foul-smelling pits, where men tread and rinse skins in nauseous liquids and dyes. In small lean-to buildings, you will find other artisans scraping and stretching the skins.

Located close to the seasonal water from the river, the Oued Issil, the odorous tanners were kept on the edge of the city with plenty of water and space to expand away from residential areas. Tanning in Marrakech is still a pre-industrial process, alive and functioning not far from the heart of the medina – even though the traditional dyes have largely been replaced with chemical products.

You may be told that there are two tanneries: one Arab, the other Berber. In fact there are several, and workforces are fairly ethnically mixed. There do remain specialities, however, with one set of tanners working mainly on the more difficult cow and camel skins, and the others on goat and sheep skins. You can get a view of the area from leather shop terraces next to Bab Debbagh – again you will be charged for the privilege.

### Ramparts & gates

Map: Marrakech, p72.

The extensive ramparts of Marrakech, stretching for 16 km around the medina, were mostly built by the Almoravids in the 12th century, although they have been extensively restored since. The reconstruction is a continual process as the *pisé*-cement walls, made of the red earth of the Haouz plains, gradually crumble. A ride in a horse-drawn *calèche* is a good way to see the ramparts; much of the route is now planted with rose gardens.

**Located close to the seasonal water from the river, the Oued Issil, the odorous tanners were kept on the edge of the city with plenty of water and space to expand away from residential areas.**

Grand gates punctuate the wall, including **Bab Rob**, near the buses and grands taxi on the southwest side of the medina. From the Almohad era, it is named after the grape juice which at one time was brought through this gate. **Bab Dabbagh** (the Tanners' gate, on the east side) is an intricate defensive gate with a twisted entrance route and wooden gates, which could shut off the various parts of the building for security. **Bab el Khemis**, on the northeast side, opens into the Souk el Khemis (Thursday market) and an important area of mechanics and craftsmen. Check out the junk

market here on a Sunday morning. There is a small saint's tomb inside the gate building. **Bab Doukkala**, on the northwest side by the bus station, is a large gate with a horseshoe arch and two towers. The medina side has a horseshoe arch and a cusped, blind arch, with a variation on the *darj w ktaf* (step and shoulder) motif along the top. A newer road across the palm grove north of Bab Doukkala completes the circuit of the ramparts.

**Bab Rob.**

# Virgins, death & pigeon poo

### Founding myths

The tanners are said to have been the first to settle in Marrakech at its foundation and a gate is named after them, the only one to be named for a craft corporation. 'Bab Debbagh, bab deheb' – 'Tanners' Gate, gold gate' – the old adage goes, in reference to the tanners' prosperity. One legend says that seven virgins are buried in the foundations of the gate (sisters of the seven protector saints of Marrakech) and women who desire a child should offer them candles and henna. Another story claims that Bab Debbagh is inhabited by Malik Gharub, a genie who dared to lead a revolt against Sidna Suleyman, the Black King, only to be condemned to tan a cowhide and cut out *belgha* soles for eternity as punishment.

The tannery was considered a dangerous place – as it was the entrance to the domain of the Other Ones, and a beneficial one, since skins were a symbol of preservation and fertility. Bab Debbagh is the eastern gate into the city, and there was a symbolism based on the sun rising in the east and skin being reborn as leather. The tanners, because they spend their days in pits working the skins, were said to be in contact with the unseen world of the dead; they were also seen as masters of fertility, being strong men, capable of giving a second life to dry, dead skin.

### Cycles & processes

The traditional process of tanning starts with soaking the skins in a sort of swamp – or *iferd* – in the middle of the tannery, filled with a fermenting mixture of pigeon poo and tannery waste. Fermenting lasts three days in

Above: Skins laid out to dry.

Tanneries at Dar Debbagh, Marrakech.

summer, six in winter. Then the skins are squeezed out and put to dry. Hair is scraped off before the skins go into a pit of lime and argan-kernel ash. This removes any remaining flesh or hair, and prepares the skin to receive the tanning products. The lime bath lasts 15-20 days in summer, up to 30 in winter.

Next the skins are washed energetically, trodden to remove any lime, and any extra bits are cut off. Next the skins spend 24 hours in a *qasriya*, a round pit of more pigeon poo and fresh water. At this stage the skin becomes thinner and stretches. There follows soaking in wheat fibre and salt, for 24 hours, to remove any traces of lime and guano.

Then begins the actual tanning process. Traditional tanneries used only plants – roots, barks and certain seeds and fruits. In Marrakech, acacia and oak bark are used, along with *takkut*, the ground-up fruit of the tamarisk. A water and tannin mix is prepared in a pit, and the skins get three soakings.

After this, the skins have to be prepared to receive the dye. They are scraped with pottery shards, beaten and coated with oil, alum and water. Then they are dyed by hand, with the dye traditionally being poured out of a bull's horn, and left to dry in the sun. The characteristic yellow of leather for belgha slippers is traditionally derived from pomegranates. Finally, the skins are worked to make them smoother and more supple, stretched between two ropes and worked on smooth pottery surfaces.

## Tanning symbolism

The process of tanning skins is strongly symbolic – the tanners say that the skin eats, drinks, sleeps and 'is born of the water'. When the skin is treated with lime, it is said to be thirsty; when it is treated with pigeon poo, it is said to receive *nafs*, a spirit. The *merkel* (treading) stage prepares the skin to live again, while the *takkut* of the tanning mixture is also used by women to dye their hair. At this point, the skin receives *ruh* (breath). Leather is thus born from the world of the dead and the *ighariyin*, the people of the grotto, and is fertilized in the swampy pool, the domain of the dead.

# Southern medina

South of Jemaa El Fna the character of the medina changes somewhat: it is a more varied part of the city, with swanky palaces old and new interspersed with narrow, dirty streets and snippets of modernity. Rue de Bab Agnaou and Rue Ben Marine are busy, pedestrianized streets filled with banks, shops and glitz. To the east, Rue Riad Zitoun El Khedim and Rue Riad Zitoun El Jedid are long and unusually straight roads with more in common with the northern medina. Two museums devoted to Moroccan artistry, Dar Si Said and Maison Tiskiwin, both in attractive traditional settings, sit close together at the southern end of Riad Zitoun el Jedid. Beyond are the sparkling spaces of the Bahia palace and the crumbling openness of the El Badi palace. The nearby Saadian tombs are an intricately filigree example of aristocratic Moroccan design, whereas the attractively dishevelled Mellah area retains some of its poor Jewish roots, complete with synagogues and a large Jewish cemetery.

## Dar Si Said

*T0524-442464.*
Wed-Mond 0900-1200, 1600-2100 summer,
1430-1800 winter, 30dh.
Map: Marrakech, G5, p72.

Built by Si Said, Visir under Moulay El Hassan and half-brother of Ba Ahmed Ben Moussa (the former slave who built the nearby Palais de la Bahia, see below), Dar Si Said is a late 19th-century palace housing the Museum of Moroccan Arts and Crafts. The palace itself makes a visit worthwhile: an intimate and ornately decorated place, it has two storeys with rooms around arcaded courtyards.

The collection includes pottery, jewellery, leatherwork and Chichaoua carpets. It is particularly strong on Amazigh artefacts such as curved daggers, copperware and jewellery. On the first floor is a salon with Hispano-Moorish decoration and cedarwood furniture, while around the Andalucían-influenced garden courtyard you'll find old window and door frames. Look out for a primitive four-seater wooden ferris wheel of the type still found in *moussems* (country fairs) in Morocco.

Other highlights include a large 10th-century carved marble bath for ablutions, the carved cedar, octagonally domed ceiling in the reception room, and antique carpets from the Atlas.

## Maison Tiskiwin

*8 Rue de la Bahia, T0524-389192.*
15dh. Map: Marrakech, G5, p72.

Between the Dar Si Said and the Bahia Palace, a few streets further south is the fantastic Maison Tiskiwin (the House of the Horns), home to a fine collection of items related to Northern African and Saharan culture and society. This small museum was lovingly put together by the Dutch art historian Bert Flint, who still lives here, though he has given the museum to Marrakech University. Flint still spends some of the year travelling and gathering objects to add to the collection and there is a strong sense of enthusiasm for the artefacts here, in strong contrast to some of the state-run museums. There are crafts

from the Rif and the High Atlas, though the collection focuses primarily on the Sahara, and includes jewellery and costumes, musical instruments, carpets and furniture. The building itself, around a courtyard, is an authentic and well-maintained example of a traditional riad. There are excellent and copious notes in English. Groups tend to visit in the morning – if you go along in the afternoon you may get the museum all to yourself. Don't miss the beautiful Saharan leatherwork.

## Palais de la Bahia

*T0524-389221.*
Sat-Thu 0845-1145 and 1445-1745, Fri 0845-1130 and 1500-1745. 10dh.
Map: Marrakech, G5, p72.

Further to the south is the Bahia Palace (the name means 'brilliant'). It was built in the last years of the 19th century by the Vizir Ba Ahmed Ben Moussa, or

Palais de la Bahia.

## Around the city

Bou Ahmed, a former slave who rose to a position of power under sultans Moulay Hassan and Abd el-Aziz. Sunlight shines through wrought-iron bars creating beautiful patterns on the *zellij* tiles, and in the courtyard water ripples over green tiles around a beautiful fountain, surrounded by trees. There are tour groups, but there are also plenty of quiet corners in which lingering until they've passed is a pleasure. The palace is a maze of patios planted with fruit trees, passageways and empty chambers with painted ceilings. Guides will tell you that each wife and concubine had a room looking onto the patio. The story goes that Bou Ahmed was so

**Palais de la Bahia.**

hated that, on his death in 1900, his palace was looted and his possessions stolen by slaves, servants and members of his *harem*. Subsequently, the building was occupied by the French authorities. Bareness is still a feature of the palace, but it is one that accentuates the beauty of the architecture and space.

### Mellah

Map: Marrakech, G6, p72.

One of the city's most labyrinthine areas, the tight, enclosed streets of the Mellah are an atmospheric part of Marrakech, where riads and gentrification are only starting to make low-key inroads. South of the Bahia and east of the El Badi Palace, the *mellah*, or Jewish neighbourhood, was created in 1558. The second such area in Morocco, it was set up at around the same time as the ghetto in Rome. Despite the similarities of separation along religious lines, Moroccan Islamic attitudes seem to have been generally more tolerant towards Judaism than those in Christian Europe. Today the Jewish community has all but vanished, but there remain some signs to tell you of its former role in the life of Marrakech – many of the tall houses have distinctive enclosed balconies overlooking the narrow streets and you may be able to find some Hebrew lettering here and there. At one time there were many thousands of Jewish people living here, with several synagogues, and under the control of the rabbis, the area had considerable autonomy. Until the 1930s there were only two doors out into the rest of the medina. It's hard to get far down a Mellah street without someone offering to show you one of the synagogues. It's worth a visit, but agree a price first and expect double "donation to the synagogue"/"donation for the guide" requests. There are probably fewer than 150 practising Jewish people left in the Mellah and the remaining synagogues can be rather sad places, though the oldest, **Synagogue Lazama** (Sun-Fri), is still well looked after, with potted plants in its blue-painted and tiled courtyard.

## Tip...

Taxis can't get to most of the medina. Good places to catch taxis or be dropped off include Dar El Bacha, Bab Taghzout and Palais de la Bahia.

Miaâra Jewish cemetery.

## Miaâra Jewish cemetery

*Rue Iman El Khezoli.*
Sun-Fri approximately 0630-1900.
Map: Marrakech, H5, p72.

To the east of the Mellah, two friendly brothers act as caretakers for the city's 17th-century Jewish cemetery. Visitors are welcome to wander among the old stones and the caretaker may also tell you about Jewish life in Marrakech. You'll probably find a dog or two lazing atop the weather-worn tombstones and shrines. It's a strangely affecting place: a bubble of complete calm around which the medina and the mountains crowd, it feels a little like a remnant of a lost civilisation. The smaller stones mark the resting places of children.

## Place des Ferblantiers & around

Map: Marrakech, G5/6, p72.

The traditional hub of the city's metalworkers, this square was once known as the Place du Mellah and was a part of the Jewish souk. These days, roses and lantern makers line its sides. Bar and restaurant Kosybar (see page 128) has an upstairs terrace that makes a good viewing platform from which to look down on the action below.

The **Grand Bijouterie**, the jewellery souk, is just to the northwest of the square, facing the entrance to the Palais de la Bahia. Its elaborate and glittering silver and gold are in marked contrast to the largely run-down Mellah. Other notable retail-based sights nearby include the dingy market stalls of **Souk Hay Essalam**, piled high with spices and cheap plastic tat (the entrance is directly opposite the jewellery souk) and, to the west, the **Marché Couverte**, the place to go should you want to purchase a live chicken.

## Palais El Badi

0830-1145 and 1430-1745 (Ramadan 0900-1600), 10dh plus another 10dh to see the Koutoubia minbar. Map: Marrakech, G6, p72.

The huge barren spaces of the ruined 16th-century El Badi Palace come as a bit of a shock after the cramped streets of the Marrakech medina. Orange trees grow in what were once enormous pools in the central courtyard, and storks nest noisily on the ruined walls. For five days in July, El Badi comes alive for the annual **Festival National des Arts Populaires** (see page 47). Most of the year, however, it is a quiet sort of place, the high thick walls protecting the vast courtyard from the noise of the surrounding streets.

The palace was built by the Saadian Sultan Ahmed al Mansur ed-Dahbi (the Golden) between 1578 and 1593, following his accession after his victory over the Portuguese at the Battle of the Three Kings at Ksar el Kebir in northern Morocco. It marks the height of Saadian power, the centrepiece of an imperial capital. In its day it was a lavish display of the best craftsmanship of the period, using the most expensive materials, including gold, marble and onyx. The colonnades were of marble, apparently exchanged with Italian merchants for their equivalent weight in sugar.

The palace was largely destroyed in the 17th century by Moulay Ismaïl, who stripped it of its decorations and fittings and carried them off to Meknès. No austere royal fortress, the Badi was probably a palace for audiences – and it was at one of these great court ceremonies that the building's fate was predicted: "What do you think of this palace?" asked the sultan El-Mansour. "When it is demolished, it will make a big pile of earth", replied a visionary. El-Mansour is said to have felt a chill sense of foreboding.

The ruins on either side of the courtyard were probably summer houses, the one at the far end being called the **Koubba el Khamsiniya** (The Fifty Pavillion) after either the 50 cubits of its area, or the fact that it once had fifty columns.

The complex contains a small museum which includes the restored *minbar* (the sacred staired Islamic equivalent of a pulpit, from which the Imam delivers sermons) from the Koutoubia Mosque. Mark Minor, one of the conservators from the Metropolitan Museum of Art in New York who carried out the restoration, called it "one of the finest works of art in wood created by mankind". Constructed in Cordoba in Spain in 1139, it is covered in around 100 carvings. The minbar remained in use until 1962. The scattered ruins of the palace, with odd fragments of decoration amidst the debris, also include stables and dungeons.

## Palais Royal Dar El Makhzen

Map: Marrakech, G6/7, p72.

To the south of the El Badi Palace is the **Dar el Makhzen**, the modern-day Royal Palace, one of the late King Hassan II's favourite residences. It is closed to the public, however, and out of favour with the current king, who has had a new palace constructed, close to the Hotel Mamounia.

## Kasbah

*Follow Rue Bab Agnaou south from Jemaa El Fna, or enter the medina at Bab Rob.*
Map: Marrakech, F7, p72.

**Bab Agnaou**, meaning the gate of the black people, marks the entrance to the Kasbah quarter from the west. The 12th-century gate is one of the city's most handsome, as well as one of its oldest structures. The Kasbah quarter dates from the reign of the Almohad Sultan Ya'qub al Mansour. The gateway was probably decorative rather than defensive, and would once have had a tower at each side, marking the entrance to the Almohad palace. It is surrounded by a series of arches within a rectangle of floral designs, with a shell or palmette in each corner and an outer band of Kufic inscription.

The road from the gate leads to Rue de la Kasbah, on which is the much restored **El Mansour**, or Kasbah Mosque, built at the end of the 12th century. It is one of the few remaining Almohad structures in the city, though rebuilding has given it a rather modern appearance. The minaret has original Almohad motifs on a background of green tiles, above which is a band of coloured tiles. The three balls on top are commonly known as the golden apples, though they are actually made of brass. The entrance to the Tombeaux Saadians (see opposite) is directly to the right of the mosque.

## Tip...

Popular sites in Marrakech, such as the Tombeaux Saadiens and the Jardin Majorelle, tend to have a lull in crowds around lunchtime, as groups head off to lunch.

## Tombeaux Saadiens

0830-1145 and 1430-1745
(Ramadan 0900-1600), 10dh.
Map: Marrakech, F6, p72.

The unrestrainedly opulent 16th-century
Saadian Tombs were discovered thanks to aerial
photography in 1917. The final resting place of the
Saadian family, a dynasty from the Draa valley that
came to rule Morocco, the tombs were sealed
off by Moulay Ismaïl in the 17th century in a vain
attempt to condemn the Saadian rulers to oblivion.
The claustrophobically narrow passage that leads
to the tombs still emphasizes their hidden past.

Inside there are two mausoleums, containing a
series of chambers set around a small garden and
intricately decorated with an extraordinary

**Below: Saadian Tombs.**
**Opposite page: Flower heads being dried in the Kasbah.**

profusion of Italian Carrara marble, carved
cedar and plasterwork. A contrast to the much
simpler Almohad style, the tombs contain some
of Morocco's most striking Islamic architecture.

The *mihrab* (the niche indicating the direction
of Mecca) in the first burial chamber is particularly
impressive, supported by fine white marble columns.
In this first room is the tomb of Prince Moulay Yazid.
Known as the mad sultan, he was shot in the head by
an uprising in 1792 and was the last to be buried here,
after the tombs had been sealed off. The room was
probably a prayer room before being used for burials.

The elaborate, domed second room is known
as the Hall of 12 Columns and contains the central
tomb of Ahmed al Mansour himself, the most
famous of the Saadi rulers (1578-1603). Either side
lie his descendants. It is a dramatic space, faintly lit
from above, with beautiful *zellij* tiling.

The second, older and plainer mausoleum was
built by Ahmed al Mansour for the tombs of his
mother, Lalla Messaouda, and Mohamed esh
Sheikh, founder of the Saadians. In the slightly
dilapidated garden and courtyard are the tombs of
more than 100 other princelings and members of
court. Try to visit early in the day as the place can
get overcrowded with tour groups.

### Jardins de la Mamounia

*Av Bab Jedid, T0524-388600, mamounia.com.*
Map: Marrakech, D5, p72.

Not just any old five-star hotel, La Mamounia
(see page 114) is a byword for Moroccan opulence.
After a long refurbishment it reopened in 2009,
its 1920s Art Deco style spruced up for the 21st
century. The 13 ha of formal walled gardens,
beloved of Winston Churchill, give their name
to the hotel. Once royal playgrounds, they were
given as an 18th-century wedding gift to Prince
Moulay Mamoun by his father, King Sidi Mohamed
Ben Abdellahand. The pavilion here is older, dating
back as far as the Saadian empire in the 16th
century. To the southwest of the Koutoubia, just
inside the city walls, the gardens can be visited if
you're smartly dressed and pop in for a pot of tea.

# Ville nouvelle & the gardens

Guéliz, the suburb laid out by the French in the 1920s, is a world apart from the medina. All glossy new apartment buildings and traffic, there are few sights but it is worth a wander for its cafés, upmarket boutiques and food market and it has many of the city's best restaurants. Moroccans dressed in smart Western clothes promenade up and down the main thoroughfare of Avenue Mohamed V in the evenings and lounge over long cups of coffee outside streetside cafés. There's a refreshing absence of hassle, but at times it's also easy to forget that you're in Morocco at all.

To the south, Hivernage offers a bigger, brasher version of the same, with wider streets and large hotels interspersed with occasional cafés, cocktail bars and casinos.

One of the most distinctive features of Marrakech is its gardens, and three in particular, around the peripheries of the city centre, are worth visiting.

## Guéliz

Map: Marrakech, A2, p72.

For a few remnants of French colonial architecture and a taste of a modern, buzzing Moroccan cityscape, Guéliz is worth a visit, though there are not really any conventional sights. Cafés and restaurants abound, however, and it's the place to come for many of the city's designer boutiques and commercial contemporary galleries (see page 100). Place du 16 Novembre is where the busiest roads (Avenue Mohamed V and Avenue Hassan II) converge; the most interesting parts of Guéliz are to the north of here, as is the Marché Municipale, a market with food stalls. The new, Charles Boccara-designed Théâtre Royal, opposite the (even newer) train station, is worth a look – work on the place seems to have stalled but the guardian will probably be happy to show you around. The building is a good example of the incorporation of traditional Moroccan elements into contemporary architecture.

## Jardin Majorelle

*Avenue Yakoub El Mansour, jardinmajorelle.com.*
Jun-Sep 0800-1800, Oct-May 0800-1700, 30dh, plus 15dh for the museum.
Map: Marrakech, D1, p72.

A small tropical garden, this verdant splash of colour was first laid out by a French artist, Louis Majorelle, in 1924. A member of a family of

Jardin Majorelle.

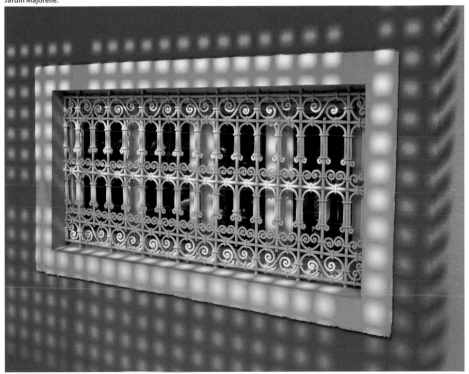

# Marrakech galleries

Away from the kitsch tourist-focused art of noble-savage blue-clothed figures standing, staff in hand, in orange desertscapes, the city has a burgeoning contemporary art scene, with abstract and semi-abstract painting and some interesting photography. The following galleries, all in Guéliz, are some of the best, though Dar Cherifa (see page 87) also has excellent contemporary art shows. Those in the Musée de Marrakech (see page 85) are more mixed.

### Galerie 127
*2nd floor, 127 Ave Mohamed V, T0524-432667.*
Tue-Sat 1400-1900.
One of only a handful of photography galleries in Africa, this place features many French as well as local photographers.

### Galerie Bleue
*119 Blvd Mohamed V, T0666-192129.*
Daily 1000-1300 and 1600-2000.
This gallery showcases French and Moroccan contemporary artists, with mostly figurative painting.

### Galerie Rê
*Résidence Al Andalous III, Angle Rues de la Mosquée et 3 Ibn Toumert, T0524-432258, galerie-re.com.*
Mon-Sat 1000-1300 and 1500-2000.
A wide, light space with metal stairs leading to a mezzanine, with exhibitions of mainly abstract Moroccan art.

### Matisse Art Gallery
*43 Passage Ghandouri, off 61 Rue de Yougoslavie, T0674-927925, matisse-art-gallery.com.*
Daily 0930-1230 and 1530-1930.
Rotating exhibitions of Moroccan painters and calligraphic artists in a high-ceilinged, white-walled gallery hidden away in the middle of a Guéliz block.

**The cacti are large and sculptural and strong colours and forms dominate the garden, especially the walls, buildings and plant pots, which are a particularly vivid shade of cobalt blue.**

cabinet-makers from Nancy who made their money with innovative art nouveau furniture, Majorelle portrayed the landscapes and people of the High Atlas in large, colourful paintings, some of which were used for tourism posters. The carefully restored garden belonged to Yves St Laurent, whose ashes were scattered here after his death in 2008. The cacti are large and sculptural and strong colours and forms dominate the garden, especially the walls, buildings and plant pots, which are a particularly vivid shade of cobalt blue. Bulbuls, monogamous songbirds often compared to nightingales, sing in the bamboo thickets and flit between the Washingtonia palms. A green-roofed garden pavilion houses the small **Musée d'Art Islamique** with a fine and easily digestible collection of North African art and objects from the personal collections of Pierre Bergé and Yves St Laurent, as well as works by Majorelle himself. The gardens are one of the city's most popular sights – try to visit early, late or at lunchtime to avoid the worst of the crowds.

### Jardins de l'Agdal

Map: Marrakech, H7, p72.

The large, tree-filled Agdal Gardens, stretching south of the medina, were established in the 12th century under Abd el-Moumen, and were expanded and reorganized by the Saadians. The vast expanse, over 400 ha, includes several pools, and extensive areas of olive, orange and pomegranate trees. They are usually closed when the king is in residence, but parts can be visited at other times. Of the pavilions, the **Dar al-Baida** was used by Sultan Moulay Hassan to house his harem.

The largest pool, **Sahraj el Hana**, receives occasional coachloads of tourists, but at other times is a pleasant place to relax. As with the other gardens, swimming, however, is not allowed.

## Ménara Gardens

Map: Marrakech, A7, p72.

From the medina and the Agdal Gardens, Avenue de la Ménara leads to the Ménara Gardens, a large olive grove centring on a rectangular pool. The green-tiled pavilion beside the pool was originally built by the Saadian dynasty in the 16th century, and was renovated in 1869 by Sultan Abderrahmane. With palm trees and the Atlas Mountains as a backdrop, it is one of the city's prettiest sights and features on many Marrakech postcards. The large expanse of water generates a microclimate that is slightly cooler than the surrounding streets, and, being a short moped hop from central Marrakech, the gardens are popular with locals for picnics and romantic assignations. Together with the Agdal Gardens, the Ménara is listed as a UNESCO World Heritage Site.

## Tip...

Many shops and sights open for a limited time during Ramadan. Bars and restaurants, especially those aimed mainly at tourists, generally stay open.

Above: Ménara Gardens. Opposite page: Matisse Art Gallery.

# Around Marrakech

Especially in summer, Marrakech can be a stifling place. The reservoir of Lalla Takerkoust, surrounded by the foothills of the High Atlas, makes a good retreat from the heat and the insistences of *babouche* sellers. Through the trees of the palmery and out into the countryside are rural retreats such as Beldi and La Pause, where you can stay, but also just visit for the day, have lunch and sit by the pool. At some places activities are organized, while others go for a beach club vibe, with plenty of space for the sort of expansive swimming pools and lounging areas which aren't possible in the city centre. The northern flanks of the High Atlas mountains (see page 176) and Essaouira (see page 142) are also doable as day trips, though they make more sense as places to stay at least for a night. Some of the hotels in the High Atlas, such as Kasbah Toubkal, encourage day trips from the city and organize visits to the surrounding areas as well as lunch. A hire car, or better still, a car and driver, is the easiest way to reach many of these places; some also lay on free transport.

Nearer to the city centre, across the river Oued Issil, in places the ancient palm groves are becoming increasingly suburbanized, though you can still find a sense of semi-rural Morocco.

## Lalla Takerkoust

Often referred to as 'the lake', Lalla Takerkoust, 40 km to the southwest of the city, is actually a reservoir, formed by a hydroelectric dam (the Barrage Lalla Takerkoust) which provides Marrakech with a good portion of its electricity. It is a popular swimming and picnicking place for Marrakchis wanting to escape the oppressive heat of the city. Lapping at the red-earth foothills of the High Atlas, and with the high peaks as a backdrop, it's a strikingly beautiful place, and there are a couple of places to stay and eat (see page 120) too. If you have a car, or a driver, the route across the Kik plateau from here to Asni has extraordinary panoramic views across the high pastures to the Atlas peaks beyond. Catch a grands taxi from Bab Er Robb.

## La Pause

*Douar Lmih Laroussiène, Comune Agafay, GPS N 31° 26' 57", W 08° 10' 31", T0661-306494, lapause-marrakech.com.*
Day visits by reservation. Lunch €35 per person, horse riding €35, mountain biking €25, cross golf €25, quad biking €100.

Around 28 km southwest of Marrakech, La Pause is a great place to stay (see page 121) in the arid wilderness, but also makes a good destination for a day trip, with huge views of the surrounding Agafay hills and the High Atlas beyond. As well as lunch in the oasis setting, there are plenty of chances for activities, from camel riding and desert golf. The food is excellent and the feel is of an upmarket desert retreat, though it's also child friendly.

**La Pause.**

Lalla Takerkoust.

### Beldi

*Km 6, Route du Barrage, T0524-383950, beldicountryclub.com.*

With a spa, restaurant and pool just outside Marrakech, Beldi makes a relaxing, high-end escape from the city. The dark-tiled pool is long and thin and surrounded by mature olive trees and sun loungers. There are views of the Atlas Mountains and a showroom of local arts and crafts for sale.

### Plage Rouge

*Route de l'Ourika, Km 10, T0524-378086, laplagerouge.net.*
1000-0100. Free bus from outside the Palais des Congres.

A huge 80 x 40 m swimming pool is the centrepiece of the Plage Rouge. DJs spin tunes and there are draped 'Balinese bed' loungers, a bar and restaurant. Trying hard to conjure up a Marrakech version of Ibiza, there's not much of Morocco left except for the palm trees and the Atlas views.

### Nectarome

*BP142 Tnine Ourika Haouz, T0524-482447, nectarome.com.*

A beautiful organic cooperative near the foothills of the Atlas, Nectarome produces essential oils for its cosmetics and aromatherapy products (available in Essence des Sens in the medina, see page 136). Visits, by appointment, give an insight into the production of argan oil, black cumin, apricot kernel oil and other traditional products.

### Oasiria

*Km 4, Route d'Amezmiz, T0524-380438, oasiria.com.*
Free minibus from the Koutoubia car park at 0930, 1015, 1100, 1145, 1330, 1415 and 1500; open all year.

A water park that is especially good for kids, Oasiria also has verdant gardens and a restaurant. There's a pirate ship, water slides and a wave machine and it's a surprisingly pleasant place just to hang out and soak up some sunshine.

### Earth Café Farm

*Book trips through Earth Café (see p127), 2 Derb Zawak, Riad Zitoun Kedim, T0661-289402, earthcafemarrakech.com.*
1000-2300 daily.

In the Haouz Valley, 16 km from Marrakech, this is a simple, earthy, unpretentious, organic farm, where you can get a taste of rural Moroccan life. Trips out here include lessons on how to make Moroccan bread, and vegetarian lunches. Chickens scratch around the rudimentary swimming pool and you can take an educational tour of the 2½ ha olive grove which supplies the farm's delicious oil. It may be possible to stay in exchange for work on the farm.

### The Palmeraie

Marrakech's palmery is not quite the oasis it once was, with the encroachment of smart homes and hotels turning much of the ancient irrigated Almoravid agricultural powerhouse into a well-off suburb. Reduced in size since the 1930s from around 7500 ha to 3000 ha today, it's still possible to get a feel for the place by taking a horse-drawn *calèche* tour. Petit taxis will also be happy to offer a look around, or you could book an afternoon camel tour, complete with pancakes, mint tea and blue Touareg robes, through **Locaquad** (T0524- 314444, locaquad-incentives.com).

Earth Café Farm.

# Sleeping

The term riad is, strictly speaking, architectural, and refers to a Moroccan house built around a courtyard garden. These days it is often used to refer more generally to a guesthouse, or *maison d'hôte*, converted from an old Moroccan house. Marrakech has seen an explosion in the availability of riads like nowhere else in the country. Estimates vary of the total number, but there are probably more than 500. Many offer a fantastic opportunity to stay in elegant, stylish places in the heart of the old city with a level of service substantially higher than that found in many top hotels. A stay in a riad will be a highlight of a visit to Morocco and unless your budget is very tight, or you are wedded to the facilities that only large hotels can provide, such as gyms or big swimming pools, a riad should be your first choice, at least for a night or two.

There is a lack of mid-range hotels in the medina with a modicum of style – those that do exist are mostly grouped around Riad Zitoun el Kedime, to the southeast of Jemaa El Fna, but they tend to fill up far in advance. There are, however, some good medium priced hotels in Guéliz, the centre of the ville nouvelle.

The vast majority of cheaper hotels are five to 10 minutes' walk from Jemaa El Fna, in the alleys off Bab Agnaou, Riad Zitoun el Kedim and the Kennaria neighbourhood behind the Café de France.

Many of the larger, more upmarket hotels are located in Guéliz and Hivernage, where they are often huge modern complexes. These are a short taxi ride into the old town. It is a good idea to reserve rooms, as demand can outstrip supply of accommodation in Marrakech, especially around Christmas and Easter holidays.

## Riad agencies

### Fleewinter
*49 Stilehall Gardens, London, W4 3BT, T(+44) (0)20-7112 0019, fleewinter.co.uk/morocco.*
A London-based agency with knowledgeable service, a great website and a guarantee that prices are the same as if you book directly. Fleewinter offer a great range of riads and plenty of helpful advice too, on all aspects of your trip, from the practicalities to the best places to eat. There's also a good online itinerary system.

### Marrakech Riads
*8 Derb Chorfa Lakbir, Mouassine, T0524-391609, marrakech-riads.net.*
Small, friendly agency that owns and runs eight excellent riads in the city, including the simple Dar Sara and the beautiful Al Jazira. The riads have a sophisticated Moroccan style, with contemporary art and splashes of colour, but less of the fussiness that can sometimes complicate the design of European-owned riads. Rooms range from 415dh-960dh per room. The agency's headquarters, the beautiful Dar Cherifa (see page 127), a 17th-century house converted into a gallery space and literary café, are worth a visit in their own right.

### Habibi Homes
*T011-409984 or T072-091886, habibihomes.com.*
Run by a Dutch-American partnership, one of whom set up the Café du Livre, Habibi Homes offer entire homes for rent, from chic little riads to family estates. They are often high-end private homes not otherwise offered as accommodation. Some are owned by architects and designers and tend to be especially well looked after. Sandra and Caitlin's service is personalized, they'll happily advise on the best things Marrakech has to offer. Prices from 5000dh to 50,000dh a night per property.

# Riad rental agencies

Before you book your riad accommodation, it may pay to shop around and see what is offered by riad rental agencies – usually these make their money by adding a commission to the price, but they can also have special offers available, and some match the riads' direct prices. Those listed here are some of the best.

## Hip Marrakech

*UK: T(+44) (0)871-663 4304,*
*Morocco: T0668-518349,*
*hipmarrakech.com.*
Most riads have staff that can speak English, but Hip Marrakech specialize in English-owned places. They have a particularly informative website and an excellent online availability and booking system. As with Fleewinter, Hip Marrakech promise that their prices are the same as if you book directly with the riads. Sister site hipmorocco. com also has accommodation in Essaouira and Oualidia. They plan to offer tours soon.

## Jardins de la Koutoubia €€€€

*26 Rue de la Koutoubia,*
*10524-388800,*
*lesjardinsdelakoutoubia.com.*
Map: Jemaa El Fna &
the Souks, p81.
On the site of one of Marrakech's finest palaces, Dar Louarzazi, Les Jardins has a spectacular and elegant central courtyard with a large square pool, off which the lights sparkle at night. As well as the pool there is a spa, an underground car park and a rooftop restaurant with great views. Its size – there are 72 rooms and suites – means that service can be a little impersonal but you're right at the heart of the action.

## La Maison Arabe €€€€

*1 Derb Assehbe, Bab Doukkala,*
*T0524-391233,*
*lamaisonarabe.com.*
Map: Marrakech, E3, p72.
Once one of Marrakech's best restaurants, La Maison Arabe is now converted into a very swish hotel, run by an Italian who grew up in Tangier. Seventeen rooms still retain something of a private house atmosphere despite extension. Some have fires; suites have private terraces. Amenities are those of a hotel: TVs, minibars and air conditioning; bathrooms are styled in granite or marble. A shuttle bus runs to the hotel's swimming pool, set in gardens

10 minutes outside the city. Cookery classes (see page 137) are recommended, or you can just eat at one of the two restaurants. There's a high quality hammam and two courtyards overflowing with flowers.

### Maison MK €€€€
*14 Derb Sebaai, Quartier Ksour, T0524-376173, maisonmk.com.*
**Map: Jemaa El Fna & the Souks, p81.**
Vibrant, bright and exceedingly hip, the six suites of Maison MK combine riad decoration standards – *tadelakt* and wrought iron – with contemporary black and white photos and rubber ducks. The 21st-century building takes the traditional riad format and replaces most of the sharp angles with curves. So funky is the place that even the mint teapots are brightly coloured and two-toned. The playroom has a 2½-m cinema screen and popcorn as well as an Xbox and you can put in advance requests for what you'd like in your minibar. Earthy tones and Arabic writing decorate the walls and a spliff-smoking camel head keeps an eye over the cocktail lounge. Rooms come with iPods and guests get a mobile to phone back in case they get lost. Drinks and a barbecue on the roof terrace can be enjoyed with a great view across the Marrakech rooftops to the Koutoubia. For around 15,000dh you can rent out the whole place.

### Riad 72 €€€€
*72 Arset Awsel, Bab Doukkala, T0524-387629, riad72.com.*
**Map: Marrakech, E3, p72.**
Italian run, Riad 72 is an exceptionally stylish riad – traditional *tadelakt* and tiles are used but the colour palette is more muted than most, with lots of greys along with splashes of red. There are only four rooms, but plenty of space, with huge banana palms in the courtyard, a small pool, a hammam and a roof terrace with great views across the medina. The same people run the equally chic Riad Due and Riad 12.

### Riad Charaï €€€€
*54 Diour Jdad, Zaouïa, T0524-437211, riadcharai.com.*
**Map: Marrakech, E1, p72.**
The former residence of the Pacha of Marrakech's secretary, this riad now sleeps up to 16 people in elegant surroundings, full of velvet tones and sultry low level lighting. The entrance corridor is spectacular, especially at night, when candles are lit beneath the trees, standing sentinel either side of the path. There's a hammam, a massage room, a spectacular, turquoise pool (4 by 9 m – unusually large for a riad) surrounded by high walls and a huge garden patio. Rooms themselves are restrained but generously large and the roof terrace has good views across the city.

### Riad El Cadi €€€€
*86/87 Derb Moulay Abdelkader, Dabachi, T0524-378655, riyadelcadi.com.*
**Map: Jemaa El Fna & the Souks, p81.**
The 12 rooms and suites around five courtyards in seven conjoined houses make the cultured Dar el Cadi one of the medina's biggest riads. It was also one of the first riads in the city to open its doors to guests and the years of practice have paid off. Service is efficient and friendly, and cool, simple and scholarly decoration is the order of the day. There's a library, Wi-Fi, and a tented roof terrace.

### Riad El Fenn €€€€
*Derb Moullay Abdullah Ben Hezzian, Bab El Ksour, T0524-441210, riadelfenn.com.*
**Map: Marrkech, E4, p72.**
Possibly Marrakech's most spectacularly luxurious riad, El Fenn also does the simple things well. The design is striking – deep red walls coexist with more classic riad style and a fine collection of contemporary art adorns the walls. There are 22 rooms, most of which have private fires, and one of which has a private, glass-bottomed rooftop pool, through which sunlight streams into the room below. English owned but run with laconic French style, El Fenn has some great ecological policies: they use solar panels, and have their own organic garden outside the city which provides the riad with fresh produce.

### Riad el Ouarda €€€€

*5 Derb Taht Sour LakbirTaht es
Sour, Zaouia el Abbasia,
T0524-385714,
riadelouarda.com.*
Map: Marrakech, F1, p72.
Around two courtyards, the
larger of which has a small pool,
Ouarda has four double rooms
and five suites, all with their own
theme. There's a modern feel to
the place – plain white walls and
low furniture laid out with
pebbles combine with restrained
use of traditional Moroccan tiles
and fabrics. On the northern side
of the medina, it's a fair way from
the majority of tourists.

### Riad Enija €€€€

*9 Derb Mesfioui, Rahba Lakdima,
T0524-440926, riadenija.com.*
Map: Jemaa El Fna &
the Souks, p81.
Fifteen rooms and suites
with fabulously extravagant
metal-framed and four-poster
beds around a truly jungliferous
courtyard. Swiss and Swedish
managed, every room is done in
a different style, though all share
a sense of exotic romance –
modern European touches mix
with an extravagance of tiles,
arches, carved plaster and
draped fabrics. Not all rooms
have en suite bathrooms,
though some have their
own private terrace.

### Riad Zolah €€€€

*114-116 Derb El Hammam,
T0524-387535, riadzolah.com.*
Map: Jemaa El Fna &
the Souks, p81.
Exemplary service sets Zolah
apart. There are complimentary
*babouches*, a mobile phone is lent
to guests in case they get lost in
the medina, and the welcome is
as warm and friendly as they
come. It's also exceptionally
beautiful: one courtyard has
four orange trees, the other
a plunge pool and the 17th-
century building retains some
original plasterwork. Alan
Keohane's black and white photos
of Morocco decorate the place,
there's a selection of Moroccan
wines, three rooms have working
fireplaces and spectacular silk
drapes and romantic lighting add
to the special atmosphere. Free
Wi-Fi and a TV with Premiership
football, should you wish.

### Dar Hanane €€€

*9 Derb Lalla Azzouna, T0524-
377737, T0663-839292 (mob),
dar-hanane.com.*
Map: Marrakech, G3, p72.
Ipod docking stations, free Wi-Fi
and an honesty bar all contribute
to the open, friendly attitude at
Dar Hanane, near the Medersa
Ben Youssef. There's one suite and
four rooms, all elegantly stylish
but also homely and unfussy.
A superb terrace view tops the
place off. If it's full, the owners
have two more riads in the city,
Riad Tzarra and Dar Bel Haj

Dar Rocmarra.

### Dar Rocmarra €€€

*29 Derb el Halfaoui, Bab
Doukkala, T0524-388081 or
T(+44) (0)7738-294100 (UK mob),
darrocmarra.com.*
Map: Marrakech, E2, p72.
A warm welcome awaits at
this bijou riad, well placed near
Dar El Bacha, that opened in 2008.
Rooms are variously themed: the
Sahara room has cracked
kasbah-style walls and a high,
wooden frame bed, whereas the
Berber room has exposed beams
and a hanging wood carving. In
general the decor is simple and
unfussy; fresh flowers and the
ubiquitous scattered petals add
some colour. The spacious suite
has an open fire and the *tadelakt*
bathrooms are immaculate.
Chameleons live in the olive tree
in the centre of the courtyard,
where water bubbles into a pool.

The excellent roof terrace has views not just over Marrakech, but of an eccentric dovecote next door constructed out of the city's flotsam and jetsam. Staff are extraordinarily polite and eager to please and Jamila will rustle up a delicious meal on request too.

### Dar Tamkast €€€
*10-12 Derb Sidi Bou Amar, Zaouiat Lahdar, T0524-384860, T0663-445795 (mob), tamkast.co.ma.*
Map: Jemaa El Fna & the Souks, p81.
With just three rooms, Tamkast feels personal and intimate, yet there's plenty of space, especially on the multi-level roof terrace. The ground floor room has a private courtyard, strewn with cushions, across from which is a bathroom big enough to swing several cats in. Decoration – white carved plaster and cedarwood – is simple but elegant. One smaller room is particularly good value.

### Riad Chergui €€€
*53-54 Derb El Halfaoui, T0524-383334, riadchergui.com.*
Map: Marrakech, E2, p72.
Though it calls itself a riad, Chergui has something of the feel of a small hotel: it's a little less personal than some riads, and has a good-sized pool in one of its two courtyards, and satellite TV in the salon. It's a stylish place, right at the top of this price bracket, with spacious rooms and a

restrained French stylishness: staff float about clad in white, the Berber rugs are worn just the right amount, the pale walls are punctuated by beautiful arches and plants climb towards the open sky. Not all staff are fluent in English, so you may want to book through Fleewinter in the UK (see page 106).

### Riad Edward €€€
*10 Derb Marestane, Zaouia Abbassia, T0524-389797.*
Map: Marrakech, E1, p72.
Bohemian, laid-back and antique, Riad Edward is, relatively speaking, an old-timer on the Marrakech riad scene, and the benefits of the years of experience show. The seriously cool stylishness here seems to come effortlessly. Battered green walls, a big courtyard pool surrounded by mature trees, rugs

on bare floors and whimsical touches such as antique radios and an old accordion all add to the hippy chic quotient. It's a large, labyrinthine riad, with 10 bedrooms spread around and a generous living room. The food is good and photographers and fashionistas populate the place. A tortoise and a cat called Couscous complete the family.

### Riad El Zohar €€€
*56 Derb El Hammam, Mouassine, T0524-391636, elzohar.com.*
Map: Jemaa El Fna & the Souks, p81.
Probably as near to the very centre of the medina as it's possible to be, El Zohar was the house of the sister and brother-in-law of the Glaoui in the 1930s, and retains some of its aristocratic atmosphere, though it's also a friendly, down-to-earth

Riad Edward.

place to stay, with no boutique pretensions. A pool in the courtyard is, unusually, just about long enough to swim in, looked over by a centaur sculpture. Now owned by an English-French couple, the antique cedarwood ceilings are intricately decorated and a homely feel is created by the good supply of books, fresh flowers and the olive wood logs that burn on the open fire in winter. Of the five rooms, four have four-poster beds and large black and white photos add a touch of contemporary style.

### Riad Elizabeth €€€
*Derb El Baroud, Hart Essoura,*
*T0524-383558,*
*riadelizabeth.com.*
Map: Marrakech, G2, p72.
Striking black and white design elements with splashes of red give Elizabeth a chic, contemporary, up-market feel, though prices are very reasonable. The large courtyard has a decent-sized pool, watched over by Dobbin, a wooden carousel horse; bedrooms, named after the family's six daughters, have more in the way of traditional Moroccan style. The English owners live in Marrakech and give guests a warm welcome. The large, terracotta-red roof terrace doesn't have great views but there's an honesty bar and the home-cooked food is delicious – try the monkfish tagine if you get the chance. A large salon and

dining room downstairs has an open fire, making it an excellent all-year-round option.

### Riad Magellan €€€
*62 Derb El Hammam, Mouassine,*
*T0661-082042, riadmagellan.com.*
Map: Jemaa El Fna &
the Souks, p81.
French-run Magellan, in the centre of the medina, has a mix of Parisian and Moroccan furnishings and a light, contemporary feel. Massage and meals are available on request and cooking courses can also be organized. Stefanie also runs Kifkif, a nearby craft shop. The six rooms are simple and stylish, with art deco touches alongside the *tadelakt* and arches.

### Riad Porte Royale €€€
*84 Diour Jdad, Zaouia Sidi bel*
*Abbes, T0524-376109,*
*riadporteroyale.com.*
Map: Marrakech, E1, p72.
Owned by an English writer, Porte Royale brings a touch of British

elegance to the northern edge of the medina. There's no over-the-top decoration or wild kaleidoscope of colours here, just pristine white walls, a few carefully chosen pieces of furniture, and occasional rare fabrics. The stylish reserve of the decoration serves to emphasize the beauty of the building and contributes to an atmosphere of serenity. The location puts you in a beautiful part of the medina that few tourists reach and service is superbly friendly and attentive. Both refined and very good value.

### Riad Sara €€€
*120 Derb Arst Awzel,*
*Bab Doukkala.*
Map: Marrakech, E3, p72.
One of the riads owned and run by Marrakech Riads (see above), Sara is striking and classy, with none of the fussiness often found in European-owned riads. Spacious and carefully thought out, the contemporary Moroccan design includes great use of bold

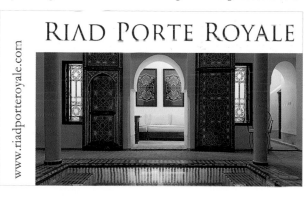

colours and good contemporary art, which contrasts nicely with the classic Marrakech simplicity of the riad. Nine rooms and multiple tree-filled courtyards make it one of the bigger riads around and there's a large if rather bare roof terrace. Rooms have deep-pile red rugs and bright white walls and there's a pool and a hammam too. The riad is in a quiet street, not too far from Dar Al Bacha, and is excellent value, though staff are more laissez-faire than in many other riads.

Top: Riad Sara. Above: Riad Tizwa.

### Riad Tizwa €€€
*26 Derb Gueraba, Dar el Bacha, T0668-190872 or T(+44) (0)7973-115471 (UK), riadtizwa.com.*
Map: Marrakech, E2, p72.
Stylish and good value, the Bee brothers' Marrakech riad is an elegant place near Dar el Bacha. Well designed without being fussy, the six bedrooms, primarily white with splashes of colour, open into a central courtyard with a small fountain. Effortlessly classy, the place also has a distinct sense of fun: antique tiles are mixed with pop art-style displays of Moroccan packaging and the roof terrace has copious candles, sun-faded cushions and a chess set; rooms come complete with iPod docks. Huge beds are exceptionally comfortable and the dressing areas are a great design feature – bring plenty of clothes in order to make full use of the inventive hanging space behind enormous *tadelakt* headboards. Bathrooms are luxurious, with innumerable

thick towels and soft hooded dressing gowns you may never want to get out of.

### Riad Zamzam €€€
*107 Rue Kaa El Machraa, Zaouia El Abbassia, T0524-387214, riadzamzam.com.*
Map: Marrakech, E1, p72.
In the very furthest northern point in the medina, Zamzam is far from the noise and hubbub in a heavily residential area; ideal if you want an escape, less so if you want cafés, restaurants and shoe-sellers on your doorstep. English-owned and relatively new on the scene, Zamzam offers a post-colonial style, with early 20th-century influenced furniture, African masks in alcoves and a zebra skin in the dining room. There are modern touches too, such as satellite TV and Wi-Fi. Ornate lamp shades cast filigree shadows on the ceilings, rose petals rotate around a plunge pool, and

there's a rooftop barbecue and a hammam. Rooms come with fresh fruit, Egyptian cotton and handmade mattresses adorn the king-sized beds and bathrooms are done out in finest *tadelakt* and marble. Service is both friendly and immaculately professional and it's a good place for families. The food is superb, with international touches on a Moroccan base and a good choice of wines.

Riad Yima.

### Dar Najma €€
*18 Derb El Ferrane, Riad Laarouss, T0524-375610, darnajma.com.*
Map: Marrakech, F2, p72.
From the same management as Riad tlaatawa-sitteen, Dar Najma takes the same pared down approach to create a simple place, stylish but with more of an emphasis on value than frills. Prices are per person, meaning that it's especially good value if you're travelling on your own.

### Les Jardins Mandaline €€
*55 Derb Ferrane Riad Laarouss, T010-412347, lesjardinsmandaline.com.*
Map: Marrakech, F2, p72.
This French-run, good value riad in the centre of the medina has eight differently decorated rooms, all with private bathrooms. There's a plunge pool and a pretty *tadelakt* hammam too. Fresh flowers punctuate the mainly white decoration and the salon has chess and a collection

of DVDs. The roof terrace doesn't have any views, but it's quiet and there are sun loungers.

### Marianis €€
*26 Derb el Firane, Riad Laarouss, T0524-383696, T0676-961618 (mob), riad-marianis.com.*
Map: Marrakech, F2, p72.
*Tadelakt*, long narrow rooms and heritage Moroccan rugs and drapes tick all the riad boxes. There's also a good roof terrace and excellent food is cooked to order. What sets the relaxed Marianis apart is the warmth of the welcome. It's also very good value; check the website for occasional special offers.

### Riad Tlaatawai-sitteen €€
*63 Derb El Ferrane, Riad Laarouss, T0524-383026, T0663-599223 (mob), tlaatawa-sitteen.com.*
Map: Marrakech, F2, p72.
At €50 for a room, tlaatawa-sitteen is remarkably good value

for a riad. You don't get all the polished edges that come with most riads, but you still get a stylish place to stay in the heart of the medina. Homeliness is emphasized, and the option to go to the market or to a hammam with the staff makes a stay here feel almost like being part of a Moroccan family. There's a salon with books and music and a kitchen for guests to use. The grey-green colour scheme and Moroccan tiles give the place a young, hip feel.

### Riad Yima €€
*52 Derb Aarjane, Rahba Lakdima, T0524-391987, T0665-167554 (mob), riadyima.com.*
Map: Jemaa El Fna & the Souks, p81.
Artist photographer and designer Hassan Hajjaj has created this personality-filled riad using local materials and an unusual pop art approach. There's a rare lightness and sense

of humour to the place, from the backlit cupboard doors to the cinema posters and creative uses for old flour sacks and tin cans. If you just want to buy some of Hassan's recycled objets d'arts, the riad incorporates a small boutique selling his designs. All rooms are en suite, with more traditional *tadelakt* bathrooms. One larger room would be good for families.

### Equity Point Hostel €
*80 Derb el Hammam, Mouassine,*
*T0524-440793, equity-point.com.*
**Map: Jemaa El Fna &**
**the Souks, p81.**
Just 300 m from Jemaa El Fna, this is a hostel by name but a riad in style, with lamps and arches, sofas and cushions, big mirrors and shiny red-walled bathrooms. You can stay in an en suite double for about the same price you'd pay in a riad proper (1000dh), or go budget in an eight-bed dorm for a much cheaper 150dh. It's open 24/7 and breakfast and internet is included.

### Southern medina

While many of the mid-range riads are in the north of the medina, the south has more at the extremities of the spectrum: from the highest end luxury to the bargain basement.

### Jardins de la Koutoubia €€€€
*26 Rue de la Koutoubia,*
*T0524-388800,*
*lesjardinsdelakoutoubia.com.*
**Map: Jemaa El Fna &**
**the Souks, p81.**
On the site of one of Marrakech's finest palaces, Dar Louarzazi, Les Jardins has a spectacular and elegant central courtyard with a large square pool, off which the lights sparkle at night. As well as the pool there is a spa, an underground car park and a rooftop restaurant with great views. Its size – there are 72 rooms and suites – means that service can be a little impersonal but you're right at the heart of the action.

### La Mamounia €€€€
*Av Bab Jedid, T0524-388600,*
*mamounia.com.*
**Map: Marrakech, D5, p72.**
A Marrakech institution, the Mamounia was one of the first hotels in the city, built within the walls a couple of minutes' walk from the Koutoubia. Originally owned and run by Moroccan railways in the 1930s, it has always been patronized by the rich and famous, from Charlie Chaplin through Ronald Reagan to Nelson Mandela and Tom Cruise. The hotel has been undergoing extensive renovation during recent years, but reopened in September 2009. Three years of work, led by interior designer Jacques Garcia, has expanded the hotel to

La Mamounia.

136 rooms, 71 suites and three separate riads, each with three bedrooms, private terraces and private swimming pools. Four restaurants are run by two Michelin-starred chefs and supplied by the hotel's own vegetable gardens. Taking tea at Le Menzeh glacier and patisserie in the 200-year-old gardens (see page 97) is a good way to get a glimpse of Moroccan grandeur at its most spectacular. Moroccans still talk about the Mamounia in hushed, awestruck tones and it looks set to continue as the country's most luxurious hotel for some time.

### La Sultana €€€€
*403 Rue de la Kasbah,*
*T0524-388008,*
*lasultanamarrakech.com.*
**Map: Marrakech, F6, p72.**
Four conjoined riads make up this luxury hotel overlooking the Saadian tombs, in the Kasbah

area of the city. From the outside you'd hardly know it was there but inside 21 rooms and suites open up off enormous corridors and there are 1200 sq m of roof terrace with a bar. There's a heated pool, a jacuzzi and a salon de massage too. Decoration is ornate, with chandeliers, rich sultry colours and the pervasive tinkling of water.

### Les Jardins de la Medina €€€€
*21 Derb Chtouka,*
*T0524-381851,*
*lesjardinsdelamedina.com.*
Map: Marrakech, F7, p72.
This hotel in a refurbished palace that once belonged to a cousin of the king has 36 air-conditioned rooms, a heated pool surrounded by trees and good restaurants. While it lacks something of the individuality of a riad, it makes up for it with an extremely high standard of service, exceptional facilities and an exalted setting, with copious space for lounging in grand style. There are English newspapers, a licensed bar, lots of books, beautiful gardens overlooked by fitness machines, a hammam, a beauty centre, a jacuzzi and a cookery school, where you can spend a morning learning how to make your own Moroccan tagine.

### Riad Assakina €€€€
*14 Derb Alaati Allah, Hay Salam,*
*T0524-380552, riadassakina.com.*
Map: Marrakech, G5, p72.
In a remarkably short period of time, the English owner of this Mellah riad has turned her stylish place from an ex-brothel into one of the city's most popular accommodations. A background as an interior designer helps, but it's the exceptional welcome and attention to detail that really sets Assakina apart. The Mellah may be the next growth area for riads in the medina but for the moment it's still almost entirely ungentrified, yet conveniently close to some of the city's best sights. Fresh flowers, ceramics, antique wall-hangings and crisp Egyptian cotton add touches of refinement to the bedrooms and the fine two-level roof terrace overlooks the Bahia Palace. There's a courtyard pool, as well as a splash pool on the roof. Suites also have satellite TVs.

### Villa des Orangers €€€€
*6 Rue Sidi Mimoun, T0524-384638, villadesorangers.com.*
Map: Marrakech, E5, p72.
Just south of the Koutoubia, the Villa des Orangers is a chic hotel in a 1930s building. Carved plasterwork and tiles give it a traditional riad flavour, while televisions, a heated pool and minibars remind you that this is more than a maison d'hôte. Musicians play every night in one of the two courtyards,

surrounded by fountains and trees. The high prices include some extras, such as airport transfers and tea and pastries.

### Dar One €€€
*19 Derb Jamaa El Kabir, Hay Salam, T0661-306328, riad-dar-one.com.*
Map: Marrakech, G5, p72.
One of Marrakech's most successful riads, the muted toned rooms of French-owned Dar One are often booked well in advance. Modern and friendly, it's fashion-shoot-photogenic and sophisticated, not afraid to mix darker shades with splashes of colour. Every room is different – chocolate brown *tadelakt* is carefully lit by warm red lamps in one; berry coloured velvet furniture contrasted against natural stone-coloured walls in another. The sound of trickling water fills the courtyard, the generous roof terrace is well used and the Mellah setting gives an edge of adventure. There are plenty of modern touches too, such as Wi-Fi, Hi-Fi and plasma TV

### Riad Akka €€€
*65 Derb Lahbib Magni, Riad Zitoun Jdid, T0524-375767.*
Near the Bahia Palace, this French-run riad is strikingly decorated in reds and blacks, with cacti, contemporary art and Far East influences. There's a good- sized and fairly pool in the courtyard downstairs, a

Dar One.

pretty roof terrace and good modern facilities too: air conditioning and Wi-Fi plus huge flat-head showers. The owners speak very good English and, in contrast to the slightly clinical decor, the riad has a homely, lived-in atmosphere.

### Hotel Assia €€
*32 Rue de la Recette,*
*T0524-391285,*
*hotel-assia-marrakech.com.*
Map: Jemaa El Fna &
the Souks, p81.
Halfway between a riad and a budget hotel, the good value Assia has *tadelakt*, tiles, plants and a fountain, though service can be on the slow side. There are 26 comfortable rooms – those downstairs are dark. Book and money exchange are both available from reception.

### Hotel Belleville €€
*194 Riad Zitoun el Kedime,*
*just after Hotel de France,*
*T0524-426481,*
*hotelbelleville@yahoo.fr.*
Map: Jemaa El Fna &
the Souks, p81.
Four-poster beds are squeezed tightly into some of the 10 en suite rooms in this small hotel not far from Jemaa El Fna. There's lots of wrought iron, a roof terrace with tent and a heated Moroccan salon too, though there's too much gold lamé for the quality of the styling to match the chic riads it is trying to impersonate.

### Hotel Gallia €€
*30 Rue de la Recette,*
*T0524-445913.*
Map: Jemaa El Fna &
the Souks, p81.
At the cheap end of the city's stylish places to stay, the Gallia is clean and conveniently located in a 1930s building with a beautifully planted courtyard, a huge tree and caged birds. There's plenty of hot water and the three floors have carved plaster, peach-painted walls and Moroccan tiles. Though rooms aren't overly fancy, they have good beds, and, at 500dh for a double including breakfast, it's good value. Heading down Rue Bab Agnaou from Jemaa El Fna, the Gallia is at the end of a narrow street on the left. Popular, so reserve well in advance.

### Hotel Jnane Mogador €€
*116 Riad Zitoun Kedime,*
*T0524-426324,*
*jnanemogador.com.*
Map: Jemaa El Fna &
the Souks, p81.
So popular that management advise booking six months in advance, Jnane Mogador fills a gap in the market between grotty budget hotels and stylish but expensive riads. Theirs is a blueprint that others in Marrakech are now starting to follow, but still nobody else does it quite this well. The 17 rooms aren't large but they have attractive drapes and rugs, and turquoise bathrooms. There's a pretty courtyard with a petal-filled fountain, free internet access, a hammam with massage and a salon with both air conditiong for summer and a fire for winter.

### Hotel Sherazade €€

*3 Derb Djama, T0524-429305, hotelsherazade.com.*
**Map: Jemaa El Fna & the Souks, p81.**
Beds are big, fabrics are bold and striped, there's lots of greenery and the vibe is friendly in this hotel southeast of Jemaa El Fna. It's spotlessly clean and the 23 rooms are arranged around large courtyards. Breakfast is an extra 50dh for a buffet on the roof terrace. The owners also have two bungalows for rent 14 km north of the city. The street is the third narrow one on your left as you head down Riad Zitoun el Kedim from Jemaa El Fna. Good value and very popular, so book well in advance.

### Hotel Ali €

*Rue Moulay Ismail, T0524-444979, hotel-ali.com.*
**Map: Jemaa El Fna & the Souks, p81.**
An old travellers' favourite, just off Jemaa El Fna. It's a decent base for those intending to go climbing/trekking as it is run by people from the Atlas and there are usually guides to be found hanging out here. Don't expect anything stylish – it's steadfastly ugly and rooms have as many beds squeezed into them as possible – but it's fairly comfortable and there's cheapish Moroccan food. Discounts for a week's stay. There are two entrances, the main one facing Jardin Foucault, the back one on the Rue Bani Marine.

### Hotel Essaouira €

*3 Derb Sidi Bouloukate, T0524-443805.*
**Map: Jemaa El Fna & the Souks, p81.**
Essaouira has clean, simple rooms with coloured glass, basins and mirrors. Shared bathrooms are good and clean and hot showers are included in the price. Tiles and old painted woodwork give the place some style and there are tents, plants and a kitchen on the roof terrace, assuming you can get up the steep spiral stairs. A suite would be a good option for a family.

Hotels south of Jemaa El Fna.

### Hotel Ichbilia €
*1 Rue Bani Marine,*
*T0524-381530.*
Map: Jemaa El Fna &
the Souks, p81.
The best of the 32 rooms here
have balconies overlooking the
street, though these can be
noisy. Beds are comfortable but
there's little style. Rooms without
air conditioning or en suite
bathrooms are cheaper.

### Hotel La Gazelle €
*13 Rue Bani Marine,*
*T0524-441112,*
*hotel_gazelle@hotmail.com.*
Map: Jemaa El Fna &
the Souks, p81.
The eponymous Gazelle sits
on a shelf in the light and pretty
courtyard of this friendly budget
option south of Jemaa El Fna.
Pink walls predominate and
there's a roof terrace, though the
beds are rather old and sagging.
Rooms have basins, with showers
on corridors.

### Hotel Medina €
*1 Derb Sidi Bouloukate,*
*T0524-442997.*
Map: Jemaa El Fna &
the Souks, p81.
Sixteen simple but perfectly
adequate rooms are arranged
around a small courtyard. The
place is cool, with turquoise walls
and a good terrace, where it's
possible to sleep for 30dh.
Showers are shared but hot and
free and the 100dh per person
prices make it especially good

value for single travellers.
Breakfast is an extra 20dh and
evening meals are also available.
The Medina has the same owners
as the Hotel Aday, with which it
also shares much of its style.

### Sindi Sud €
*109 Derb Sidi Bouloukate,*
*T0524-443337,*
*sindisud@caramail.com.*
Map: Jemaa El Fna &
the Souks, p81.
Just around the corner from
the Aday and Medina, Sindi Sud
has one room on each floor (€€)
with private shower and air
conditioning/heating. Tiled
rooms are very clean and
standard rooms have washbasins
with shared showers (5dh) on
the corridors. There are some
nice design touches, such as
decorated doors and even some
carved plasterwork. The roof
terrace has plants and a laundry
area. Even breakfast (15dh) is
good value.

## Ville nouvelle – Guéliz & Hivernage

### Dar Rhizlane €€€€
*Av Jnane el Harti,*
*T0524-421303, dar-rhizlane.com.*
Map: Marrakech, B5, p72.
Nineteen air-conditioned rooms
and suites in this Hivernage hotel
are decorated in the riad style
but the ville nouvelle setting
gives an extra spaciousness you
don't usually find in the medina,
as well as a good pool and a

garden with roses. There's
free Wi-Fi and all rooms come
equipped with satellite TV and
open fires as well as terraces.

### Diwane €€€
*24 Rue Yougoslavie (on the*
*corner with Rue moulay Ali),*
*T0524-432216, diwane-hotel.com.*
Map: Marrakech, A1, p72.
One of the most human of the
city's super-hotels, Diwane has a
good pool with grassy surrounds
and a boutique which actually
sells some useful maps and
books alongside the usual
tourist tat. The 115 rooms are a
cut above the usual big hotel
standard too – they have
generous desks, balconies and
fridges and tiles and *tadelakt* in
the bathrooms for some local
style. A good option if you want
a big hotel with all the trimmings
and don't mind sharing it with
tour groups. Two hammams,
sauna, gym, hairdresser.

### Ryad Mogador Opera €€€
*Av Mohamed VI,*
*T0524-339390,*
*ryadmogador.com.*
Map: Marrakech, A3, p72.
Once the building works next
door have finished, a good
option for those who want a
resort-style hotel. There are
111 rooms here, around an
octagonal central atrium with a
giant chandelier. Breakfast is a
steep additional 80dh – making
it worth venturing out to find
coffee and some pancakes in a

café. Painted wood gives a small touch of local style. There's a good big pool and a spa. Ryad Mogador Menara offers more of the same just down the road.

### Hotel du Pacha €€
*33 Rue de la Liberté, T0524-431327, hotelpacha@wanadoo.net.ma.* Map: Marrakech, B2, p72.
On a quiet corner of Marrakech's ville nouvelle, Pacha is a good value mid-range option, though a little way from the heart of the action. Rooms are freshly painted and have Moroccan fabrics; some have small balconies. Bathrooms are tiled and clean, the lobby has carved plaster and reception is very helpful. Fresh flowers in reception and alcohol in the bar are added bonuses and there's a restaurant too, with a 150dh menu, or mains á la carte for 55-80dh.

### Hotel Fashion €€
*45 Av Hassan II, T0524-423707, fashionhotel@menara.ma.* Map: Marrakech, B3, p72.
Don't be put off by the ugly exterior, or the naff name – the friendly Hotel Fashion combines something of riad style with a convenient location and contemporary mid-sized hotel advantages such as a rooftop pool (albeit a small and rather shallow one – you may bang your knees), a hammam and a good café downstairs.

Spacious and fairly plush rooms, on five floors, are decked out in warm yellows and reds, with comfortable sofas, big desks and good beds. Showers have the habit of going suddenly very hot, so it may be a good idea to make use of the baths. It's on a busy road, but noise in the rooms isn't a problem. The good ground-floor café is open to all-comers and a buffet breakfast is served here for guests.

### Hotel Toulousain €€
*44 Rue Tarik Ibn Ziad, Guéliz, T0524-430033, geocities.com/hotel_toulousain.* Map: Marrakech, B2, p72.
Downstairs rooms open onto a quiet garden courtyard with climbing plants, decorated in pink and blue. There's car parking and it's a friendly, laid-back place, and very handy for the excellent Café du Livre next door. First floor rooms can be hot in summer. Rooms without private shower are cheaper.

### Moroccan House Hotel €€
*3 Rue Loubnane, T0524-420305, moroccanhousehotels.com.* Map: Marrakech, B1, p72.
The fifty rooms in this modern hotel are decorated in a rather over-the-top recreation of riad style. There are four-poster beds and lots of purple and bright colours, creating an overall sense of fun. There's a good pool and a big roof

terrace for breakfast, plus a more traditional hammam in the basement. Service, in contrast to the garish decor, is staid and professional. Some tour groups.

### Hotel des Voyageurs €
*40 Blvd Mohamed Zerktouni, T0524-447218.* Map: Marrakech, A1, p72.
Almost opposite Café Les Négociants, the Voyageurs is well situated at the heart of Guéliz. Some of the 26 rooms have no en suite shower and these are cheaper. Beds sag, but the welcome is friendly and rooms are well sized and have some sturdy old pieces of furniture. Ground floor rooms are dark but the hotel is surprisingly quiet for these parts. One of the best aspects is a vine-entwined garden, shady and cool. Good value for the price.

### Hotel Farouk €
*66 Av Hassan II, near the main post office, T0524-431989.* Map: Marrakech, B3, p72.
A long-established Marrakech address with the same management as Hotel Ali. Some rooms are very noisy at weekends from the nightclub next door and cleaning is inconsistent at best, but there's a roof terrace and breakfast at the streetside café downstairs, with delicious pancakes cooked freshly right beside the tables. Reconfirm if you reserve, as bookings can get lost.

### Around Marrakech

In the Palmeraie, north of the centre, the old palm groves are increasingly being taken over by smart hotels. These can feel a bit far from the action, though there is usually the advantage of large pools and gardens, and many provide transport into the city centre. To the south, a few rural hideaways also exist.

**Amanjena Resort €€€€**
*Km 12 Route de Ouazarzate, T0524-403353, amanjena.com.*
The Amanjena is a top-end complex centring on a large reflecting pool. Luxurious accommodation starts at €716 per night for a 'pavilion' and goes up to €2420 for a 'maison' with a private pool. Everything is spectacularly grand and spacious, but, despite the use of local materials, the newness of the place is hard to hide and it therefore lacks something of the soul of a genuine riad. Nevertheless, wood burning fires, candle lanterns, a gym, clay tennis courts and hammams make the sky-high prices seem a little less extortionate.

**Dar Ayniwen €€€€**
*Tafrata, Palmeraie, T0524-329684, dar-ayniwen.com.*
Luxury of the ornate, antique sort is on offer at this palm grove guesthouse. Very different to the minimalist riad chic usually found in such places, the decoration creates a more lived-in, but no less elegant atmosphere. 'House cars' with drivers are available to take you wherever you desire in the city. There's a pool, a 20-acre garden with fruit trees, and a hammam. High season prices start at 3,000dh a night.

**Jnane Tamsna €€€€**
*Douar Abiad, Palmeraie, T0524-329423, T0661-242717 (mob), jnanetamsna.com.*
Well away from the bustle of downtown Marrakech, the 24 rooms here are spread over five villas in a walled herb, vegetable

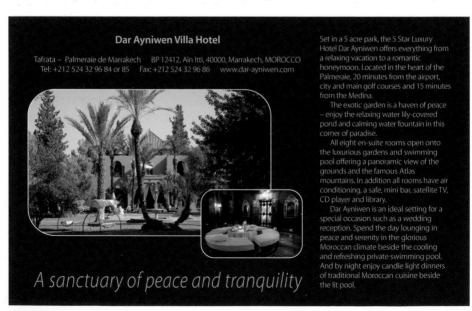

**Dar Ayniwen Villa Hotel**

Tafrata – Palmeraie de Marrakech    BP 12412, Aïn Itti, 40000, Marrakech, MOROCCO
Tel: +212 524 32 96 84 or 85    Fax: +212 524 32 96 86    www.dar-ayniwen.com

Set in a 5 acre park, the 5 Star Luxury Hotel Dar Ayniwen offers everything from a relaxing vacation to a romantic honeymoon. Located in the heart of the Palmeraie, 20 minutes from the airport, city and main golf courses and 15 minutes from the Medina.

The exotic garden is a haven of peace – enjoy the relaxing water lily-covered pond and calming water fountain in this corner of paradise.

All eight en-suite rooms open onto the luxurious gardens and swimming pool offering a panoramic view of the grounds and the famous Atlas mountains. In addition all rooms have air conditioning, a safe, mini bar, satellite TV, CD player and library.

Dar Ayniwen is an ideal setting for a special occasion such as a wedding reception. Spend the day lounging in peace and serenity in the glorious Moroccan climate beside the cooling and refreshing private swimming pool. And by night enjoy candle light dinners of traditional Moroccan cuisine beside the lit pool.

*A sanctuary of peace and tranquility*

and fruit tree garden. The whole ensemble makes an elegant, sophisticated and peaceful place to stay. The design is traditional Moroccan, with lots of personal touches, such as old photos and furniture designed by the owner, Meryanne Loum-Martin. The roll-call of celebrity visitors bears testimony to the highly personalized service and extras such as organic food, botanical workshops, cooking classes, tennis coaching and five swimming pools. Meryanne and her husband Gary, who set up the Global Diversity Foundation, are currently working on a new project, Jnane Ylane – a boutique hotel and natural spa with 30 bedrooms spread over five villas – which promises to be just as enticing when it opens in 2010.

### Les Deux Tours €€€€
*Douar Abiad, Palmeraie,*
*T0524-329525,*
*les-deuxtours.com.*
Out in the palm groves, this small development was originally designed by local architect Charles Boccara as second homes for Moroccans tired of the big city. The 36 traditional rooms all have balconies and are surrounded by palms. Each has its own plunge pool and Moroccan style (tiles, fabrics, antique desks) are combined with mod cons. There's a good swimming pool too, set in verdant and extensive gardens, though the place has

had some mixed reports about the quality of its service and food.

### La Ferme M'barka €€€
*Km 20 Douar Driaat BP84,*
*Tamesloth, Km 20, T0661 315063,*
*lafermembarka.com.*
Describing itself as a countryside bed and breakfast, La Ferme M'barka is a hippy chic farm on a 15-ha plot of land that was bought by the owner in 2006. Accommodation is in one of three lofts or the douria, a separate dwelling. All sleep at least four people, making it an ideal rural getaway for families or a group of friends. Waxed concrete floors, *tadelakt* and whitewashed walls give a calm feel to the place, while carefully chosen and faintly eccentric objets d'art give a nice personal flavour. Ducks, rabbits, dogs and a pig roam the farm, which also produces organic fruit and vegetables for the kitchen. There's a pool, and cookery classes and excursions are organized.

### Le Flouka €€
*BP45, Barrage Lalla Takerkoust,*
*T0664-492660.*
Fourteen rooms are scattered around Le Flouka, right at the water's edge of Lalla Takerkoust. Comfortable rooms are simply decorated with lamps and rugs and there are bare beams and open fires. There are also simpler tents and a de luxe 'tente de pacha', which comes with a built-in bathroom. Of the two

pools, one is reserved for hotel guests, though you can just as easily head straight out into the lake. Swimming straight towards the Atlas mountains is hard to beat. There is a restaurant (€€) right beside the lake, serving dishes such as steak or mozzarella and tomato salad, as well as a bar, but it's generally a peaceful spot, big enough to absorb its visitors with laid-back ease.

### La Pause €€€
*Douar Lmih Laroussiène,*
*Comune Agafay, GPS N 31° 26'*
*57", W 08° 10' 31", T0661-306494,*
*lapause-marrakech.com.*
At the end of dusty tracks out in the parched hills of the Agafay desert, La Pause makes a good place to visit for a day (see page 103) but for the full effect you should come to stay. Prices are full board, a good thing since there's nowhere around from which to grab a sandwich.

Accommodation is in well decked out traditional *pisé* (mud and straw) rooms, simple but cosy with thick rugs and lanterns. The fine food can be eaten outside on one of the terraces, or, in the evenings, served by attentive staff in a Bedouin tent. Hammocks are strung through the olive groves and camel treks, mountain biking and desert rock golf are some of the activities on offer. Suprisingly, it's only 30 km from Marrakech, but that's still plenty of space to get lost in if you have a driver who's not quite sure of the way.

# Eating

### Villa Dinari €€€
*Alpha 41, Lots Bouzaoui,*
*Commune al Ouidane,*
*T0524-328922, villadinari.com.*
Set in beautiful gardens
13 km southeast of the city, the
high-class post-colonial luxury of
Villa Dinari is a private house, the
fruits of an English-Moroccan
partnership. Guests are
wonderfully well looked after
– many arrive with ambitious
plans to explore and then seldom
stray far from the poolside. The
food, a mix of European, Asian
and Moroccan, is home-cooked
and well received and breakfast
can be served whenever you
want. There is an aperitif on the
terrace at 1900, as well as an
honesty bar for all other times of
the day. Verdant lawns and gravel
paths are interspersed with olive
and fruit trees, and should you
feel especially active there's a
gym and a boules court. The
immaculately well looked after
rooms are done out in a muted
Moroccan style, with rugs, iPod
docks and minibars adding to the
pampering quotient.

### Villas Fawakay €€€
*T0673-187346, villasfawakay.com.*
The three Fawakay villas are set in
the grounds of the house of the
Boys-Stones family, east of
Marrakech. Guests can rent a
room or a whole villa, making it a
good option for families. There's a
good pool and a tennis court and
the layout allows as much privacy
or socialising as you desire. Half

board is available but the villas
also have kettles and fridges. One
comes with a summer house at
the end of a gravel path, another
with a Berber tent. The design is
strikingly contemporary on the
outside, with more homely
traditional touches within, such
as drapes, filigree lanterns, carved
wood and *tadelakt*. There's a
barbecue area by the pool and
a table tennis table too.

### Jardin D'Issil €€
*Km 13 Route de l'Ourika,*
*BP26, Tassoultant,*
*T0524-485711, jardinsdissil.com.*
Jardin D'Issil's accommodation is
in 15 large themed tents dotted
around palm tree- and flower-
filled gardens that centre on a
beautiful swimming pool. The
tents are big, solid and permanent
enough to be more like chalets,
and there is a slight air of Butlin's
circa 1950 in the piped music and
forced smiles. It's a great spot for
families though, spacious, good
value and 20 km from Marrakech,
the minarets of which you can
make out on the horizon as you
watch the sunset from the
rooftop. Not much English is
spoken, so unless your French is
good, book through Fleewinter in
the UK (see page 106).

It's possible to wander the streets
of Marrakech for hours without
seeing any eateries other than
hole-in-the-wall tagine outlets.
More up-market riad restaurants
in restored houses with garden
courtyards are generally well
hidden, marked only with a
discreet wall plaque, or not at all
– taxi drivers generally know
where they are, or someone from
the restaurant will come to
accompany you. Reservations are
generally a good idea. Riads are
usually happy to make these
reservations for you. Riads
themselves usually serve up
excellent food with a little
advance warning, and some are
happy to cater for non-guests too.
Mid-range places in the medina
are thin on the ground. For a
much wider range of
contemporary eating, the ville
nouvelle has plenty of good
cosmopolitan options, and,
whatever your budget, you
shouldn't miss the experience
of dining with the locals at the
cheap benches in Jemaa El Fna
at least once.

### Jemaa El Fna & the northern medina

### Dar Moha €€€
*81 Rue Dar el Bacha, T0524-386400.*
Map: Jemaa El Fna &
the Souks, p81.
One of the best medina riad
restaurants, Dar Moha offers
unusually inventive Moroccan
cuisine, such as a sea bass tagine

or a quail pastilla with lentils. It's easier than most to locate, on the busy Rue Dar el Bacha. In summer, try to get a table outside by the pool in the much-photographed garden courtyard, where petals float around at the feet of a statue. There's a good selection of Moroccan wines and lots of candles make it a romantic evening spot, though it can get crowded.

### Dar Zellij €€€
*1 Kaasour, Sidi Ben Slimane, T0524-382627, darzellij.com.*
Map: Marrakech, F1, p72.
Converted from accommodation to a restaurant, Dar Zellij now offers one of the most spectacular settings in the city in which to enjoy an evening meal. It's not easy to find but is well worth the effort. Waiters seem to float around the tree-filled courtyard in long white gowns and the live music is subtle rather than intrusive. Tables come sprinkled with petals, there's an open fire,

dark red walls, candles, enormous high ceilings, curtains and calligraphic art. The traditional Moroccan food is good too, though at times it can't quite match the extravagance of the surroundings or the service. Set menus from 300-600dh.

### Kousina €€€
*64 Derb Arset Awzel, Dar El Bacha, T0524-387700.*
Map: Marrakech, E3, p72.
A smart new place recently converted from a riad into a swish restaurant, Kousina has an intimate, romantic and glamorous feel, with lots of mirrors behind the bar, candles, and the ubiquitous petals floating in the fountain. Moroccan music plays and dancing is planned, as is a new roof terrace. The food is good, if fairly standard, with a *tanjia* (like the tagine, this slow-cooked lamb dish is named after the earthenware pot in which it is cooked) expertly shaken and served at the table.

### Ksar Essaoussan €€€
*3 Rue des Ksour, Derb El Messoudyenne, T0524-440632, essaoussane.com.*
Evenings only; closed Sun and Aug. Map: Jemaa El Fna & the Souks, p81.
An intimate 18th-century patrician home where Bach plays in an antique-filled interior, Ksar Essaoussan contrasts with the Las Vegas dazzle of some of the medina places. The cooking is reliable, with three menus (300-500dh) including a half-bottle of wine and mineral water. There are good photo opportunities from the terraces. Off Rue Fatima Zohra, where somebody will meet you with a lamp to guide you in. Reservations recommended.

### Le Foundouk €€€
*55 Souk Hal Fassi, Kaât Ben Hadid, T0524-378190, foundouk.com.*
Noon to midnight.
Map: Marrakech, G3, p72.
For those for whom insipid, overcooked tagines have become a chore, the succulent, well-spiced versions at Fondouk will be something of a welcome

Kousina.

Restaurant
## Dar Zellij

### Moroccan Cuisine

*Take time out in the Arabo-Andalusian fashion for a dinner in an authentic 17th century riad.*

1,Kaa Essour, Sidi Ben Sliman, 40000 Marrakech
Tel: 00212 (0) 524 38 26 27 - Fax: 00212 (0) 524 37 54 41
www.darzellij.com

*Five of the best*

# Special restaurants

❶ **Al Fassia** A stylish, all-woman run, traditional Moroccan restaurant in the ville nouvelle.

❷ **Café du Livre** Links with a Michelin-starred chef has given this laid-back café a justifiably sophisticated reputation.

❸ **Dar Zellij** The complex theatre of being served almost matches the spectacular riad setting.

❹ **Fondouk** Chic and contemporary take on Moroccan food in the most traditional of riad settings of the medina.

❺ **Riad des Mers** Seafood is freshly shipped in from the coast to this sumptuous little place in the north.

surprise. Near the Medersa Ben Youssef, the licensed Fondouk, in a converted riad, is one of the most elegant restaurants in Marrakech. There are roses in glasses on the tables, contemporary art and mirrors on the walls, and modern jazz plays while a white, dark brown and burgundy colour scheme gives the place an air of sophistication. As well as the tagines (for around 130dh) there's European food too – try the terrine de foie gras or the duck with pineapple chutney. Evening reservations recommended.

## Le Tobsil €€€
*22 Derb Abdallah ben Houssein, Ksour, T0524-444052.*
**Evenings only; closed Tue.**
**Map: Marrakech, E4, p72.**
Elegant Moroccan cuisine is cooked and served with more subtlety than usual in this ochre-walled little riad. The menu is fixed price, and though it's expensive (600dh), you get quantity as well as quality for your money. Reservations are essential as there are not very many tables, and it can get a little cramped. Live music adds to the atmosphere.

## Riad des Mers €€€
*411 Derb Sidi Messaoud, Bab Yacout, T0524-375304.*
**Evenings only.**
**Map: Marrakech, F1, p72.**
Off the beaten track in the north of the medina, Riad des Mers offers a welcome change from meaty tagines: sophisticated French and Moroccan seafood in and around a beautiful tree-filled courtyard, heated in winter. Fresh fish is specially brought in every day from the coast. The razor-clam provençale and the bream with aniseed are both very good, but leave some room for the fantastic apple tart. The only downside is the truly awful easy listening music. Three fixed price menus from 250-550dh.

## Villa Flore €€€
*4 Derb Azzouz, Mouassine, T0524-391700, villa-flore.com.*
**Map: Jemaa El Fna & the Souks, p81.**
Pale, slender arches opening onto a beautiful courtyard create a great setting for this sophisticated French restaurant in the heart of the medina. The cuisine is a creative Moroccan-French fusion, with well-presented dishes such as a tasty starter of artichoke and prawn samosas and a parmentier de canard. Glass-topped tables, candles and professional service create an unusually reserved atmosphere for the medina – if it's theatricality you're after, this is probably not for you, but for subtlety it does very nicely.

## Bougainvillea €€
*33 Rue el Mouassine, T0524-441111.*
**Map: Jemaa El Fna & the Souks, p81.**
In a simpler, café-style take on the riad restaurant, Bougainvillea serves up international dishes in a sunken courtyard near the Mouassine mosque. Round tables fill the patio under cascading plants, while inside contemporary art hangs on the walls, and the whole place is decked out in pinks and whites. Popular with families, there's no alcohol, but the smoothies are excellent and there's a wide range of pasta, sandwiches and pizzas as well as Moroccan dishes.

### Les Premices €€

*Jemaa El Fna, T0524-391970.*
Map: Jemaa El Fna &
the Souks, p81.
At the southeast edge of the
square, a bit away from the main
action, Les Premices is a cut
above much of its competition.
There are two levels of terrace
overlooking the square or you
can sit inside. Try the tasty
European dishes such as
mozzarella salad or fried sole
or go for standard Moroccan
tagines or couscous.

### Les Terrasses de l'Alhambra €€

*Jemaa El Fna, T0524-427570.*
Map: Jemaa El Fna &
the Souks, p81.
Almost opposite the Café
de France is this popular
contemporary place for
reasonably priced pasta, pizzas
and salads. The latter are a good
option, including smoked
salmon and avocado. If you're in
the mood for something more
Moroccan, tagine and pastilla
feature too. It's a slick and fairly
smart operation compared to
many of the places around the
square with a loungey
atmosphere and two terraces
with views over this part of the
square. Also good for a drink or
ice-cream stop during the day.

### Terrasse des Épices €€

*15 Souk Cherifa, Sidi Abdelaziz,*
*T0524-375904 or T0676-046767*
*(mob), terrassedesepices.com.*
Map: Jemaa El Fna &
the Souks, p81.
A new venture in 2008 from the
owners of the successful Café
des Épices, the titular terrace is a
surprisingly expansive and open
space on the first floor of a
building in the middle of the
souks. Comfortable, shaded
tables and private booths are
spaced around the edge, there's
a bar and daily specials are
marked up on a board. In the
evening the place becomes
especially atmospheric, as the
sun sets and lanterns light the
place. The food is excellent –
as well as a traditional 100dh
Moroccan menu there are
inventive options such as
caramalised prunes with goat's
cheese crème fraiche. And the
chocolate mousse is worth
saving some room for. It's not
simple to find, though it is
unusually well signposted.

### Chez Bahia €

*Rue Riad Zitoun el Kadim, just off*
*Jemaa El Fna, T071-525224.*
Map: Jemaa El Fna &
the Souks, p81.
Being just off Jemaa El Fna, Chez
Bahia gets fewer tourists, and
also offers better value than
some of its competitors right
on the square. Tagines are only
25-40dh and it's also a good spot
for breakfast, with freshly cooked

pancakes and *bisara*. It's clean,
bright, basic, good value and
very Moroccan.

### Chez Chegrouni €

*46 Jemaa El Fna, T0524-6547615.*
Map: Jemaa El Fna &
the Souks, p81.
Just to the left of the Café de
France, Chez Chegrouni is
well-known for its good
couscous. That, combined
with its seats out the front and
upstairs terrace – both great
places to watch the world go by
– mean that it's popular, and
you'll have to turn up early for
the best seats. It's still very good
value though, a vegetable
couscous only 30dh. It's also
widely regarded as one of the
best places for vegetarians, since
they don't use meat stock for
their vegetarian dishes.

### Jemaa El Fna food stalls €

Evenings from around 1800.
Map: Jemaa El Fna &
the Souks, p81.
One of Marrakech's great
experiences, eating in Jemaa El
Fna is not to be missed. Piles of
salads and steaming tagines are
set up under hissing gas lamps
from early evening onwards. Each
stall has a different variety of
cooked streetfood, from sheep
heads to snails to fried fish to
simple bowls of lentil soup. It is
best to go for the food cooked to
order while waiting and the most
popular places obviously have a
faster turnover of food. In general,

# Jemaa El Juice

Ask people about their impressions of Jemaa El Fna and they'll mention the snake charmers, the food, the acrobats, the swarming mass of humanity, but also the orange juice. Around the edges of the square, from dawn to dusk and beyond, their stalls piled high with immaculately stacked oranges, a 3dh glass of refreshing juice from the army of drink vendors is an important part of the Jemaa El Fna experience. Depending on which stall you get it from, it may come slightly watered down with squash, and the locals complain when there's no sugar added, but it's invariably delicious, and absurdly cheap. Expect to pay 10dh if it's freshly squeezed (and therefore entirely unadulterated) in front of you, or for grapefruit.

however, eating here is no less safe than in most Moroccan restaurants, and there shouldn't be any problems. Walking along between the stalls is an experience in itself – you will be cajoled onto benches from all sides by young Moroccans who have somehow picked up a surreal repertoire of Jamie Oliver impressions and mock cockney patter. Generally, more than 50% of customers are Moroccan, and you'll be squashed onto rickety benches with large families out for the evening and sweaty labourers getting a bite after a day's work. Don't necessarily expect to be given cutlery or napkins, though just about anything you want will appear if you ask. Prices are low and

overcharging is rare, but you may find that you're given more dishes than you asked for – be firm if you don't want something.

### Snack Toubkal €
*Jemaa El Fna.*
Map: Jemaa El Fna & the Souks, p81.
A good spot for a snack stop or a light lunch, Toubkal is an old-fashioned place beloved of travellers that does cheap and quick omelettes, salads and drinks. The tables out the front are the most coveted, with a view of the comings and goings in the southeastern corner of the square.

## Cafés
### Café des Epices
*75 Rahba Lakdima, T0524-391770, cafedesepices.net.*
Map: Jemaa El Fna & the Souks, p81.
The open space of Rahba Kedima, thronged with hat, basket and live reptile sellers, makes a great setting for the medina's best café. In a small, and usually overflowing, building, the Café des Epices offers good sandwiches and salads over three floors, with comfy seats, interesting photos on the walls and a chilled and friendly atmosphere. The roof terrace is especially popular and there's free Wi-Fi.

Above: Jemaa El Fna food stalls. Opposite: Earth Café.

## Cafés with views

Around Jemaa El Fna there are lots of cafés which exist primarily because of their terraces overlooking the square. None are licensed, and none would be great cafés in other locations, but they are all rightfully popular, especially late in the afternoon, for the ability to survey the frenzy below from the relative calm of a terrace.

As a response to the hordes of tourists coming up to these cafés just to take photos, many will only let you onto their terraces after you've bought a drink.

### Café-Restaurant Argana

North of the food stalls, is a strategic meeting place, as no one can miss the large red Argana sign on top of the restaurant. Good views from the top terrace.

### Café de France

Has several levels and an excellent panorama over the square and the medina beyond.

### Café Glacier

On the southeast edge of the square, has perhaps the best views of sunset through the rising smoke from the food stalls below.

### Les Princes

*32 Rue Bab Agnaou, T0524-443033.*
Map: Jemaa El Fna &
the Souks, p81.
On the pedestrian street south of Jemaa El Fna, Les Princes has an excellent selection of pastries and petits fours, though the ice-creams aren't great. Mint teas come in different varieties in a salon du thé at the back.

## Tip...

**Cyber Parc Moulay Abdeslam**, a green space just inside Bab Nkob, has Wi-Fi and internet terminals around the park. Cafés and riads often also have Wi-Fi.

### Dar Cherifa

*8 Derb Charfa Lakbir, Mouassine, off Rue Mouassine, T0524-426463.*
Map: Jemaa El Fna &
the Souks, p81.
It's hard to find and when you do you'll probably need to ring the bell to be let in, but that adds to the rarefied air of this cultured gallery café in a tall, spacious, spectacularly beautiful riad. Downstairs is the city's best contemporary art space (see page 07), while the quiet café spreads onto the roof terrace upstairs. There are two lunch menus (80/120dh) and the mint tea is exemplary. Look out for occasional cultural evenings.

### Earth Café

*2 Derb Zawak, Riad Zitoun Kedime, T0661-289402, earthcafemarrakech.com,*
1000-2300 daily.
Map: Jemaa El Fna &
the Souks, p81.
Claiming to be Morocco's first and only vegan café, this intensely colourful if slightly dusty place does a good line in veggie food as well as great mint tea served with complimentary bread and their very own organic olive oil from a farm just outside the city. Good also for more substantial veggie burgers, spring rolls or filo pastry with prunes, fennel and spring onions. Ask about trips to see the farm (see page 104), where you can learn to cook Moroccan bread, make bricks, swim and chill out with the chickens.

### Marra Book Café
*53 Derb Kabada (just off Av des Princes), T0524-376448.*
Map: Jemaa El Fna & the Souks, p81.
'Oriental' cuisine, water pipe, tarts and crumbles are the order of the day at this café above a rather touristy bookshop just south of the square. Sandwiches and even a tagine or two are on offer if you're hungry and there's reggae, fans, comfy seats and black wood and glass tables. The coffee is not as good as it should be but they do a mean

tart. Books – mainly coffee table photography, cookery and cheap classic novels – can be taken upstairs to read. If you want an altogether superior literary café, go to Café du Livre in the new town, but this is a convenient spot to wind down for half an hour.

### Venezia Ice
Map: Jemaa El Fna & the Souks, E4, p81.
Opposite the Koutoubia Mosque, Venezia Ice has a large selection of ice-cream flavours which are served in freshly made cones for 6dh a scoop.

#### Southern medina

### Kosybar €€€
*47 Place des Ferblantiers, T0524-380324.*
Map: Marrakech, G5, p72.
A good spot from which to watch the square below, Kosybar, like many Marrakech venues, is multi-functional: both a good bar (see page 132) and a restaurant. On several floors, slickly designed, colourful rooms with heavy wooden furniture are spread around a tall central space, with a bar on the ground floor as well as on the roof terrace. The chef is Japanese, and Asian dishes such as teriyaki roast chicken with Cantonese Rice are combined with more European choices, such as verrine of sea bream in persimmons with vanilla oil, and desserts such as lemon soufflé.

### Le Tanjia €€€
*14 Derb J'did, Hay Essalam, Mellah, T0524-383836, letanjia-marrakech.blogspot.com.*
Mon-Sun 0800-0100.
Map: Marrakech, G5, p72.
Describing itself as a brasserie, le Tanjia brings something of chic Paris to the Marrakech medina – dark wood round tables and leather chairs are combined with Moroccan lanterns and palms. Food is either Italian or high quality Moroccan, with unusually good salads, excellent tagines and good vegetarian options. The terrace and the ground floor bar are good spots for a drink at any time of day, whereas the roof terrace makes a great spot in the evening for watching the sunset and the nearby storks nesting. Waiters are traditionally costumed and a belly dancer performs at 2100 and 2230.

### Mamatilee €€€
*13 Derb Larsaa, Riad Zitoun Jdid, T0524-381752.*
Map: Marrakech, G5, p72.
Hard enough to find that in-the-know expats usually outnumber tourists, this well-hidden French restaurant is an elegant spot, with walls and arches painted in white and lavender and a cool black floor. The contemporary setting is matched by the artistically presented food – colourful salads on large square white plates and inventive dishes such as mushroom cappuccino and

---

## Five of the best

# Memorable views

**❶ Jemaa El Fna rooftop cafés** Rubbish cafés but great views of the square below as the evening smoke starts to rise.

**❷ Le Tanjia** From the upstairs terrace the sunset lights the sky orange behind the Koutoubia and the southern medina.

**❸ Maison MK** Many riads have great rooftop views, but the clubby bar area at the top of MK is extra chic.

**❹ Menara Gardens** With the pavilion reflecting in the water of the lake and the snow-topped Atlas behind, this view features on many Marrakech postcards.

**❺ Nid'Cigogne** Opposite the Saadian tombs, the terrace of this restaurant looks directly into the nests of storks across the road.

pea gazpacho. The homemade granite is also recommended.

### Nid'Cigogne €€
*60 Rue de la Kasbah, T0524-382092 or T0661-464786 (mob).*
Service is continuous 0900-2300.
Map: Marrakech, F6, p72.
Opposite the Saadian tombs, you climb two flights of stairs to reach this roof-terrace restaurant/café, with good salads and sandwiches. The salade Maroc is especially varied and generous for 20dh. It makes a very handy lunch spot and you can peer straight across the road into the nests of the eponymous storks.

### Cafés
### Dejeuner a Marrakech
*2/4 Place Douar Graoua, T0524-378387, dejeuneramarrakech.com.*
Map: Jemaa El Fna & the Souks, p81.
Newly opened in 2009, this smart little contemporary café and snack bar has Wi-Fi, pastries and smoothies as well as pancakes and sandwiches, not far from Jemaa El Fna.

### Ville nouvelle

While Marrakech's medina restaurants serve mostly Moroccan food, the ville nouvelle has a much wider range of eating and (especially) drinking options. Guéliz (the main ville nouvelle area) also has some good cafés, old-fashioned and modern,

straight-laced and alternative, many of which also make good eating spots.

### La Trattoria €€€
*179 Rue Mohamed el Bequal, T0524-432641, latrattoriamarrakech.com.*
Map: Marrakech, A2, p72.
The city's smartest Italian restaurant, La Trattoria is on a rather dark and dingy street, but is an elegant place, with a leafy garden and a few wannabe mafiosi. Excellent selection of wines and superb desserts.

### Le Jacaranda €€€
*32 Blvd Mohamed Zerktouni (opposite Café Les Négociants), T0524-447215, lejacaranda.ma.*
Map: Marrakech, A1, p72.
A long-standing restaurant with a good reputation, Le Jacaranda specializes in elaborate French food, strong on fish and creamy sauces. There are good value fixed price menus at around 100dh during the day, more expensive at night, or you can eat à la carte. At the very centre of the ville nouvelle, the outside terrace can be noisy.

### Al Fassia €€
*55 Blvd Zerktouni, T0524-434060, alfassia.com.*
Map: Marrakech, A2, p72.
This excellent Moroccan restaurant is run by a women's cooperative, and all the staff, once you're past the doorman, are female. You can dine à la

carte and there's an excellent choice of tagines – for example lamb with aubergine and chicken with caramelised pumpkin – for 110dh. Other good options include vegetable couscous and seafood pastilla and there's a long wine list too. The interior is elegant with silk tablecloths and napkins, snug corners and a central area where sunlight filters down in daytime. Reservations recommended.

### Casanova €€
*221 Av Yacoub El Mansour, T0524-423735, T0661-381615 (mob).*
Map: Marrakech, B1, p72.
On the corner with Rue Ibn Toumert, this is a friendly Italian restaurant, which often seems full of genuine Italians. There are good pasta dishes from 70-100dh and specials up to 180. Generous salads too.

### Catanzaro €€
*11 Rue Tarik Ibn Ziad, next to the Hotel Toulousain, T0524-433737.*
Closed Sun.
Map: Marrakech, B2, p72.
An Italian that's a bit of a Marrakech institution, with excellent wood-fired pizzas alongside other more complex dishes and meat grills. Booking is a good idea, but you can usually also turn up and queue.

## Listings

### Kechmara €€
*3 Rue de la Liberté, T0524-422532. kechmara.com.*
0700-0000 daily.
Map: Marrakech, A2, p72.
Like a very cool café of the future with a good wine list and exciting food, Kechmara is unlike almost all other eating options in Marrakech. The tea menu includes blue and green varieties from Vietnam and there are omelettes and panini plus free Wi-Fi for daytime stops. Contemporary art hangs on the white walls and upstairs there's a laid-back roof terrace. It's the evening when the place really buzzes though, with Marrakech's bright young things sitting on big comfy plastic chairs ordering contemporary European food of the highest order. There's Moroccan Flag beer on tap, and, in a recent development, live music on Wed, Thu and Fri nights from 2000.

### Le Chat qui Rit €€
*92 Rue Yougoslavie, T0524-434311.*
Closed all day Sun, and Mon lunchtime.
Map: Marrakech, A3, p72.
The owner will probably greet you personally on entry to the laughing cat. There's a good menu of French/Italian options, including some excellent pasta dishes and fish. There are, however, better pizzas to be had elsewhere. Just up from Ave Hassan II.

### Le Lounge €€
*24 Rue Yougoslavie, T0524-433703.*
1000-0100.
Map: Marrakech, A1, p72.
Le Lounge has cocktails but also a 100dh daily fixed menu of French Moroccan fare, in a suitably loungey environment, with dimly lit reds and blacks and a vaguely art deco feel. It's on one of the ville nouvelle's rare segments of pedestrianized street too, so the outside terrace is relatively peaceful.

### Rôtisserie de la Paix €€
*68 Rue Yougoslavie, T0524-433118.*
Map: Marrakech, A2, p72.
Bow-tied waiters bustle around this popular spot, offering good, freshly grilled meat with a few fish options. There are also pizzas and tagines on the menu, but the whole point is really the meat. In the summer the garden fills up quickly with a mix of expats and tourists and in winter there's an open fire inside.

### Yellow Sub €€
*82 Av Hassan II, T0672-569864.*
Tue-Sun 1900-0100.
Map: Marrakech, B3, p72.
A new restaurant done up in 1960s retro style, with stylised portraits of the Beatles on the walls, Yellow Sub is a dark place, serving carefully presented Italian and international food such as a platter of smoked salmon or macaroni cheese.

### Bar L'Escale €
*Rue Mauritania, no phone.*
Closed Sun.
Map: Marrakech, B2, p72.
A gritty, male environment, Bar L'Escale is famed for its charcoal-grilled coquelet and chips with your Flag beer. Note that if you eat at one of the few tables on the pavement you'll have to forego alcohol.

### Pizzeria Niagara €
*Route de Targa, T0524-449775.*
Map: Marrakech, A1, p72.
Generally considered Marrakech's best pizza place, Niagara is not exactly central – it's probably worth taking a taxi. It gets crowded in the evenings with chic locals dining on the covered terrace, so reservations are essential, though it's one of a clutch of pizza places so if you can't get a spot, there are other options nearby.

#### Cafés
### Adamo
*44 Rue Tarik Idu Ziad, T0524-439419, traiteur-adamo.com.*
Map: Marrakech, B2, p72.
The exquisite smells of French baking wafting across the most bijoux area of the ville nouvelle should draw you to this little French patisserie, which also does splendid coffee.

### Café du Livre

*44 Rue Tarik Ben Ziad, T0524-432149, cafedulivre.com.*
Mon-Sat 0930-2100.
Map: Marrakech, B2, p72.
Depsite the name, Café du Livre is a fully fledged restaurant as well as a café, with some of Marrakech's most expertly prepared international food in a real haven of culture and epicurean treats. There are books to browse, free Wi-Fi, exceptionally good coffee in many guises and equally special chocolate tart. There's a relaxed but eminently stylish and intellectual atmosphere and it's popular with expats as well as in-the-know travellers. There's an open fire for winter and dark wood furniture and antique framed fabrics on the walls add to the sophisticated feel. It's also a good place to pick up

Café du Livre.

information about what's going on in the city. Up a flight of stairs, you have to enter a courtyard off the street to find it. The 'tapas' menu gives you choices from a range of Moroccan delicacies, or you could go for the delicious brochettes with pumpkin couscous, or the smoked salmon on a bed of leaves.

### Café Les Négociants

*Corner of Av Mohamed V and Blvd Mohamed Zerktouni, T0524-435762.*
Map: Marrakech, A2, p72.
In Guéliz, this busy intersection has popular cafés on each side, but this is the granddaddy, the old-timer still at the heart of ville nouvelle life and the place to come for important conversations, for long, lingering mint teas and to watch the world go by.

### Grand Café de la Poste

*Corner of Blvd El Mansour Eddahbi and Av Imam Malik, T0524-433038.*
0800-0100 daily.
Map: Marrakech, B2, p72.
Built in 1925, the extravagant Grand Café has immaculately restored 1920s colonial styling and has a very pleasant outdoor terrace under umbrellas. It's a place people come to be seen but they pay inflated prices for the privilege.

### Le 16

*Place du 16 Novembre, T0524-339670.*
Map: Marrakech, C2, p72.
Along with Kechmara, the welcoming 16 is one of a new breed of café-restaurants in Marrakech. Its tables spilling onto the central Place du 16 Novembre, it's hard to miss in the very heart of the ville nouvelle, and is worth a visit for its fantastic (and often very imaginatively unusual) ice-creams. Try the fragrant bergamot tea flavour or the wonderfully warm pastry scents of corne de gazelle flavour. It is famous for its rainbow of colourful macaroons and it also makes an excellent lunch spot, with good salads and light meals. Everything is made on site, with natural ingredients.

### Le 6

*Av Mohamed VI, T0524 449159.*
Map: Marrakech, B5, p72.
One of a strip of cafés facing the big hotels across Mohamed VI. There's a breakfast menu on the blackboard outside but Le 6 is most popular as a hangout for Marrakech's beautiful people later in the evening.

### Around Marrakech

Many of the hotels around the city, such as Le Flouka (see page 121), also have restaurants and actively encourage visitors

# Entertainment

to come for the day and have lunch. Also see the section on excursions around Marrakech (see page 102) as many of these, such as Beldi or La Pause, would also make fine culinary destinations outside the city.

### Bô & Zin €€€
*Km 3½, Route de l'Ourika, T0524-388012, bo-zin.com.*
**Mon-Sun, evenings only from 2000.**
Just beyond the edge of Marrakech, Bô & Zin (strapline 'drinking and fooding') is one of the city's trendiest spots, with a verdant garden and DJs spinning hip tunes. The theme is vaguely colonial and staff are attentive. The international fusion food pulls in influences from just about everywhere – you could start with a platter of sushi, followed by red curried squid and finished off with a crème brûlée. There are plenty of places to lounge, either at the bar or on comfy seats in the garden, surrounded by palms and bamboo and the place morphs into something approaching a club after about 2200.

## Bars & clubs
Dedicated bars are thin on the ground in the city – your best bet for a drink is often somewhere that also functions as a licensed restaurant but stays open late, of which there are a few. Some, such as Le 6 and Bô & Zin come very close to fully blown nightclubs once the plates have been cleared away. Superclub Pacha has brought hipness on a whole new scale to the city's nightlife.

### Café Arabe
*184 Rue Mouassine, T0524-429728, cafearabe.com.*
Conveniently located on one of the main routes through the medina, Café Arabe offers good, if slightly unimaginative, Moroccan and Italian fare on the ground floor in a lush riad setting. Upstairs is where Café Arabe really comes into its own, with a rare medina bar and a relaxing rooftop terrace.

### Chesterfield pub
*115 Blvd Mohamed V, T0524-446401.*
In the Nassim hotel, the Chesterfield is not especially pub-like, but the cosy bar is a good spot for a drink nevertheless. Dark wood, bar stools, lamps with frills and large amounts of leather give it more of an American feel, though the TV does often have British football on. There's beer on tap, Western music, bar snacks and you can take your drink and sit by the pool.

### Guepard
*Av Mohamed V, T0524- 439123, T0661-301534 (mob).*
**0700-0100.**
In daytime, as a restaurant, Guepard is rather overpriced, and the macho hustling to get customers in is off-putting. In the evenings, however, the licensed bar inside is a stylish place, with mood lighting and modern music, while outside there's a courtyard with large metal cats.

### Kosybar
*47 Place des Ferblantiers, T0524-380324.*
On several levels on the square traditionally taken up by Marrakech's metal workers, Kosybar functions as a restaurant and café (see page 128) but its roof terrace is a great place to hang out with a drink.

Kosybar.

# Shopping

### Le Comptoir Darna
*Av Echouhada, T0524-437702,*
*comptoirdarna.com.*
1600-0200 daily.
Muted lighting and elegant
waitresses in caftans set the tone
for this popular, if pricey, drinking
spot. There's a restaurant too but
the licence, the live music, the
belly dancers and the weekend
DJs make it better suited to
late-night cocktails. The
Comptoir has become a
Marrakech institution over
recent years and there's even
a little boutique.

### Pacha
*Blvd Mohamed VI, T0524-388400,*
*pachamarrakech.com.*
A big dancefloor, a laid-back
chillout bar, a restaurant and a
swimming pool – Marrakech
may not be the most obvious
place for an Ibizan club franchise,
but the Moroccan outpost works
well. It claims to be the biggest
club in Africa.

### Theatro
*Hotel Es Saadi, Av El Kadissa,*
*theatromarrakech.com.*
Top DJs spin their stuff at
weekends at this hip club
in an ex-theatre in the
Hivernage district.

### Casinos
### Grand Casino de la Mamounia
*Mamounia Hotel,*
*Av Bab Jedid, T0524-448811,*
*grandcasinomamounia.com.*
2100-0400.
Twenty live games and
200 gambling machines in
a grand art deco setting.
No jeans or trainers.

### Cinemas
The major cinemas showing
films in French are the Colisée,
Blvd Mohamed Zerktouni, and
the Regent, Av Mohamed V.
Try also the Institut Français
(see below).

### Cultural & language centres
### Institut Français de Marrakech
*Route de la Targa, Guéliz, ifm.ma.*
Daily 0830-1200 and 1430-1830
except Mon.
With a café, open-air theatre and
pleasant garden, the French
Institute shows films and holds
exhibitions and other cultural
events. The library has a small
stock of books in French on
Morocco-related subjects.

Demand from riad owners and
from visitors wanting their homes
to look a little more like riads
keeps an enormous quantity of
Marrakech retailers in business.
Craft production is a big industry,
with a huge range of products in
metal and ceramics, leather and
wood. Antique dealers sell
beautifully decrepit old doors,
and chic boutiques deal in
expensive clothes, leather and
inventive crafts that meld
Moroccan craft traditions with
Western aesthetics. Get a feel for
prices by visiting the Coopartim
Ensemble Artisanale, on the right
past the Koutoubia as you head to
Guéliz: here prices are fixed, and
slightly more expensive than in
the old city. However, it's a tame
experience compared to the
sights and sounds of the souks
(see page 82) – the pulsing heart
of the city's exhilarating shopping
experience.

Man selling antiques in the medina.

## Art & antiques

Marrakech has a handful of good contemporary galleries (see box, page 100) and you'll find plenty of art, albeit rather derivative, in the souks. Old black and white photos are also on sale in the souks – there are some nice images but watch for bad reproductions. Antiques are also easy to pick up – there's a steady trade in wooden carvings, old doors, rugs and fabrics. **Bazar Miftah Elkhair** (see crafts, below) is one of the best places.

## Books

It's worth trying the literary cafés, **Marra Book Café** (see page 128) and **Café du Livre** (see page 131), both of which sell books. The latter is also a great source of information. Foreign newspapers, a day or two old, can be bought from the stands along Av Mohamed V – the one next to tourist information has a good selection.

### Librairie Chatr
*19/21 Av Mohamed V,*
*T0524-447997.*
Under the arcades at the top end of Av Mohamed V in Guéliz. The best choice of books in the city, from coffee table books to novels in English and Atlas Mountain guidebooks.

### Librairie Dar El Bacha
*2 Rue Dar El Bacha, T0524-*
*391973, marrakechlibrarie.com.*
A small but well-stocked shop with maps and guidebooks on its green shelves in the medina.

## Crafts & interiors

Many come in search of rugs; other good items to buy in Marrakech include wooden boxes, painted wood mirrors, ceramics and elaborately framed mirrors. Each of the souks has their own speciality, at least nominally (see page 82).

If you're in the market for serious home decoration, you may want to take a taxi about 12 km out of town to **Sidi Ghanem** (Safi road, sidighanem. com), an industrial zone where many contemporary Marrakech designers have showrooms and outlets. Many make their money from export and sales to the hotel trade, but most places are also open to casual visitors Monday-Friday, 0930-1300 and 1430-1800. Pick up a map of the zone from one of the shops – most will also be happy to call a taxi for you back into town.

### Bazar Miftah Elkhair
*9 Bis Kissariat Miftah Alkhair,*
*Rue Lekssour, T0666-737793.*
With fair, fixed prices and large rooms piled high with mountains of carpets and rugs and dusty shelves full of antique pieces, this is a great source. There's little or no information or

sales pitch, and the profusion on offer could be overwhelming, so it may help to come with a clear idea of what you want, or someone who can point you in the right direction. It's the first left off Rue Mouassine after you leave Place Bab Fteuh.

### Kif Kif
*8 Rue de Ksour, Bab Laksour,*
*T0661-082041, kifkifbystef.com.*
A colourful selection of jewellery, accessories, textiles and toys in a shop run by a local expat and designer. Many items have more of a European feel than the Marrakech norm.

### Moor
*7 Rue des Anciens Marrakchis,*
*T0524-458274.*
Closed Mon am and Sun.
Minimalist elegant French design in any-colour-as-long-as-it's-pale shades fill this off-shoot of the successful and more colourful Akbar Delights. Moor is not just paler, it's also more contemporary and more artfully conceived. Prices are high but the huge round lanterns and embroidered shirts are very special.

### Riad Yima
*52 Derb Aarjane, Rahba Lkdima,*
*T0524-391987, riadyima.com.*
Designer Hassan Hajjaj creates imaginative and highly original objets d'art, from bags to T-shirts and frocks, using recycled local materials and a Moroccan pop art approach. His riad (see

page 113) incorporates a small boutique selling his excellent designs.

## Tresor des Nomades
*Arzet Aouzale 142, Bab Doukkala, (near Dar al Bacha).*
Behind unmarked wooden doors, Mustafa Al Blaoui will happily ship his treasures abroad: lanterns kilims, pottery and mirrors. He also has a stock of magnificent old doors and frames from India.

## Zenobie
*Souk Kchachbia 7/9, in front of Souk Attarine, T0666-078087.*
Opened by a Parisian designer in 2009, this shop sells china teapots, tea glasses and bric-à-brac as well as embroidered tops, bags and jewellery.

### Clothing & bags
Leather bags and *babouches* (shoes or slippers, depending on the soles) are two of the most popular shopping targets in Marrakech, but you can also find some great kaftans and shirts, traditional and contemporary, if you seek them out.

## Akbar Delights
*Place Bab Fteuh, T0671-661307, akbardelights.com.*
Closed Mon.
Printed, embroidered and bead-adorned fabrics, cushions and accessories are squeezed into this much-loved little medina

Top: Pigments for sale. Above: Marché Couvert.

shop. French designer touches gild traditional Moroccan basics.

## Aya's
*11 Bis, Derb Jedid Bab Mellah, T0524-383428, ayasmarrakech.com.*
Clothes, jewellery, *babouches* and antique postcards. Elegant contemporary kaftans are a speciality.

## Beldi
*9-11 Rue Laksour, T0524-441076.*
A good selection of traditionally tailored clothes, Beldi caters for both women and men. High quality for reasonable prices.

## Choumissa
*Appt 23, 3rd floor, Imm Asmae, Av Mohamed V, T0667-478287, choumissa.net.*
Tue and Thu 1000-1300 or by appointment.
Well-designed and made clothes and accessories for babies and toddlers, plus some colourful bags too.

## Kasbek
*216 Rue Riad Zitoun El Jedid, T0663-775690, studio@kasbekaftans.com.*
1000-1900.
Named after its Australian owners Kassie and Rebecca, this boutique has a fine line in colourful kaftans, which they refashion from vintage garments, and some beautiful chunky jewellery.

## Michèle Bacconnier
*6 Rue du Vieux Marrakchi, T0524-449178, ilove-marrakesh.com/baconnier.*
Mon-Sat 0930-1300, 1530-1930.
An international collection of high-end fashion, this French boutique in Guéliz has some of the city's most delectable *babouches* as well as clothes and jewellery mixing colourful origins and influences from as far afield as Uzbekistan and Turkey as well as Morocco.

## Mohamed Amine
*83 Ryad Zitoun Lakdim, T0655-125992.*
There is no shortage of traditional leather satchels, handbags and shoulder bags in Marrakech. Mohamed Amine's bags are completely different: great, creatively designed, colourful shoulder bags made with sewn patchwork of brightly coloured and hard-wearing plastic in funky, contemporary designs.

## Warda La Mouche
*127 Rue Kennaria, T0524-389063.*
Just off Jemaa El Fna, this little boutique combines 1960s European chic with Moroccan style to create funky clothes and accessories for both men and women.

## Cosmetics
Many places around the city sell a range of traditional cosmetics and remedies. Also common are more contemporary products using traditional ingredients, such as argan oil, similar to olive oil but ascribed many additional health-giving properties by its devout fans.

## Essence des Sens
*52 Fhal Chidmi, Mouassine, T0676-963107.*
Natural cosmetic products, some of which originate in the Nectarome cooperative (see page 104) outside the city.

## Herboriste du Paradis
*93 Place Ben Youssef, T0524-427249.*
0800-1930 daily.
A Berber pharmacy opposite the Musée de Marrakech with a good selection of spices, perfumes, cosmetics and miracle cures.

## Naturelle
*5 Rue Sourya, T0524-448761, naturelledargan.com.*
Beauty products and other argan oil based products as well as a carefully chosen smattering of handicrafts such as the exquisite inlaid teaspoons found in several riads in the city.

## La Savonnerie
*26 Rue el Baroudine, near the Musée de Marrakech, T0668-517479.*
Often used by riads, Badr's handmade soaps and shower gels are 100% natural products and essences.

# Activities & tours

### Food & drink

On the Casablanca road, the vast **Hypermarché Marjane** stocks just about everything; you can buy alcohol here during Ramadan.

Opposite the bus station at Bab Doukkala, **Aswak Assalam** is another supermarket, handy for stocking up if you're heading out on a trip.

There are various **food markets** around the city, mostly aimed at locals: three of the best are on the east side of Jemaa El Fna, near the Badi Palace and behind Place du 16 Novembre in Guéliz. You'll also find stalls selling spices, sweets and olives throughout the souks and dried fruit sellers in Jemaa El Fna.

**Country markets** outside Marrakech serve local needs, although you'll also find a few tourist-targeting trinket pushers. Men from the mountain villages come down on mules, bikes and pick-up trucks to stock up on tea and sugar, candles and cigarettes and agricultural produce, and maybe have a haircut or a tooth pulled. This is the place to sell a sheep, discuss emigration or a land sale.

**Monday**: Tnine; **Tuesday**: Amizmiz, Tahanaoute, Ait Ourir; **Wednesday**: Tirdouine; **Thursday**: Ouirgane, Setti Fatma, El-Khemis; **Friday**: Aghmmat, Tameslohte; **Saturday**: Asni; **Sunday**: Chichaoua, Sidi Abdel Ghiat.

Riads are often your best bet for arranging activities – almost anything is possible, and most places have a network of contacts and recommendations. Also see Activities & tours, page 60, for agencies that organize tours and trips all over the region.

### Adventure tours

**Mountain Safari Tours**
*64 Lot Laksour, Route de Casa, Guéliz, T0524-308777, mountainsafaritours.com.*
An established Marrakech-based company, Mountain Safari Tours organize treks, mountain biking, 4WD tours, skiing trips and camel treks. They can also help organize wedding ceremonies.

### Ballooning

**Ciel d'Afrique**
*15 Rue Mauritanie, Guéliz, T0524-432843, T0661-137051 (mob), cieldafrique.info.*
Since 1990, huge balloons owned by Ciel d'Afrique have been drifting across the pale blue early morning skies north of the Marrakech Palmeraie. For about an hour the balloon floats over Berber villages between the Oued Tensift and the Jbilet mountains, with views of Marrakech and the Atlas to the south. Passengers are picked up at their hotel at around 0600 and taken to the launch site, where the balloon is readied for take-off. After landing and, hopefully, being found by the 4WD support vehicles, mint tea is taken in a nearby village. For two people the cost of a flight is €205 each; for an extra €55 you can have champagne on board. Ciel d'Afrique also organize balloon trips further afield in the south of the country.

### Cooking

Many riads offer cookery lessons – often these will be informal sessions with riad staff after a trip to the local market to buy produce and spices. The **Earth**

# Hammams

The Islamic requirement for ablutions and the lack of bathrooms in many Moroccan homes means that the city's hammams are still well used. They cost around 8dh per person. Massage and black soap scrubs cost extra but are not expensive.

Try one of those on Riad Zitoun el Kedim or **Hammam Dar el Bacha**, Rue Fatima Zohra. This is a large hammam dating from the early 1930s. The vestibule has a huge dome, and inside are three parallel marble-floored rooms, the last with underfloor heating. Many riads have private hammams, though these offer a different sort of experience compared to the real thing. Riad staff may be happy to accompany you to the local hammam.

Segregation of the sexes is the rule at the hammam. Some establishments are only open for women, others are only for men, most have a shift system (mornings and evenings for the men, all afternoon for women). The hammam, along with the local zaouïa or saint's shrine, is an important place for women to gather and socialize, whereas for men the experience tends to be practical.

Very often there are separate hammams for men and women next to each other on the ground floor of an apartment building. A passage leads into a large changing room/post-bath area, equipped with masonry benches for lounging on and (sometimes) small wooden lockers. Undress under a towel here.

Hammam gear today is usually shorts for men and knickers for women. If you're going to have a massage/scrub down, you take a token at the cash desk where shampoo can also be bought. The next step is to proceed to the hot room: five to 10 minutes with your feet in a bucket of hot water will have you sweating nicely and you can then move back to the raised area where the masseurs are at work.

After the expert removal of large quantities of dead skin, you go into one of the small cabins or *mathara* to finish washing. (Before doing this, find the person bringing in dry towels so that they can bring yours to you when you're in the *mathara*). For women, in addition to a scrub and a wash there may be the pleasures of epilation with *sokar*, a mix of caramelized sugar and lemon. Men can undergo a *taksira*, which involves much pulling and stretching of the limbs. And remember, allow plenty of time to cool down, reclining in the changing area.

## Hotel hammams

### Riad El Fenn
*T0524-441210, riadelfenn.com.*
This riad in the Mouassine area of the Marrkech medina, owned and designed by Vanessa Branson, is a calm, exquisite oasis with individually designed rooms. The *gommage* treatment here ends with two halves of a fresh orange being squeezed over your body, and a jar of wonderful-smelling rosewater poured over your head and face. See page 108.

### Riad Farnatchi
*T0524-384910, riadfarnatchi.com.*
Daily 1600-1900.
Riad Farnatchi in Marrakech has a gorgeous white marble hammam. There are *gommage*, massage or beauty treatments on offer, and a small pool with an underwater jet stream (heated in the winter).

### Riad El Cadi
*T0524-378655, riadelcadi.com.*
The hamman at this funky riad has rich red walls and there's a small solar-heated pool and a jacuzzi you can dip into afterwards. See page 108.

### Kasbah Tamadot
*T+44 (0)20 8600 0430, virginlimitededition.co.uk.*
Located in Asni, in the High Atlas, this place has a hammam a few steps away from a lovely dark blue swimming pool. See also Spas and retreats, page 190.

حمام للرجال

*Bain*

*pour l'hommes*

Café (see page 127) offers lessons in traditional bread-making as a part of its visits.

## Maison Arabe
*1 Derb Assehbé, Bab Doukkala, T0524-387010, lamaisonarabe.com.*
The city's most professional cookery lesson set-up is in the Maison Arabe hotel (see page 107). They also have a facility for lessons at the hotel's out-of-town swimming pool. Rates start at 50dh and depend on the number of people in a group. See also Les Jardins de la Medina, page 115.

## Souk Cuisine
*Derb Tatah 5, T0673-804955, soukcuisine.com.*
Run by Gemma Van de Burgt, a Dutch woman, a day at this new cookery school in Marrakech

Maison Arabe cookery school.

starts with shopping for produce in the local markets, before cooking and eating traditional Moroccan dishes. Mint tea as you cook and a couple of glasses of Moroccan wine as you eat are included, for €40 per person. There are also occasional culinary weeks.

## Football
### Kawkab
*Stade al Harti, Rue Moulay el Hassan, Hivernage.*
The KACM football club of Marrakech is one of the best in Morocco.

## Golf
### Royal Golf Club
*6 km south off the Ouarzazate road (P31), T0524-444341.*
**Daily, per round 300dh, club hire 100dh.**
A beautiful, colonial-style 18-hole course set among orange and apricot trees. The oldest golf club in Morocco, Winston Churchill once played here. It's 6200 m, par 72. There's also a good buffet lunch.

## Horse Riding
### Les Cavaliers de l'Atlas
*lescavaliersdelatlas.com, T0672-845579.*
Just outside Marrakech is a new, professional stables that organizes rides through local countryside and villages. Half-day rides cost €50 per person, full-day rides with lunch €90 per person.

## Rafting
### Splash Rafting Morocco
*19 Bis Rue Fatima Zahra Rmila, T0659-346703, moroccoadventuretours.com.*
The best rafting conditions are in the winter and spring. Class three and four white water rafting takes place in the Ourika Valley, Moulay Ibrahim Gorge and the Tizi-n-Test Gorge. Splash also run canyoning and river tubing at other times of the year.

## Wellbeing
Hammams are scattered throughout the medina, often little more than local washrooms, though black soap rub-downs are part of the experience (see box, page 138).

### Les Bains de Marrakech
*2 Derb Sedra, Bab Agnaou, Kasbah, T0524-381428, lesbainsdemarrakech.com.*
A hammam and spa that combines authenticity with an unintimidating atmosphere. A 45-minute hammam with a traditional black soap body scrub costs 150dh.

# Transport

Walking is the only practical way to get around the medina. For journeys between Guéliz and the medina, petit taxis are a good bet. For journeys outside the city, buses or shared grands taxi are the most economical. Hiring a car with driver is the most stress-free option, and most riads will have a driver they recommend who will pick you up from the door and deliver you back again later. Marrakech is at the end of the train line from the north. Riads and many hotels will be happy to book transport for you.

### Drivers

Two recommended transport companies with good, English-speaking drivers are **Tahar** (T0667-413984) and **Tabarac** (T0610-171057). Reckon on around 700dh for a day.

### Grands Taxi

Moroccans usually pay for one place in a grands taxi, and six passengers are squeezed in before it will set off. You can also pay for more than one place, or indeed a whole taxi. For the whole car, Essaouira costs around 350dh, Setti Fatma around 200dh and you'll pick one up in the centre of the city. If you just want a place in a shared taxi, they leave from different places, depending on the destination. For the Ourika Valley, Asni and Ouirgane, they depart from Bab Rob. For Essaouira, from Bab Doukkala, and for destinations east from Bab Doukkala or Bab el Khemis.

### Buses

The main bus station (*gare routière*) is just outside **Bab Doukkala**, T0524-433933, easily reached by taxis and local buses. **CTM** departures can also be caught from the office near the Cinéma Colisée in Guéliz.

The best option to Essaouira is with **Supratours**, whose deluxe buses leave from outside the old train station. If they're full, CTM also run good quality buses. Buses to the Ourika Valley and Asni run from Bab Rob.

Asni, 10 daily, 1½ hours; Essaouira, six Supratours buses daily, plus frequent others, 3-3½ hours; Oualidia two or three daily, four hours; Ouarzazate, around 15 daily, six hours; Zagora around six daily, 10 hours.

**Rush hour congestion Marrakech style.**

# Contents

145 Introduction
146 *Map: Essaouira medina*
148 Medina & harbour
152 Beach & coast
156 Sidi Kaouki
158 Oualidia
160 Listings:
160 Sleeping
168 Eating
172 Shopping
173 Activities & tours
174 Transport

Sunset on Essaouira beach.

Essaouira & coast

# Introduction

Just three hours from the dusty heat of Marrakech, cool winds blow off the Atlantic onto the coast. The fishing town of Essaouira is the pretty, whitewashed and sand-blown highlight. A ontime military port, it was rebuilt as an international trading centre in the 18th century. International commerce has long since passed it by, but otherwise it hasn't changed much since. The walls are white, the windows and shutters cracked and faded blue, while stray cats and backpackers rest at the feet of sandy camel-brown arches and columns. Windsurfers and fanciful Jimi Hendrix myths hint at Essaouira's hippy heyday, the vestiges of which live on in a few cafés and a generally chilled pace to life. New flights to the airport may further reduce Essaouira's isolation though for the time being most visitors still arrive by bus or taxi from Marrakech. Foreigners continue to buy up picturesque property, continuing a creeping gentrification as well as the supply of good quality accommodation and there are two successful music festivals. To the south, the chilled surfing playground of Sidi Kaouki has a huge expanse of beach, some camels and very little else, bar a clutch of new family-friendly hotels. To the north, foodie Oualidia is a different sort of beach resort, with the focus on its stunning natural lagoon and its famous oysters and seafood restaurants.

Street, Essaouira.

## What to see in...

**... one day**
Start with a coffee on **Place Moulay Hassan** and then take a look at the port as the overnight fishing boats come in. The ancient Portuguese **Skala du Port** gives good views across to the Essaouira walls and the Illes Purpuraires. Wander the **medina** streets, taking in the fish and spice souks, doing some shopping and visiting in a gallery or two before spending the afternoon on the beach, returning to the **Skala de la Ville** to watch the sunset over the Atlantic.

**... a weekend or more**
For deeper exploration of Essaouira's streets, try the poor but atmospheric **Mellah** district before heading out to the wilder northern beach of **Plage de Safi**. Alternatively, catch a bus or taxi down south to the huge open sandy beach at **Sidi Kaouki** for some surf, camel riding or serious chilling.

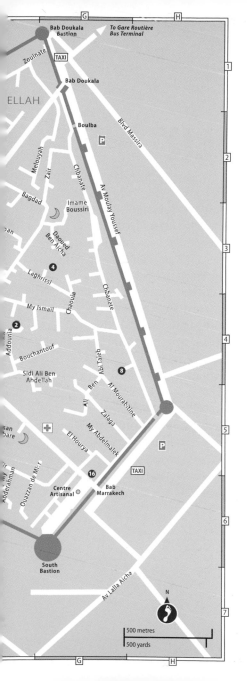

# Essaouira medina listings

## ● Sleeping

1 Casa Lila *94 Rue Mohamed El Qouri* F5
2 Dar Liouba *28 Impasse Moulay Ismaïl* F4
3 Dar Loulema *2 Rue Souss* B5
4 Essaouira Hostel *17 Rue Laghrissi* G3
5 Hotel Beau Rivage *Place Moulay Hassan* B5
6 Hotel Cap Sim *11 Rue Ibn Rochd* B5
7 Hotel Dar l'Oussia *4 Rue Mohamed Ben Messaoud* D7
8 Hotel Emeraude *228 Rue Chbanate* G4
9 Hotel Riad Nakhla *12 Rue d'Agadir* D5
10 Hotel Villa Maroc *10 Rue Abdallah Ben Yassin* C6
11 Jack's Apartments *1 Place Moulay Hassan* B5
12 La Maison des Artistes *19 Rue Laâlouj* B4
13 Lunetoille *191 Rue Sidi Mohamed Ben Abdullah* E2
14 Madada Mogador *5 Rue Youssef el Fassi* C7
15 Océan Vagabond *4 Boulevard Aïcha* B7
16 Palais Bleu *2 Rue Ibn Batouta* G5
17 Palazzo Desdemona *12-14 Rue Youssef el Fassi* C6
18 Riad De La Mer *7-9 Rue Khalid ben Oualid* D2
19 Riad El Mess *14 Rue Oujda* D3
20 Riad Lalla Mira *12 Rue de l'Iraq* E4
21 Riad Le Grand Large *2 Rue Oum-Rabia* D3
22 Riad Lotus Ô Marine *17 Rue Abderrahmane Eddakhil* C3
23 Riad Watier *16 Rue Ceuta* C3
24 Sofitel Essaouira *Av Mohamed V* B7
25 The Tea House *74 Derb Laalouj, La Skala* B3
26 Villa de l'Ô *3 Rue Mohamed Ben Messaoud* D7
27 Villa Garance *10 Rue Eddakhil* D3

## ● Eating & drinking

1 After 5 *5 Rue Youssef el Fassi* C7
2 Café des Arts *56 Av Istiqal* D4
3 Café Taros *2 Rue de Skala* B6
4 Chez Sam *Port* C7
5 Dar Al Houma *9 Rue El Hajjali* C5
6 Dar l'Oussia *4 Rue Mohamed Ben Messaoud* D7
7 El Minzah *3 Av Oqba Ibn Nafia* C5
8 Elizir *1 Rue Agadir* D5
9 Ferdaouss *27 Rue Abdesslam Lebadi* D4
10 Fish stalls *Port* B7
11 Gelateria Dolce Freddo *Place Moulay Hassan* B5
12 La Cantina *66 Rue Boutouil* E2
13 L'Artisan Pizzas *4 Rue El Fatouaki* C5
14 La Triskalla *58 Rue Touahen* B3
15 Le Patio *28 Bis, Rue Moulay Rachid* B5
16 Les Alizés *26 Rue de la Skala* B4
17 Océan Vagabond *Bld Mohamed V* C7
18 Restaurant La Découverte *8 Rue Houmman* C5
19 Samarkand *9 Rue Abderrahmane Eddakhil* C3
20 Souk el Hout *Marché de Poissons et Epices* E3

# Medina & harbour

Enclosed by walls with five main gates, the salty streets of the medina itself are Essaouira's major attractions, and apart from trips to the beach, many visitors have little reason to leave the old centre. An irregular square shape, Essaouira has a main street that bisects it diagonally from the wide open space of Place Moulay Hassan in the southwest to the gate of Bab Doukala in the northeast, changing names as it goes; it's about a 15-minute walk from one corner of town to the other. At the very centre of Essaouira are the fish, spice and jewellery souks. Mohamed El Qouri leads southeast from here to Bab Marrakech, another of the main gates; most of the conventional 'sights' lie to the west of here. The northeastern quarter of the town is the poorer Mellah, where a few remnants of the Jewish population which once comprised 40% of the town remain. The active fishing port, to the southwest of Place Moulay Hassan, supplies the open-air fish shacks here – one of the town's culinary highlights. To the north is the sea, waves crashing at the very edge of the town. Some of the fortifications along the town's seaward sides can be walked along, with fine views out over the sea, especially impressive at sunset.

## Place Moulay Hassan

Map: Essaouira medina, B7, p146.

The town's main square and social space, pedestrianized Place Moulay Hassan has views over the sea and along the skala, the sea fortifications. This is one of the main spaces for the summer gnaoua festival, and a popular spot with both visitors and locals for sitting, sunning and chatting for the rest of the year. At the square's northern end it tapers into a wide street lined with cafés.

## The Harbour & Skala du Port

*Entry to the Skala du Port via a kiosk close to the Porte de la Marine.*
0830-1200 and 1430-1800, 10dh.
Map: Essaouira medina, A7, p146.

Southwest from Place Moulay Hassan is the small harbour. Once known as the Port of Timbuktu, due to the enormous quantity of trade that passed through, it is now busy only with the comings and goings of its fishing fleet. The sardine boats generally come into port, laden with their catch, in the morning. Between the port and the square, the open-air restaurant stalls serving grilled fish have been considerably smartened up in recent years but are still a great spot for lunch. The sea gate (**Porte de la Marine**) which serves to link the harbour with the medina was built in 1769, it is said by an Englishman converted to Islam, during the reign of Sidi Mohamed Ibn Abdallah. The gateway is built of stone in the classical style and the year of its construction (1184 of the Hegira) is inscribed on the pediment. It is connected to the ramparts on the **Skala du Port**, an old Portuguese sea defence and battery, by a bridge which spans small primitive dry docks.

From the top of the bastion there are good panoramic views of the harbour and the offshore islands, the **Iles Purpuraires** (see page 153).

## Skala de la Ville

Map: Essaouira medina, A3, p146.

Along Rue du Skala from Place Moulay Hassan it is possible to get onto the ramparts of the Skala de la Ville, one of Essaouira's most picturesque spots. Entry here is free and crenellated walls protect a 200 m-long raised artillery platform and an array of decorated Spanish and other European cannons. This is a great spot from which to watch the sun set over the sea. From the tower of the North Bastion there are fine views of the old *mellah*, the white buildings and blue shutters of the medina and the coastline to the north of Essaouira. The woodworkers' souks, where you can watch the extraordinarily fine work of artisans inlaying wood, are in the arches under the ramparts. Some beautiful boxes can be bought here; prices are not exactly fixed, but bargaining may not get you very far.

## Avenue de l'Istiqlal

Map: Essaouira medina, D5, p146.

From Bab El Minzah beside Place Moulay Hassan, Essaouira's main street starts off as Avenue Oqba Ibn Nafiaa, passing on the right the so-called new

Kasbah quarter, built in the 1860s to accommodate an influx of rich foreign merchants. The original Kasbah area is on the other side of the clock tower. Don't miss cute little Place Chefchaoni through an arch on the left. Through Bab Moulay Youssef the road becomes Avenue de l'Istiqlal and passes the Ben Youssef mosque on the right before passing through more gates to reach the central souks (see below). Beyond here, now called the Avenue Mohamed Zerktouni, Essaouira's high street becomes more of a shopping strip, with market stalls and a few artists' studios at the end around the final gate, Bab Doukala. This is the loading-up point for the distinctive blue trolleys that carry produce through the town's narrow streets.

### Musée Sidi Mohamed Ibn Abdallah

*Darb Laalouj, T0524-472300.*
0830-1200 and 1430-1800, except Fri 0830-1130 and 1500-1830, closed Tue, 10dh.
Map: Essaouira medina, B4, p146.

Essaouira's museum, just off Avenue de l'Istiqlal, houses a collection of traditional art and heritage

Top: Skala de la Ville. Above: Seafront next to Place Moulay Hassan. Opposite page: Scarves, Rue Souk Jedid.

of Essaouira. The house, once the home of a pasha, has an impressively grand staircase , and even if you don't understand the French information, there's enough here to make it worth a quick half hour visit. The ethnographic collection includes stringed instruments such as a *rbab*, a sort of violin, beautifully decorated with marquetry and complete with an intricately designed bow. The costume section is rather dull but alongside artefacts from Essaouira's Jewish community – such as a beautiful coffee pot with a six-pointed star – there are some fine examples of inlaid thuya wood. The Roman and Phoenician remains are not much more than fragments; more interesting is a 1767 map of Mogador and some early 20th-century photos of the port and a man firing a gun inexplicably out to sea.

## Galerie Damgaard

*Av Oqba Ibn Nafiaa, T0524-784446, galeriedamgaard.com.*
0900-1300, 1500-1900, free.
Map: Essaouira medina, C6, p146.

Essaouira's biggest art gallery is a good place to see the town's own art movement, 'free art'. Naïve and colourful, it takes elements of Berber and African tribal myths and incorporates them into graphic and patterned pieces that share something with Australian Aboriginal art. Look out for the works of sculptor-painter Abdellatif Akjait, whose pieces have a playful Gaudiesque shapeliness, or for the enigmatic exuberance of the paintings of Mostafa El Hadar. Other private galleries around town tend to be a little derivative, but if you're interested in buying something a little cheaper try **La Petite Galerie**.

## Souk Jedid

*The town's souks are mainly located around the junction between Rue Mohamed Zerktouni and Rue Mohamed El Qouri.*
Map: Essaouira medina, E3, p146.

On one side is the Marché de Poissons et Epices: the fish souk and the spices souk, both very photogenic, and both pungent, in their own way. The fish market has benches in the far corner which make a great, if very basic spot for lunch (see page 170). In marked contrast to the benches near the port, this fishy eating spot has seen no prettification. On the opposite side of the main drag, Place Marché des Grains, the grain souk, is these days taken over by cafés and shops, though La Joutia, the jewellery souk, a symbol of Essaouira's Jewish past, retains its original function. The woodworkers' souk is north of here, inside the **Skala** walls to the north of Place Moulay Hassan. There are also craft workshops in the **Centre Artisanal**, just inside Bab Marrakech. Don't miss the giant, 400-year-old tree here, in a courtyard off to the right.

## Mellah

*At the northeast end of Rue Zerktouni, close to Bab Doukkala.*
Map: Essaouira medina, F1, p146.

The much decayed Mellah, the old Jewish quarter, was once home to around 15,000 Jewish people. Although the Jewish community no longer remains, it made a substantial contribution to the commercial and cultural development of the town. Talk of it being a dangerous area for foreigners is exaggerated but it's notably dirtier, grittier and less gentrified than the western parts of town. Some Hebrew inscriptions can be found and you'll also see distinctive balconies opening onto the street.

# Beach & coast

To the south of Essaouira's medina, hotels and other modern buildings line a wide sweep of beach that stretches 2½ km to the mouth of the river Oued Ksob, and the village of Diabat. The fine, dry sand is easily blown and it's often too windy for comfortable sunbathing, but there's plenty of action in the sea, with windsurfers and kite-surfers vying for the best waves. It's also a popular place for a horse- or camel-ride. Beyond, Diabat is a village on the next promontory. To the northeast, the Plage Safi is a wilder spot, harder to reach but worth the effort.

Beach time in Essaouira.

## La Plage

Essaouira has fine beaches. The wind, known as the *alizée*, stirs up a lot of sand, and makes it cold and choppy for swimming, but ideal for wind- and kite-surfing, though not great for surfing.

South of the town, the wide beach is great for football and there are usually games going on here. At the far end, Club Mistral, attached to Océan Vagabond (see page 171), is the place to head if you want to take windsurfing or kite-surfing lessons, or hire some kit. Around the sand dunes at this end of the beach are also lots of men pushing camel and horse rides. Past the Oued Ksob, you will see the waves breaking against the remains of **Borj El Baroud**, an old watchtower built by the Portuguese in the 18th century. The building is said to have been swallowed by the sand after the people of the Sous put a curse on it as their trade was being ruined.. Stories linking the ruins with Jimi Hendrix's *Castles Made of Sand* are spurious – the song was released 18 months before the singer visited Essaouira. The incoming tide makes the Oued Ksob below Diabat into an impassable river.

Contemporary **Diabat** is being swallowed up by Essaouira's new golf course (see page 173). A walk up the road from Diabat will bring you to the crossroads with the P8 road from the south, which runs back into town.

## Iles Purpuraires

Settled by the Phoenicians for military reasons and used by the Romans to extract purple dye from the shellfish found there, these islands are now a nature reserve and home to the rare Eleonora's falcon. The birds winter in Madagascar before flying thousands of kilometres across the continent . Members of the hobby family, their long pointed wings can grow to a span of up to a metre. It is possible to see the falcons from the end of the jetty using a good telescope. One particular area frequented by the falcons is the mouth of Oued Ksob to the south of the town. The river mouth is also noted for a large colony of yellow-legged herring gulls and a variety of migrating

**Tip...**

Essaouira's northern beach is much quieter than the main beach but is a little way from the medina. Take a petit taxi or rent a bike.

seabirds including black, little, sandwich, whiskered and white-winged terns. The remains of a 19th-century prison can be seen on Ile de Mogador, the main island.

Boat trips around the islands can be arranged from the little shack of the Sociéte Navette des Iles in the harbour. A 90-minute trip around the islands is 80dh per person. They also run 3-hour fishing trips (200dh per person).

## Plage de Safi

The northern Plage de Safi, much less frequented than the main beach, can also be a little more sheltered. Backed by scrubby dunes, there are sometimes dangerous currents . From Bab Doukala it's a 2-km walk along Boulevard Moulay Hicham (not one of the nicest parts of town), bearing left at the end, to reach the beach. There are usually lots of taxis hanging around Bab Doukala.

## Consul's cemetery

Outside Bab Doukkala, Boulevard Moulay Hicham passes between the Jewish cemetery on the right and the Consul's cemetery on the left. The latter was for the British officials who died here converting Mogador into a trading post with close British links. Charles Alfred Payton, British consul at the end of the 19th century, is one of the names visible here. Behind a high wall opposite (the guardian will let visitors in) the Jewish cemetery also holds the bodily remains of notable inhabitants of the past, possibly including family members of Leslie Hore-Belisha, the erstwhile British transport minister who introduced the driving test and the Belisha beacon. However, few of the old inscriptions are still legible.

## Surfing the garden

Just on the northern fringe of the town of Safi lies one of the world's most enigmatic, yet terrifyingly perfect, point breaks. Le Jardin, the 600-m-long, 3-m reeling point offering endless barrel sections, has gone from a jealously guarded secret to a worldwide star since the 1990s. But what makes this wave so special? Looking across to the harbour at Safi, a long headland curves away to the northwest, acting as a foil to the huge swells that angle in from the North Atlantic. This is a wave that can work from 1 m to over 3½ m. Breaking over a rock reef covered with a smooth deposit of Saharan sands, the swell jacks as it reaches the outside edge of 'The Garden' and throws into a fast hollow, reeling barrel. This outside section is particularly treacherous and difficult, breaking close to the rocks.

Once through the outside section the wave wraps into the middle and inside sections, both of which can be big and hollow, before breaking onto the beach on the inside. Luckily for the travelling surfer, its reputation as a place where there were tensions with locals has now eased and respectful surfers can enjoy some of the longest, most hollow waves in the whole of the country.

# Sidi Kaouki

'Sans Stress', the hand-painted signs advertise, and they're not wrong. Sidi Kaouki is on the verge of comatose: apart from an occasional frisson of competition between the cluster of shack café bars around the centre of the village, and the to-ing and fro-ing of surfers across the gargantuan beach, there's very little going on here. And apart from the occasional young man with a camel politely enquiring if you're interested in a ride along the beach, there's a refreshing absence of hassle.

Sidi Kaouki is a huge surf beach, essentially, with a few scattered cafés and restaurants along the road. There are a couple of new hotels going up but there's a long way to go before it becomes anything like developed. If Essaouira's slower pace is still too frantic, and if the oyster bars of Oualidia aren't your thing, then the simple, seriously chilled pleasures of Sidi Kaouki might be the way forward.

Mausoleum of Sidi Kaouki.

Sidi Kaouki beach.

## La Plage

The hub of Sidi Kaouki is a dusty patch behind the crumbling, whitewashed Mausoleum of Sidi Kaouki, resting place of a 19th-century local holy man with supposed powers to cure the infertile. From here the sandy beach stretches south for several kilometres, backed by dunes which shift shape and location through the seasons. The surf shack (see page 174) is a good place for renting boards or getting lessons and you don't have to hang around for long before you'll be offered a camel ride – some options are the half-hour trip north to Taguenza (50dh, see below), or the longer hour and a half or so south to waterfalls (300dh there and back). You could also just potter up and down the beach for 15 minutes. For those with transport, preferably 4WD, Iftan Plage, another isolated beach around 30 km south, would make a good destination for a day out.

## Taguenza

About half an hour's walk north from the Mausoleum, Taguenza is another beach, backed with a huddle of stone fishermens' shacks and a café which is little more than some deck chairs on the sand and some strewn cushions inside. Peaceful and idyllic, it's a great spot for a picnic, a swim, wild camping or an alfresco fish meal straight out of the sea. The walk can mostly be done barefoot along sand and over rocks at the edge of the waves.

# Oualidia

Oualidia (pronounced 'wa-lid-ee-a') has abundant natural beauty and is a restful beach resort, except in July and August when Moroccan tourists descend on it in their hordes. New holiday bungalows are beginning to cascade down the hillside but for most of the year it remains a chilled haven with few sights and relatively few visitors, a good spot for families or a relaxing post-Marrakech seaside sojourn.

Named for the Saadian Sultan El Oualid, who built a kasbah there in the 1630s, the village is best known today for its oysters and its restaurants. There are caves, a big lagoon, safe swimming and migrating birds in autumn and spring. It's also popular with surfers, and, increasingly, kite-surfers, who ride the calmer waters in the lagoon.

The Oualidia oyster beds came into production in the late 1950s, and annual production is around 200 tonnes, mainly for local consumption. Early fruit and vegetables, in particular tomatoes, are produced in the area under plastic for local and European markets.

North of the industrial town of Safi, Oualidia is a fairly simple 2½-hour hour bus or car journey from Marrakech. The bus drops off in the main village, where there's a cash machine. The hotels are down the hill behind the lagoon.

## Lagoon and beach

The hotels and restaurants of Oualidia form a crescent around the peaceful lagoon, entered by the sea through two breaches in a natural breakwater. To the south, outside the protection of the breakwater, Atlantic waves roll onto a long sandy beach and locals fish from the rocks or from a small fleet of boats. The lagoon and beach provide an ideal sheltered location for sailing, kite-surfing, windsurfing. Surfland (T0523-366110), between the road and the lagoon, offer surfing courses and other outfits set up in season on the beach.

## Kasbah

Above the beach, the skyline on the wooded hillside is dominated by the semi-ruined kasbah built in 1634 by Saadian Sultan El Oualid to defend the potentially useful harbour against the Portuguese. A track off the S121 opposite the turning to Tnine Gharbia leads up to the building. Below it is the now disused royal villa built by King Mohamed V as a summer palace.

## Caves

At the far end of the beach to the south of the town, about a 10-minute walk, rocky outcrops are threaded with caves, some of which have been artificially enlarged over the years, especially during times of war, when they made useful hideaways and lookouts. If you walk down this way, Mustapha, who is usually to be found fishing on the rocks here, may well offer to give you a guided tour, as well as some obligatory mint tea cooked up on a camping stove.

## Lalla Fatna

For a change of scenery, you could head for Lalla Fatna, a wide sandy beach 50 km to the south. Sheltered by cliffs from the east wind, and with big northwest swells, it's a popular surfing spot. A café or two may spring up in summer, but there is little else in the way of facilities.

**Oualidia beach.**

# Sleeping

The best place to stay in Essaouira is the medina, with its upmarket riad-style guesthouses and occasionally damp cheap hotels. The new town has bigger, more modern hotels; outside town and down the coast towards Sidi Kaouki are some smart rural hideaways and beachside surf hangouts. In the centre of Essaouira it is important to get a well ventilated room with windows, and preferably a view of the ocean; there's often little to separate bedrooms from the Atlantic and even the smarter places have problems with damp. In Oualidia many of the restaurants double up as hotels.

## Essaouira medina

Essaouira is second only to Marrakech in the quantity and quality of restored properties in the old town operating as guesthouses. Though many of these are not riads in the strictest sense, they are usually referred to as such and the style will be familiar to those who have stayed in riads in Marrakech. Ring ahead, especially during the annual Gnaoua Festival.

### Palais Bleu €€€€
*2 Rue Ibn Batouta,*
*T0524-783434, heure-bleue.com.*
Map: Essaouira medina, G5, p146.
A part of the Relais and Château network, Palais Bleu is a seriously smart hotel, with the refined air of an exclusive gentlemen's club.

The style mixes colonial era elements such as dark varnished wood, animal heads and leather with black and white photography of Morocco and a riad-style courtyard with palms and a fountain. The roof terrace has a heated pool and views over the medina and there's a billiards room, a piano bar and a high-class spa. It's a buttoned-up sort of place though, markedly stiffer and more formal than its competition.

### Casa Lila €€€
*94 Rue Mohamed El Qouri,*
*T0524-475545, casalila.ma.*
Map: Essaouira medina, F5, p146.
Exceptionally photogenic, even by riad standards, the antique Casa Lila goes big on dusty pastel shades, with lots of purples and lilacs. The 10 rooms and suites come in different colour schemes but all are pretty

– the fabrics are luscious, beds come generously sprinkled with petals and open fires, floorboards and checkered floors add to the chic quotient. There's a young, hip feel to the place too, with laid-back music playing and a hammock strung between the old stone pillars in the courtyard. Lila is beginning to show her age a little – the towels are not as dazzlingly white as they once were – and rooms on the ground floor can be damp, but it mostly remains a charming spot, with smilingly good service and a great roof terrace with views across the medina.

### Dar Liouba €€€
*28 Impasse Moulay Ismaïl,*
*T0524-476297, darliouba.com.*
Map: Essaouira medina, F4, p146.
Homely and French, Dar Liouba is a tall thin guesthouse with rooms set around an octagonal

Dar Liouba.

courtyard. The decoration is a blend of European style and Moroccan touches: bright and simple with white walls and splashes of colour, though rooms are rather small. A very warm welcome and an unusual, light and airy design. The roof terrace has sunbeds and as with most Moroccan guesthouses, if you can group together 15 friends or relations, the whole place is available for rent.

### Dar Loulema €€€
*2 Rue Souss, T0524-475346, darloulema.com.*
Map: Essaouira medina, B5, p146.
Centrally situated next to the Café Taros, Loulema has big wicker chairs, a sunny roof terrace and good rooms with air conditioning and deep red walls. Four of the rooms are suites, some of which are themed – notably Belem, which is done out in maritime kitsch but has a stunning private terrace overlooking the sea and port and a glassed-in sitting. In other rooms naive art and thick rugs feature. The second-floor terrace is especially flowery.

### Hotel Villa Maroc €€€
*10 Rue Abdallah Ben Yassin, T0524-476147, villa-maroc.com.*
Map: Essaouira medina, C6, p146.
Converted from four merchants' houses, this claims to have been the first boutique hotel in Morocco. Beautifully decorated around a central court festooned

Madada Mogador.

with plants and greenery, roof terrace with superb views. There are 17 rooms and an apartment sleeping four is available.

### Jack's Apartments €€-€€€
*1 Place Moulay Hassan, T0524-475538, jackapartments.com.*
Map: Essaouira medina, B5, p146.
A well-established agency with a good selection of serviced rooms, self-catering apartments and houses throughout Essaouira. At the top of the range is the Scala Penthouse, the grand three-bedroom, ex-British consulate building, with high ceilings and big windows overlooking the sea but Jack can also offer one-bedroom apartments and a country house outside town. Moroccan food can be delivered on request and babysitting is also organized.

### La Maison des Artistes €€€
*19 Rue Laâlouj, T0524-475799, T0662-605438 (mob), lamaisondesartistes.com.*
Map: Essaouira medina, B4, p146
There's an entertaining air of artistic eccentricity about this seven-room guesthouse overlooking the sea, with lots of conversation-point pieces of furniture and striking art among the colourful decoration. 'Le Pavilion de Cesar' has stunning wrap-around sea views, as does the roof terrace.

### Madada Mogador €€€
*5 Rue Youssef el Fassi, T0524-475512, madada.com.*
Map: Essaouira medina, C7, p146.
Laid-back and French-run, Madad Mogador is a light and airy hotel with a spectacular roof terrace with wicker chairs and views of beach. Pale, warm colours and cool contemporary jazz fill the building. Rooms use

traditional *tadelakt*, beds have huge headboards and there are spacious, stylish bathrooms. At the brilliantly equipped Atelier Madada downstairs (see page 173), cookery lessons are offered.

### Riad De La Mer €€€

*7-9 Rue Khalid ben Oualid, T(+44) (0)20-87880701 (UK) or T0660-755894, riaddelamer.co.uk.*
Map: Essaouira medina, D2, p146.
In a great central position near Place Moulay Hassan, Riad De La Mer is friendly, English-owned and simple in a classy way, whitewashed and minimalist with blue and white tiles and carefully chosen objets d'art. The roof terrace has views across the medina to the sea. Guests can use the kitchen if they want to prepare lunches. The owners opened a new Essaouira riad in 2009: Riad des Palmiers.

### Riad Lotus Ô Marine €€€

*17 Rue Abderrahmane Eddakhil, T0524-476665, riadslotus.com.*
Map: Essaouira medina, C3, p146.
Slick and contemporary with a stark colour scheme, Ô Marine is the latest jewel in the Lotus crown. Some of the art doesn't quite hit the right notes, but the spectacular chandelier cascading light down the centre of the building should take guests' minds off that. Blacks and whites are used strongly in the art deco-influenced design and

there's plenty of modern equipment in the rooms, including DVD and CD players. The atmosphere is professional and closer to boutique hotel than traditional riad but the setting in the heart of the medina (just off Avenue Sidi Mohamed Ben Abdellah) gives an injection of Moroccan authenticity.

### Riad Watier €€€

*16 Rue Ceuta, T0524-476204, ryad-watier-maroc.com.*
Map: Essaouira medina, C3, p146.
The French owner of this large and spacious riad has a boat, and may take you out fishing if you ask nicely. The building, an ex-school, is now home to a resident tortoise, a massage room, lots of plants, and state-of-the-art plumbing. White walls add to the sense of light and there are tiles, rugs, terracotta coloured *tadelakt* and big showers in the 10 rooms. The

views from the roof terrace north along the coast and of the sunset are spectacular. Master suites sleep four or five and would be good for families.

### The Tea House €€€

*74 Derb Laalouj, La Skala, T0524-783543, theteahouse.net.*
Map: Essaouira medina, B3, p146.
Despite its English name, this small guesthouse is very much in the traditional Essaouira vein. The 200-year-old house is beautifully decorated, with antiques and pale pastel painted walls. The first and second floors are available for rent, each accommodating four people and each having a kitchen, a sitting room with an open fire, two bedrooms and a large bathroom. There's a shared roof terrace too, and breakfast and firewood are included.

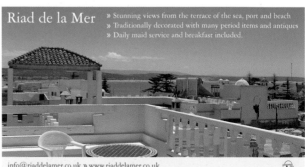

Riad de la Mer
» Stunning views from the terrace of the sea, port and beach
» Traditionally decorated with many period items and antiques
» Daily maid service and breakfast included.

info@riaddelamer.co.uk » www.riaddelamer.co.uk
T: England: (0)20 87880701 » Morocco: 00212 660755894    Riad de la Mer

### Villa de l'Ô €€€

*3 Rue Mohamed Ben Messaoud,*
*T0524-476375, villadelo.com.*
Map: Essaouira medina, D7, p146.
Twelve rooms and suites are grouped around a huge courtyard in this grand, colonial-style hotel that opened in 2008. Quiet and sophisticated, Villa de l'Ô is the most elegant accommodation in Essaouira. It's run by two enthusiastic and friendly French sisters, Celine and Caroline. Housed in a former almond store dating from the 18th century, it has kept many original features. Some rooms have sea views. Special offers are available with the new golf course (see page 173).

### Riad Amana €€€

*14 Rue khader Ghailane,*
*T0672-673026, riad-amana.com.*
With traditional tiles, white walls and powder wooden blue shutters, Amana has seven simple rooms and suites, some with balconies, and a sheltered roof terrace with chunky wicker furniture and an open fire. The fabrics are a little shiny, but rooms are generous.

### Hotel Dar l'Oussia €€

*4 Rue Mohamed Ben Messaoud,*
*T0524-783756, darloussia.com.*
Map: Essaouira medina, D7, p146.
A large place for the medina, l'Oussia has rooms around a big white courtyard. There's a

hammam and spa, and free Wi-Fi throughout. Metal-frame beds, white drapes and *tadelakt* bathrooms give the rooms some style and there's a big roof terrace with views across to the beach. Wooden sun loungers and a bar on the roof terrace make it a great spot for evenings as well as for breakfast in the morning.

### Hotel Emeraude €€

*228 Rue Chbanate, T0524-*
*473494, essaouirahotel.com.*
Map: Essaouira medina, G4, p146.
A small, attractive French-Moroccan run hotel on the dry side of the medina. Near the little gate of Borj Moulay Mohamed,

Villa de l'Ô.

to the northeast of Bab Marrakech, it's in a quiet area and has a sunny roof terrace, where breakfast is served, and eight double and two triple attractively decorated rooms all en suite. There's also guarded car parking just 40 m away. Officially a hotel, it has all the trappings and style of a riad.

### Lunetoille €€
*191 Rue Sidi Mohamed Ben Abdullah, T0524-474689; lunetoileriad.com.*
Map: Essaouira medina, E2, p146.
Low-key and good value, Lunetoille is off the beaten track in the Mellah, and you'll probably be able to hear the sea and the seagulls from your room. In places the blue and yellow colour scheme is a little jarring

Palazzo Desdemona.

but it has a genuine worn Moroccan feel, it's homely and the large apartments are a great option for families. Half price in January and February.

### Palazzo Desdemona €€
*12-14 Rue Youssef El Fassi, T0524-472227, palazzo-desdemona.com.*
Map: Essaouira medina, C6, p146.
Fifteen good-value rooms in a Moroccan-run hotel, airy and high-ceilinged with wooden beams. Walls are painted turquoise and there's internet available downstairs. The location is especially handy, near most of the Essaouira action.

### Riad El Mess €€
*14 Rue Oujda, T0524-476374, riad-el-mess@menara.ma.*
Map: Essaouira medina, D3, p146.
A riad in name but a budget hotel in price, El Mess is, despite the name, clean and tidy. There's a rather bare roof terrace with great views and a few riad signature elements: a fountain, tiles and arches. The colour scheme may be on the gaudy side of bright but this is a comfortable, good value and surprisingly comfortable base.

### Riad Lalla Mira €€
*12 Rue de l'Iraq, T0524-476744, lallamira.net.*
Map: Essaouira medina, F4, p146.
German run, Lalla Mira emphasizes its eco-credentials, and has a hammam with various

treatments which is also open to non-guests (see page 174) as well as a restaurant. Rooms have brick floors, draped beds and dark blue bathrooms.

### Riad Le Grand Large €€
*2 Rue Oum-Rabia, T0524-472866, riadlegrandlarge.com.*
Map: Essaouira medina, D3, p146.
The name is not only tautological, it's not really true, but this is a decent, colourful, and good value option, with 10 comfortable rooms, the best of which overlook the street. There's a roof terrace and a pizzeria too.

### Villa Garance €€
*10 Rue Eddakhil, T0524-473995, essaouira-garance.com.*
Map: Essaouira medina, D3, p146.
Well looked after by its French owners, Villa Garance has a pretty roof terrace with views over the sea and a plant-draped central courtyard. The eight rooms have external windows on a quiet street and a playroom and four-bedroom suite make it a good option for families.

### Essaouira Hostel €
*17 Rue Laghrissi, T0524-476481, T0661-709083 (mob), essaouirahostel@gmail.com.*
Map: Essaouira medina, G3, p146.
It's well hidden in the Essaouira backstreets, but as long as you can find it, this new hostel offers a very warm welcome, with communal meals for 20dh, a bar, a frescoed roof terrace and well

constructed dorms. Voted the second best hostel in Africa in the annual Hoscar awards (it was pipped to first place by the Equity Hostel in Marrakech), there's a great friendly vibe.

### Hotel Beau Rivage €
*Place Moulay Hassan,*
*T/F0524-475925.*
Map: Essaouira medina, G5, p146.
Some of the 21 rooms in the central hotel have balconies overlooking the main square, others have a sea view. The style is dated, but it's clean and has friendly, helpful management and a roof terrace.

### Hotel Cap Sim €
*11 Rue Ibn Rochd, T0524-785834.*
Map: Essaouira medina, B5, p146.
Clean and cheap, just round the corner from Place Moulay Hassan. The simple contemporary rooms, around a central courtyard, are very clean with tiles and coloured glass.

### Hotel Riad Nakhla €
*12 Rue d'Agadir, T/F0524-474940,*
*essaouiranet.com/riad-nakhla.*
Map: Essaouira medina, D5, p146.
Eighteen colourful rooms, all with private bathrooms, for a knockdown price. The decoration may not be quite up to the level of its riad competitors but there's a courtyard with a fountain, a roof terrace for breakfast and the whole place is attractive, comfortable and very good value.

**Outside the medina**

Outside the medina, most of Essaouira's hotels are big and too characterless to recommend, though there are a few seafront options worth considering if being within a stone's throw of the beach is important. In the surrounding countryside, rural retreats are a more restful option.

### Sofitel Essaouira €€€€
*Av Mohamed V,*
*T0524-479000, sofitel.com.*
Map: Essaouira medina, B7, p146.
Opposite the beach, this is a large and luxurious hotel, with 117 rooms decorated in a contemporary version of traditional Moroccan style. There's a big heated pool surrounded by palms and a good bar and restaurant.

### Baoussala €€€
*El Ghazoua, T0524-792345,*
*T0666-308746 (mob),*
*baoussala.com.*
Turn right 6 km south from Océan Vagabond.
A well established rural guesthouse 9 km from Essaouira with a beautiful solar-heated pool, spacious Baoussala has hammocks strung up in quiet corners and plenty of sunny spots for chilling out. Three suites and three double rooms are all beautifully decorated with a colourful organic charm. Breakfast can be taken on the roof terrace and there are generous public

areas. Eight staff keep the place functioning smoothly, with a chef producing meals using fresh local produce and transfers and car hire organized. Purpose-built by its French owners, the whole house can be rented.

### Océan Vagabond €€€
*4 Blvd Lalla Aïcha, angle Rue Moukawama, T0524-479222,*
*oceanvagabond.com.*
Map: Essaouira medina, B5, p146.
Facing the beach but only around 200 m from the medina, the Océan Vagabond hotel lacks some of the atmosphere of a medina riad and a little of the surf vibe of its sister café (see page 171) but it is attractively

Océan Vagabond.

decorated and the 14 rooms have balconies – some with sea views – and plenty of mod cons, such as large flat screen TVs. The style is international boutique, with rooms themed to match various ethnic stereotypes: Samurai, Masai, Geisha etc. There's a bar and a flowery garden, which isn't big but has a decent pool.

### Auberge Tangaro €€
*T0524-784784,*
*auberge-tangaro.com.*
A rural place with no electricity and good food, which is a good thing as half board is compulsory. The hot water can be a bit unreliable, but there are great ocean views. There are 13 rooms, six suites and camping is possible.

### La Maison du Chameau €€
*Off the Agadir road some 13 km from Essaouira, take the left turn for Marrakech, T0524-785077, maisonduchameau@yahoo.fr.*
Traditional whitewashed farm buildings have been converted into tranquil guest accommodation, but most come here for the camels – imported from Mali, these are white camels, rare in Morocco, and you can ride them here; prices go from €10 for an hour's introductory lesson up to €90 for a two-day trip along the coast.

## Sidi Kaouki

Website sidi-kaouki.com has details of other hotels, apartments and rooms for rent in Sidi Kaouki.

### Rebali Riads €€€
*Sidi Kaouki, bookings through Fleewinter in the UK: T(+44) (0)20-7112 0019; rebaliriads.com.*
Six newly built apartments offer a good option for families. The carefully designed complex shares a hammam and two good pools but offers privacy, too as well as the option of self-catering, though breakfast is included and other meals can be arranged. Two of the riads have rooms which can be booked individually; the other four are available in their entirety. Sliding roofs give the option of opening the central spaces to the sky, and though they are not strictly riads, the apartments have riad style elements, with Moroccan fireplaces and roof terraces with miles of sea views. The largest place sleeps six and has its own private pool, a huge 'entertaining space' and a cinema room. A tennis court may be added in future. A few minutes' walk from the beach, it's very peaceful: you'll mostly hear little more than waves and chickens.

### Hotel Villa Soleil €€
*Sidi Kaouki, T070-233097 (mob), T0524-472092, hotel-villa-soleil.com.*
The 11 simple rooms and suites of Hotel Villa Soleil are just a

Auberge de la Plage.

Rebali Riads.

minute from the beach. Sandy tiles, whitewash and greys are punctuated with geraniums and splashes of colour. Massage, manicure and pedicure are all offered and there's a restaurant too. Breakfast is taken on the terrace which has views and basket chairs.

### Windy Kaouki €€
*Sidi Kaouki, T0524-472279, windy-kaouki.com.*
This Italian-run place has six mini-apartments and a

good pool in the courtyard. The restaurant serves fantastic grilled fish, octopus salad and aubergines.

### Auberge de la Plage €
*Sidi Kaouki, T0524-476600, kaouki.com.*
A colourful and chilled place with Italian and German management. Of the 10 spacious rooms, five have private bathrooms. The colours all clash but solar energy and candles add to the atmosphere. The dining room has an open fire, the roof terrace has views over the sea, and horse-riding and camel excursions can be arranged.

### Hotel des Artistes €
*Sidi Kaouki, T0677-785350.*
Behind the café of the same name, facing the beach, these simple rooms are good value, with wood and stone used to good effect.

### Oualidia

Oualidia can get very crowded in high summer, when hotel reservations are essential. Prices drop in low season, from September to April. Most restaurants are also places to stay.

### La Sultana Oualidia €€€€
*Parc à Huitres 3, Bled Gaïlla, Oualidia, T0524-388008, lasultanaoualidia.com.*
A sophisticated five-star boutique hotel just to the north of the town. Sandy pastel shades and a carved stone spa set the tone and the restaurant goes big on lobster and oysters. There is painted furniture, lots of bare stone and wood and marble floors.

### Hotel Hippocampe €€€
*Route du Palais Oualidia, T0523-366108, hotelhippocampe.com.*
Bungalows around the edge of peaceful and amazingly floral gardens are set back from the lagoon. Among the profusion of geraniums and nasturtiums, the two sea-facing suites and 23 plainer rooms have wicker sofas and light contemporary furnishings. The licensed restaurant, serving lobster and the ubiquitous oysters, has patio doors opening onto a terrace with great views, and below this there's a pool. There are kayaks and pedaloes and half board is tempting for many who stay here and have no desire to leave the hotel's confines. Wi-Fi

### Issa Blanca €€
*T0523-366148, hotel-issablanca-oualidia.com.*
Along the beach road, away from the lagoon, the six simple rooms here have clean, tiled, black and white bathrooms and metal frame beds; one has a private terrace. There's an open kitchen in the French-style restaurant – try the salad Issa Blanca, with oysters, of course, and something from a good list of Moroccan wines.

### L'Initiale €€
*Oualidia Plage, T0523-366246.*
At the end of the road, this is a comfortable, modern place with a great licensed restaurant and, if you can get room five, a great sea view: sit up in bed and you'll see the waves crashing on the sand about 70 m away.

### Motel-Restaurant à l'Araigneé Gourmande €€
*T0523-366447.*
There are good views of the lagoon from some of the 15 rooms in two adjacent buildings, all of which have balconies. The popular restaurant has service with panache and offers seafood of just about every type imaginable. It's too large to have much atmosphere and groups (everyone from old-aged bus tours to kite-surfers) come here but the food is excellent. There's a good value menu for 70dh, or a 200dh version with lobster. Save some room for the succulent apple pie.

### Tennis Club de Oualidia €
*T0523-366262.*
Seven simple rooms face the courts (50dh per hour) – a convenient option for anyone who fancies a quick set before breakfast.

# Eating

### After 5 €€€
*7 Rue Youssef El Fassi,*
*T0524-473349.*
*1200-2300.*
Map: Essaouira medina, C7, p146.
Under huge stone arches and a
pink ceiling, After 5 is a distinctly
hip spot, with chilled lounge
tunes and an imaginative
Moroccan menu with Euro
tinges. There's a 'super brunch'
and modern dishes: the
carpaccio of swordfish is
flavoured with ginger and the
chicken and avocado salad
comes with orange segments
and a generous sprinkling of
toasted almonds. The place
really comes alive in the
evenings, however, when it
doubles as a bar. Both chic and
inviting, there is an open fire for

After 5.

winter, comfy cushions and free
Wi-Fi. Striking design features
include bold art and lightshades
big enough to live in.

### Chez Sam €€
*Port, T0524-476238.*
Map: Essaouira medina, C7, p146.
In the port itself with round
porthole windows and fine
views of the boats outside, Sam's
is a fish and seafood restaurant
and bar, with good food and
drink, particularly good lobster,
and excellent, although pricey,
seafood platters. Waistcoated
waiters and layers of dark varnish
give an authentically aged feel,
as does the decoration of photos
of old black and white film stars
and Moroccan pots. There is a
big menu to test your vocabulary
of French fish names and also a
handful of fishy tagines.

### Dar l'Oussia €€
*4 Rue Mohamed Ben Messaoud,*
*T0524-783756, darloussia.com.*
Map: Essaouira medina, D7, p146.
Couscous evenings on Fridays
with gnaoua music are the
highlight of the week at this
central eatery. The menu is
predominantly French with a
few Moroccan dishes – the foie
gras is spoken about in hushed
tones by French expats. With
arches, Cuban jazz, lamps and
low seats with cushions it's an
atmospheric place.

### El Minzah €€
*3 Av Oqba Ibn Nafia,*
*T0524-475308.*
Map: Essaouira medina, C5, p146.
This restaurant and piano bar
with good seafood options also
makes a mellow, sophisticated
spot for a drink. The Moroccan
fixed-price menu is good value,
or splash out three times as
much on the French one.

### Elizir €€
*1 Rue Agadir, T0524-472103.*
*From 1930.*
Map: Essaouira medina, D5, p146.
Run by a Moroccan recently
returned from living in the
foodie hotspots of Italy, Elizir is
about as good as a restaurant
can get. The creative food, for
a start, uses top-notch
ingredients and is exquisitely
prepared – try the ravioli with
ricotta, basil and pistachio, or
the organic chicken, fresh fig
and gorgonzola, but save some
room for the mouth-wateringly
delicious pear pastilla with
chocolate, served with a
cucumber sorbet. There's
good wine too. Then there's the
wonderfully eclectic decor, such
as a fibre glass mannequin used
as a lamp, the plastic robots and
the bowls of fruit. Everywhere
you look is a profusion of quirky,
colourful, often 1970s, pop
culture. The sound system is
excellent too and even the jazzy
music is exceedingly hip. Sit out
on the green and white roof
terrace when it's warm.

Samarkand.

### Le Patio €€
*28 Bis, Rue Moulay Rachid,*
*T0524-474166.*
Eves only, closed Mon.
Map: Essaouira medina, B5, p146.
Styling themselves as a 'tapas
ocean food' restaurant, funky
Le Patio is a stylish, atmospheric
little place with warm low
lighting, brick arches, drapes and
seductively flickering candles.
The food is creative and tasty,
with imaginative use of flavours
such as vanilla and cinnamon.

### Samarkand €€
*9 Rue Abderrahmane Eddakhil,*
*T0524-476665.*
Map: Essaouira medina, C3, p146.
Fusion Mediterranean/Moroccan
food is dished up at the dark and
atmospheric restaurant of Riad
Lotus Ô Marine. Aperitifs and
cocktails set the scene, to be

followed by dishes such as
marinated sardines, beef with
three peppers, and ravioli with
seafood.

### Dar Al Houma €
*9 Rue El Hajjali, T0524-783387.*
Map: Essaouira medina, C5, p146.
There's a rare vegetarian set
menu (55dh) as well as more
standard Moroccan menus at
this cosy little place just inside
the walls of the medina.

### Ferdaouss €
*27 Rue Abdesslam Lebadi, T0524-*
*473655, T0666-177023 (mob).*
Map: Essaouira medina, D4, p146.
A popular place for Moroccan
home cooking, Ferdaouss is
family run and has comfy seats
and cushions. The food is reliable
and good value, with the usual
selection of pastillas, couscous
and tagines.

### L'Artisan Pizzas €
*4 Rue El Fatouaki, T0524-784689.*
1100-1600, 1830-2200, closed Tue.
Map: Essaouira medina, C5, p146.
Eat in, take away or ring for
delivery from this very good
quality French-run pizzeria.
Bases are satisfyingly crisp and
although the cheese is a rather
yellow mozzarella-substitute the
other ingredients are top drawer.
There's a black and white
contemporary interior and a
couple of tables out on the street
too. Try a Mogador pizza, with
tuna, or one of the excellent
juices. They also do dessert
pizzas such as 'creole', with
flambéed banana.

### Les Alizés €
*26 Rue de la Skala, T0524-476819.*
Map: Essaouira medina, B4, p146.
One of the most popular places in
town, and rightfully so. You can't

L'Artisan Pizzas.

reserve, but waiting at the small tables just inside the entrance with some olives and a bottle of wine is one of the best pleasures of the place. Once you get a table you'll be plied with great Moroccan food – there's not an enormous choice but it's all good and the place is run with a rare combination of efficiency and good humour.

### Port fish stalls €
Lunch only.
Map: Essaouira medina, B7, p146.
The best cheap lunch options are the open-air fish-stall restaurants between Place Moulay Hassan and the port; usually served with a tomato salad, you can pick and choose your fish before it's cooked. Hygiene is good and prices are fixed, and written up on boards, but make sure you are clear on what you have and haven't ordered.

### Restaurant La Découverte €
*8 Rue Houmman, T0524-473158, essaouira-ladecouverte.com.*
Map: Essaouira medina, C5, p146.
A friendly little French-run place offering such delicacies as lentil salad with argan oil and vegetable gratin as well as meatier Moroccan choices. They also have Wi-Fi, in case you want to stop by for a drink with your email.

### Souk el Hout €
Map: Essaouira medina, E3, p146.
An alternative to the port fish stalls is the little fish barbecue place in Souk el Hout, the fish market in the town centre. Here you buy your fish from one of the market stalls and then take it to the kitchens at the back, where someone will prepare and cook it for you for 3dh. There's none of the checked awnings and sea views of the port, but it's an atmospheric experience.

### Cafés
There are good places for breakfast on Place Moulay Hassan, which also makes a good place to watch the evening social life pass by. Breakfast here is better value than in a cheap hotel, and no one seems to mind if you bring your own cakes. At the far end of the beach, Océan

Port fish stalls.

Vagabond (see below) is also a good all-day option.

### Café des Arts
*56 Av Istikal, T012-134742.*
Upstairs on the main street, this place has a young vibe, with live music, art and Moroccan food. Good for a light lunch or a quick snack.

### Café Taros
*2 Rue de la Skala,*
*T0524-476407, taroscafe.com.*
Closed Sun.
Map: Essaouira medina, B6, p146.
With lots of blue-painted furniture on a roof terrace overlooking Place Moulay Hassan, Taros is Essaouira's social pivot. It also ticks most boxes, with a bar, good food, and late opening. There are lots of books and magazines in the café area, and even a small boutique. *Taros* is the local name for the ocean wind. The entrance is just up the street off to the left of the Place.

### Gelateria Dolce Freddo
*Place Moulay Hassan.*
Map: Essaouira medina, B5, p146.
Right on the main square, this café does a roaring trade in decent ice cream.

### La Cantina
*66 Rue Boutouil, T0524-474515.*
Map: Essaouira medina, E2, p146.
Open for just two years on a little square at the Mellah end of the street, La Cantina already feels like an old friend. English-run and

popular with travellers' it serves fantastic banana and strawberry shakes, burgers, chilli con carne and has a great veggie selection too. Welcoming and friendly to all-comers, it has a book exchange and also acts as a good source of local info.

### La Triskalla
*58 Rue Touahen, T0524-476371.*
Map: Essaouira medina, B3, p146.
A very laid-back café indeed, with free internet and Wi-Fi, low lighting, wonky candles and a cat. A proper travellers' hangout, there is also colourful art, old cushions, low seating and scrabble. Snacks and pancakes dominate the menu and there's an extensive selection of juices, some of which are overly imaginative.

### Bars
Essaouira has little in the way of nightlife, although it livens up during the annual Gnaoua music festival. The roof terrace lounge bar of Café Taros (see above) is usually the liveliest spot after sundown. El Minzah or After 5 (see page 168) offer alternatives.

### Dar l'Oussia
*4 Rue Mohamed Ben Messaoud,*
*T0524-783756, darloussia.com.*
Football is sometimes shown in the dark and atmospheric bar here.

Outside the medina

### Océan Vagabond €
*Blvd Mohamed V, T0524-783934.*
Map: Essaouira medina, C7, p146.
A café/restaurant and surf hangout, Océan Vagabond, at the far end of the beach, has a big seating area out front with comfy seats from which to watch the world and his camel go by. The club mistral surf shop is attached, with lessons and rental available. They do breakfast as well as a great international menu of panini, salads and good daily specials, such as a tasty spaghetti with seafood. Wine and beer is available too. A fantastically chilled hangout spot, there's also a 'small hungers' menu of biscuits and crisps.

### Chalet de la Plage €€
*1 Av Mohamed V,*
*T0524-472972.*
Mon-Sat 1200-1330, 1830-2100.
Good seafood dishes such as fish soup, Qualidia oysters and grilled calamari. If the wind isn't too strong, try for a red-and-white-checked table on the terrace overlooking the beach.

### Sidi Kaouki

The café shacks at the centre of the village do sandwiches, snacks and tagines. They become briefly active at lunchtime, though you'll usually find one or two open for breakfast too. Café des Artistes,

# Shopping

attached to **Hotel des Artistes**, is another option, as is the lounge in the **Surfclub** (see page 174). For a more satisfying meal, however, go to the excellent restaurant at **Windy Kaouki** (see page 166).

## Oualidia

As an alternative to the many excellent restaurants, take a bottle of wine to the beach in the evening, and oyster and urchin sellers will approach you with the freshest catch for sale. See also the sleeping section – just about all the hotels here double up as good restaurants.

### Restaurant Ostréa II €€€
*Parc á Huitres et Coquillages No7, T0523-366451.*
1200-2330, closed Fri.
On your right as you come into Oualidia from the Casablanca direction. The sister of a very highly regarded restaurant in Casablanca, Ostréa is one of the best places to try the local oysters with a bottle of white wine and a nice lagoon view.

### Restaurant Les Roches €€
*T0519-336793.*
A small and friendly place opposite L'Initiale, painted white and blue and offering a good 90dh 'menu touristique' with various seafood dishes.

## Essaouira medina

Beautifully inlaid thuya wood objects such as chess sets and boxes constitute one of Essaouira's most active industries. Raffia sandals and shoes are another speciality of the town. Argan oil cosmetics and other products made from the fruit of the local Argan tree can also be found widely.

### Boutique Sahara
*Darb Lalouj, no phone, mohamed_saharas@ hotmail.com.*
Jewellery, antique locks, daggers and fossils – this is a dusty treasure trove.

### Gipsy Surfer
*14 Rue de Tetouan, T0524-783268.*
The place to come if your surf threads and shades don't yet match your newly found skills on a board.

Raffia shoes, M Hajoub's shop.

### Kif Kif
*Place aux Grains.*
Mon-Sat 1000-1300, 1600-2000.
Locally-made accessories, jewellery and knick-knacks.

### M Hajoub Cordonnier
*4 Rue El Hajjaine.*
Through spectacularly thick glasses, an old Essaouira man works away making colourful raffia shoes in his workshop at the back of this little shop.

### Poupa Litza
*135 bis Mohamed El Qory, T0524-783565, poupalitza.com.*
Mon-Sat 0900-1230, 1430-1900.
Designer handbags combining French style and local workmanship in bright colours.

### Raffia Craft
*82 Rue d'Agadir, T0524-783632.*
Mon-Sat 1000-1300, 1500-1900, Sun 1000-1300.
This tiny little place is the outlet of local designer Miro, whose raffia shoes have been discovered by European high-end fashionistas and are now sold in Parisian boutiques. His style is now mimicked by other places around town.

# Activities & tours

### Camel-riding

The beach at Sidi Kaouki is a great spot (see page 154) to wobble about on the back of a camel. You'll also get lots of offers at the southern end of the beach in Essaouira. If you want to get into camel-riding in a big way, La Maison du Chameaux (see page 166) is the place for you.

### Cookery courses

**L'Atelier Madada**
*7 Bis Rue Youssef El Fassi,*
*T0524-475512.*
Mon-Sat 1030-1430, 450dh course and meal.

Under the Madada hotel, this is a great place to learn the secrets of Moroccan cooking, or just to spend an enjoyable couple of hours, after which you get to enjoy the fruits of your labour. Kids' lessons are also possible.

### Golf

**Golf de Mogador**
*golfdemogador.com.*
Essaouira's new Gary Player-designed golf course opened in 2009. With views of the Atlantic, it is one of the best in Morocco, and is expected to bring a new sort of visitor into the town.

Villa de l'Ô (see page 163) offer special accommodation and golf deals.

## Cooking at L'Atelier Madada

In a former almond warehouse under the Madada hotel, a smart, well equipped kitchen is the setting for Moroccan cookery lessons. There's a maximum of eight people and everyone has their own space and equipment. Mona, the Moroccan chef, learnt from the best – her mother was a great Essaouiran cook who worked in La Mamounia in Marrakech. Dishes change every day but staff try to accommodate any special requests – for example they can adapt the program to suit vegetarians if you call the day before.

The day starts with a tour of Essaouira's fish and spices souks, and advice on what to buy and what to look for with spices and preserved lemons. Then it's back to the kitchen for a mint tea (which also comes with a how-to) before the rolling up of sleeves to start work.

The atmosphere is just right: friendly and informal, but also informative and well organised. And at the end of the morning, stairs at the back lead to a red draped dining room upstairs where you get to taste the products of your labours.

In the afternoons they also do a pastry workshop, which is especially good for kids, and if you want to leave offspring making gazelle horns and head off to the beach that's fine too.

Satisfied customers take the recipes away with them and send photos back.

# Transport

### Kite- and windsurfing
**Christophe Raynaud**
*T0664-894159,*
*kiteadventuressaouira.com.*
A qualified, English-speaking
kitesurfing and windsurfing
instructor. Rates from €90 for a
three-hour starter lesson.

### Quad biking
**Palma Quad**
*palmaquad.com.*
The most professional quad
biking outfit in Essaouira,
Palma Quad offer a two-hour
trip for 450dh.

### Surfing
The surf shop attached to the
**Océan Vagabond Café** (see
page 171) has Essaouira's best kit
for rent and will also offer lessons
and lots of information.

**Sidi Kaouki Surfclub**
*Sidi Kaouki, T0672-044016.*
**0900-2300.**
Lessons, advice and kit for
surfing, windsurfing and
kite-surfing. With plenty of
beach space, Sidi Kaouki would
be a good place to learn. The
surfclub also has a small café/
restaurant and they operate as
agents for hotels in the village.

### Tours
**Ecotourisme et randonées**
*T0615-762131.*
Walks around Essaouira
run from the Restaurant La
Découverte (see page 170).
There is an English guide.

### Wellbeing
**Hammam Lalla Mira**
*12 Rue de l'Iraq, T0524-476744,*
*lallamira.ma.*
The oldest public baths in
Essaouira are now attached
to the hotel of the same name
(see page 164) and are heated
with solar power. Free to guests
of the hotel, the hammam is also
open to visitors and locals.

**Les Massages Bérbères**
*135 Av Mohamed El Quori,*
*T0524-473130.*
0900-1300, 1500-1900,
350dh for 2 hrs.
Relaxing and professional, argan
and other traditional oils are
used in this calm and warmly
decorated massage parlour.

Buses to Marrakech (six
Supratours buses daily from
office near Bab Marrakech, many
other companies from bus
station outside Bab Doukala;
three hours). Also Safi (one
Supratours bus, others from bus
station; two hours) for onward
travel to Oualidia. Grands taxi
from Bab El Menzah, Bab
Marrakech or Bab Doukala to Sidi
Kaouki or Marrakech. Local bus
from Bab Doukala to Sidi Kaouki
every two hours, until 2000.

**Les Massages Bérbères.**

Beach at Taguenza.

# Contents

179 Introduction
180 Western High Atlas
184 Great days out:
    Walking in Toubkal
188 Eastern High Atlas
190 Listings:
190 Sleeping
194 Eating
194 Activities & tours
195 Transport

High Atlas

Grasslands near the Atlas.

# Introduction

Snow-topped for half the year, the High Atlas Mountains rise out of the plains south of Marrakech, easily visible from the city on clear days. West to east they stretch across Morocco from the Atlantic coast just north of Agadir until they fade into the desert on the Algerian border. In many ways they are the dominant feature of Moroccan geography, yet the High Atlas are very different to the Moroccan lowlands, socially as well as topographically.

In winter there is scope for skiing, in spring apple, almond and cherry blossom fills the valleys with pink and white and in summer the cooler air is a draw for escapees from the oppressive city. All year round there are good walking opportunities, from short strolls to waterfalls, to serious treks to mountain summits. Accommodation options are improving, with three excellent mountain kasbahs offering an elegant way to experience the Atlas.

In easy day-trip distance of Marrakech, the Toubkal National Park – named after Jbel Toubkal, the highest peak in North Africa – has long been an attraction for tourists. The region also has other popular destinations, including the pretty Setti Fatma In the Ourika Valley and the ski resort of Oukaïmeden. The striking, restored mosque of Tin Mal is high on the spectacular road to the Tizi-n-Test pass. Heading south is another spectacular high pass, the Tizi-n-Tichka, and the village of Telouet with its brooding Glaoui fortress.

Further east are the Cascades d'Ouzoud, Morocco's highest waterfalls, and the beautiful high valley of the Aït Bougmez.

The door to a house in the Ourika Valley.

## What to see in...

**... one day**
Setti Fatma makes a great day trip into the mountains, with opportunities for walks up the valley or to the nearby seven waterfalls. Makeshift restaurants beside the stream offer tagines with spectacular views. In winter, consider Oukaïmeden for a novel day of African skiing. In the Ourika Valley, rafting is also possible.

**... a weekend or more**
Imlil and Aremd are good bases for more serious walking into the high peaks of the Toubkal National Park. The high passes of Tizi-n-Test and Tizi-n-Tichka are the midpoints on two vertiginous and winding drives south across the mountains. Both routes pass near to extraordinary buildings: the 12th century mosque of Tin Mal and the mountain kasbah of Telouet. To the east, the tumbling waterfall of Cascades d'Ouzoud is impressive and the valley of Aït Bougmez offers truly isolated trekking. Dotted around the mountains, beautiful kasbah hotels make a more pampered break.

# Western High Atlas

Three main roads lead south out of Marrakech into the western High Atlas – from west to east, they head over the Tizi-n-Test pass towards Taroudant, up the Ourika Valley to Setti Fatma, Oukaïmeden and the Toubkal National Park, and over the Tizi-n-Tichka pass towards Ouarzazate.

On the R203 to the Tizi-n-Test, Asni is an important market town and Ouirgane a strung-out holiday destination in the hills. Further south the road curves and rises through the spectacular mountain valley to the awe-inspiring 12th-century mosque of Tin Mal, one of Morocco's most significant buildings, now partially restored. Back at Asni, a road branches south to Imlil and the Toubkal National Park, centring on North Africa's highest mountain. The landscapes are spectacular and there are some great walking routes.

The route up the Ourika Valley from Marrakech is, initially at least, a gentler one, splitting to terminate at either the village of Setti Fatma, with its waterfalls and riverside restaurants, or the ski resort of Oukaïmeden.

Most switch-back of all, the N9 climbs to cross through the Tizi-n-Tichka pass at 2260 m. Just east of here is the precipitous Kasbah of Telouet.

## Asni

After the rather nerve-racking drive through the gorges of Moulay Brahim, the approach to Asni with its poplar and willow trees comes as something of a relief. If you arrive on a Saturday, you will be able to see the souk, in a big dusty enclosure on your left as you come from Marrakech, with its accompanying chaos of grands taxi, mules and minibuses. The village is scattered in clusters in the valley and makes a good place for a quick break en route to Ouirgane, Tin Mal or Taroudant if you can deal with the attentions of the trinket sellers. There are good walking routes along the Plateau du Kik to the west of Asni, north to Moulay Brahim and southwest to Ouirgane.

A popular driving route goes from Asni up onto the Plateau du Kik and then through the villages around Tiferouine before heading some 8 km northwest across country to the settlement of Lalla Takerkoust and its reservoir lake (see page 103).

## Ouirgane

Ouirgane is another pleasant place to pause on the R203, about one hour's drive (61 km) from Marrakech. The settlement's houses are scattered on the valley sides, and some have been recently displaced by the building of a new dam on the Oued Nfiss. Ouirgane can be reached by bus from Marrakech (the Taroudant service), or by grands taxi from Asni. Hotels in Ouirgane (see page 190) have good food and offer the opportunity to explore the valley in easy rambles.

**After the rather nerve-racking drive through the gorges of Moulay Brahim, the approach to Asni with its poplar and willow trees comes as something of a relief.**

## Tin Mal

Tin Mal is about 2½ hrs drive from Marrakech, taking things easy, just past the village of Ijoukak. If you are not driving, you can take a Taroudant bus or a grands taxi as far as Ijoujak, where there are several basic cafés with rooms. At the mosque the guardian will let you in and point out enthusiastically features such as the original doors piled up in a corner. He'll also ask for a donation when you leave.

A small settlement high in the High Atlas mountains, Tin Mal was once the holy city of the Almohad Dynasty. It offers a rare opportunity for non-Muslims to see the interior of a major Moroccan mosque, with examples of 12th-century Almohad decor intact amidst the ruins. The Koutoubia at Marrakech (the Almohad capital from 1147) was modelled on Tin Mal.

**Tin Mal mosque.**

## Around the region

In 1122, Ibn Toumert, after much roaming in search of wisdom, returned to Morocco. He created too much trouble in Marrakech with his criticisms of the effete Almoravids, and shortly after, when the mountain tribes had sworn to support him and fight the Almoravids in the name of the doctrines he had taught them, he was proclaimed Mahdi, the rightly guided one. In 1125 he established his capital at Tin Mal, a fairly anonymous hamlet strategically situated in the heartlands of his tribal supporters. The rough and ready village was replaced with a walled town, soon to become spiritual centre of an empire. The first mosque was a simple affair. The building you see today, a low square structure, was the work of Ibn Toumert's successor, Abd el Mu'min – a student whom the future Mahdi had met in Bejaïa.

Tin Mal was the first ribat, as the austere Almohad fortresses were called, and subject to a puritan discipline. The Mahdi himself was a sober, chaste person, an enemy of luxurious living. All his efforts went into persuading his followers of the truths of Islam – as he conceived them. Tin Mal was subject to a pitiless discipline. Prayers were led by the Mahdi himself and all had to attend. Public whippings and the threat of execution kept those lacking in religious fervour in line. As well as prayer leader, the Mahdi was judge, hearing and trying cases himself according to Muslim law, which had barely begun to penetrate the mountain regions.

After Ibn Toumert's death, his simple tomb became the focal point for a mausoleum for the Almohad sovereigns. Standing in the quiet mosque, today mostly open to the sky, looking down the carefully restored perspectives of the arcades, it is difficult to imagine what a hive of religious enthusiasm this place must have been.

Completed in 1154, under Abd el Mumin, the Tin Mal Mosque has a simple exterior. The mihrab (prayer niche) is built into the minaret. To the left, as one stands before the mihrab, is the imam's entrance; to the right is a space for the minbar,

**Below: Tin Mal mosque. Opposite page: Landscape near Tizi-n-Test.**

the preacher's chair, which would have been pulled out for sermons. The decoration is simple: there are several cupolas with restored areas of stalactite plasterwork and there are examples of the darj w ktaf and palmette motifs, but little inscription. The technique used, plaster applied to brick, is a forerunner of later, larger Almohad decorative schemes.

When the new empire acquired Marrakech, a fine capital well located on the plain, Tin Mal remained its spiritual heart – and a sort of reliable rear base. It was to Tin Mal that Abd el Mumin sent the treasures of Ibn Tachfin the Almoravid. Even after the Merinid destruction of 1275-76, The tombs of Ibn Toumert and his successors inspired deep respect.

Eventually, the Almohads were to collapse in internecine struggles. The final act came in the 1270s, when the last Almohads took refuge in Tin Mal. However, the governor of Marrakech, El Mohallim, pursued them into their mountain fastness, and besieged and took the seemingly impenetrable town. The Almohad caliph and his followers were taken prisoner and executed and the great Almohad sovereigns, Abu Yaqoub and Abu Youssef, were pulled from their tombs and decapitated. The Almohads, one time conquerors of the whole of the Maghreb and much of Spain, were destroyed in their very capital, barely 150 years after they had swept away the Almoravids.

In the 1990s, around US$750,000 was put forward for restoration of the ruins. Work now seems to have ground to a halt, though the building is perhaps doubly impressive in its semi-ruined, semi-open-to-the-sky way.

## Tizi-n-Test

The R203 from Marrakech to Taroudant is one of the most spectacular routes in Morocco, winding its way up and then down through the High Atlas mountains, above the beautiful valleys and past isolated villages, eventually reaching the Tizi-n-Test pass at 2092m, with its breathtaking views across the Sous valley to the Anti Atlas mountains. There are buses between the two cities, but check that they are going via Tizi-n-Test. Driving has been possible since the road, a traditional trading route, was formally opened in 1928, following the work of French engineers. Some of its sections are a bit scary, but it is a highly recommended experience, particularly when tied in with visits to Asni, Ouirgane and Tin Mal. Signs on the exit to Marrakech will indicate if the pass is open.

## Imlil & the Toubkal Parc National

The most important village of the Aït Mizane Valley, Imlil is the start of the walks in the area, and also makes a good mountain hangout. In the centre of the village is the car park/taxi area with the stone-built Club Alpin Français hut. There are small cafés and shops, a good baker, a spice shop and a travel agent. Mules are 'parked' to the south of the village. When you arrive, you may be besieged by the men of the village, keen to help you in some way or other. The town's hammam has been built with money from Kasbah du Toubkal (see page 191).

Having a good local Tachelhit-speaking guide is essential on treks. The best time for walking is after the main snows, at blossom time in the spring: mules cannot negotiate the passes until March or April and summers can be too hot, with hazy visibility. From November to February It Is too cold and there is too much snow for walking. Without ropes, ice axes, crampons and experience, winter should be avoided.

# Walking in Toubkal

**N**orthern Africa's highest peak is one that many like to tick off their list, but the national park that surrounds it has plenty of other good walks, from afternoon strolls to serious treks. It's important to find a guide for longer walks here – conditions can be dangerous. The number of people who have to drop out of treks in the area due to stomach problems is high, so try to check on hygiene, when deciding who to use. If you're planning a trek in advance, Mountain Voyage, based in Marrakech (mountain-voyage.com), are recommended.

Walking options include the Aremd circuit, a refreshing hike through remote villages and past breathtaking views, and a hike to the Lac d'Ifni. Another is to walk to Setti Fatma, in the Ourika Valley.

Much more challenging is to climb Jbel Toubkal, the highest mountain in North Africa at 4167 m. It is necessary to break the walk at the Club Alpin Français Toubkal Refuge (ex-Refuge Neltner), a simple dormitory place with no meals at 3106 m. In winter this is a difficult trek and full equipment is essential. A specialist hiking book such as Richard Knight's *Trekking in the Moroccan Atlas* (Hindhead: Trailblazer, 2008) is recommended. Mules and guides can be hired in Imlil, most easily in the Refuge.

## Un stylo, un bonbon, un dirham

All over the country the sight of children begging is not uncommon. But in the mountains it seems particularly prevalent, spurred on perhaps by generations of well-meaning trekkers who have happily handed out coins, pens or sweets.

The mechanical chorus of "Un stylo, un bonbon, un dirham" will follow you, echoing through many remote mountain valleys.

In the past, the advice has been to bring a supply of pens to hand out or, in some worrying cases, medicine. Talk to local community leaders now, though, and they will almost certainly advise against giving the local children anything at all.

Even giving out pens encourages systematic begging, damaging the education system and family structures. It also detrimentally affects the way foreign visitors are seen: as resources to be mined, rather than human beings to interact with.

Talk to the local children, but save your pen money and donate it instead to organizations like the Global Diversity Foundation (globaldiversity.org.uk) or the High Atlas Foundation (highatlasfoundation.org).

### Imlil to Jbel Toubkal

Imlil is the end of the surfaced road but it is possible to reach Aremd (also spelt Aroumd) by car up the rough track. It takes about 45 minutes to walk. Café Lac d'Ifni makes a good stop here. Sidi Chamharouchouch is reached in another 2½ hours, going steadily uphill. It is important to bear right after the marabout to find the initially very steep, but later steady slope up to the Toubkal Refuge (3207 m). Allow 4½ hours from Imlil. The Toubkal Refuge, with dormitory space for 30 people, 80dh per night, 150dh in summer, is often crowded. On the plus side, the warden sells bottled water, soft drinks, and can do food (50dh for a tagine). Campers using the level site below the hut can also use the facilities.

### Jbel Toubkal by the South Cwm

This is the usual approach for walkers, a long day's walking and scrambling if you want to do up and back. The route is clearer on the map than it is on the ground. First observe the route from the rear of the Toubkal Refuge and the large boulders on the skyline. These are a point to aim for. Leave the refuge and go down to the river. Cross over and up the other side is the main path to the foot of the first of the many screes. Take the scree path up to the boulders which can be reached in just over an hour. From there is a choice: the long scree slope to the north of the summit or the shorter, steeper slope to the south of the summit ridge. Either way, allow 3½ hours.

The summit is not in itself attractive but the stone shelters make fairly comfortable overnight camping for a good view of sunrise. Views are excellent – if there is no haze – to the Jbels Saghro and Siroua but as the summit here (4167 m) is a plateau, other views are limited. Be prepared for low temperatures at this altitude and for the bitter winds that blow three out of four days in the spring and autumn. The descent is quicker, allow 2-2½ hours.

## Around the region

### Setti Fatma & the Ourika Valley

The Ourika Valley is a beautiful area of steep-sided gorges and green, terraced fields along the winding Oued Ourika, about 45 minutes' drive south of Marrakech. The accessibility of the valley makes it a popular excursion for both Marrakchis and tourists, and in summer sections of the valley get crowded with campers and day trippers happy to be away from the hot, dusty air of the plain. Just before Aghbalou the road splits, with a right-hand fork taking you up to the ski resort of Oukaïmeden. The trail-head village of Setti Fatma is reached by going straight ahead. The valley has occasional problems with flash floods, the worst of which, in 1995, destroyed most of Setti Fatma and killed many people.

The road ends at Setti Fatma, famous for its seven waterfalls and 100-year-old walnut trees. There is a small weekly market, a Bureau des Guides de Montagne and a good choice of basic accommodation and riverside tagine outlets. There is breeze-block housing among the older stone homes, but the stunning setting and the sound of the river make it an idyllic setting. The place is set up primarily for Moroccan rather than European visitors, but that gives it an unusual charm and Setti Fatma would be a good starting point for a trek (see page 184). It also makes a great day trip from Marrakech.

The main part of Setti Fatma stretches beyond the end of the road. Precarious temporary rope bridges wobble visitors and locals carrying sheep across to a large number of café-restaurants along the bank. The seven cascades are a 30-minute scramble up from Setti Fatma, following the path up behind the first café, and there are plenty of young men and kids who will help you find the way. There is another café beside the first waterfall.

### Oukaïmeden

Oukaïmeden, 'the meeting place of the four winds', is Morocco's premier ski resort, and Africa's highest. It's some 2600 m up in the Atlas and a 1½-hour drive from Marrakech, making it a good day trip from the city. The highest lift goes up to about 3250 m, and there are various runs down, not always very well marked. There are also four drag lifts and a tobogganing area. The resort is open for skiing from December to March but in summer it's less busy and many places are closed.

The quality of skiing is variable and good skiable snow cannot be counted on, though there's new investment, and there's talk of snow cannons. The hot African sun means that the snow melts, only to freeze again at night, leaving slopes icy. Instructors work in the resort, and there are ski shops that rent equipment out and donkeys to carry you between lifts.

In summer visitors can walk, climb and even paraglide. Look out for the prehistoric carvings on the rocky outcrop below the dam wall. There are further carvings on the flat rocks among the new chalets.

### Tizi-n-Tichka

Completed in 1936 by the Foreign Legion, the N9 road from Marrakech to Ouarzazate gives stunning views. It runs through the full range of Atlas environments, from the Haouz plains, through the verdant foothills of the Oued Zat, to the barren peaks of the Atlas and the arid regions to the south. Drivers need maximum concentration on this route, especially in the twilight when you

Above & top: Landscapes near Tizi-n-Tichka.
Opposite page: Sunflowers in Berber village in the Ourika Valley.

118 km from Marrakech where there is an old *agadir* (granary) to visit. Driving carefully in good conditions, Marrakech to Taddert will take you two hours, while Taddert to Ouarzazate is about another two.

## Telouet

*A narrow road, in need of resurfacing and with nasty tyre-splitting edges, takes you from the Tizi-n-Tichka road to Telouet (turn left 106 km from Marrakech). For those without their own vehicle, the trip is problematic, though there may be grands taxi up from Ighrem-n-Ouagdal, or you could hire a driver in Marrakech.*

An eagle's nest of a place, high in the mountains, Telouet is something of a legend. It has one of the most spectacular kasbahs in the Atlas. Today, it is on the tourist circuit, as the hordes of 4WD vehicles testify. Within living memory, however, its name was synonymous with the repressive rule of the Glaoui brothers.

The history of Telouet and its kasbah is short but bloodthirsty. It is the story of how two brothers of the Glaoua tribe, sons of an Ethiopian slave woman, by force of arms and character, managed to achieve absolute dominance over much of southern Morocco in the early 20th century. Gavin Maxwell's *Lords of the Atlas* describes the turbulent times in Marrakech and the mountains as first the Moroccan monarchy and then the French skirmished with the southern tribal leaders to achieve dominance. The denouement, which came shortly after Moroccan independence in 1956, was fatal to Glaoui power.

Abandoned before completion, the Kasbah of Telouet as it survives today is mainly the result of 20th-century building schemes by the last great Glaoui lord, T'hami. Generally, as you arrive, someone will emerge to show you around. The great reception rooms, with their cedar ceilings and crumbling stucco, a transposition of 19th-century Moroccan urban taste to the mountains, are well worth a visit.

will meet donkeys and flocks of sheep wandering across the road, guided by small children. Clapped out local buses break down, and there are some especially narrow and vertiginous stretches leading up to the pass after Taddert. A further hazard are the eager fossil sellers who hang out at viewpoints and café stops. Note that in winter there can be heavy cloud, snow storms and icy rain, reducing visibility and making the road extremely slippery. In such conditions, the road is not much fun at night. If snow cuts the pass, the snow barriers will be down. The total distance from Marrakech to Ouarzazate is nearly 200 km. Good places to stop include upper Taddert (very busy, 86 km from Marrakech), the Tizi-n-Tichka itself which is almost exactly halfway, or Ighrem-n-Ouagdal, about

# Eastern High Atlas

A mountainous hinterland with little of the infrastructure of the Atlas around Toubkal, the Atlas to the east of Marrakech is a wild and little-visited area. Well watered like the High Atlas of Toubkal, the High Atlas south of Azilal has a very different character, due perhaps to the inaccessibility of its valleys, hidden away in the heart of the mountains. The people here are Tamazight speaking, and more limited contact with mainstream Morocco makes them more conservative. Formal education has had little impact in the high valleys and it was only in the late 1990s that roads began to replace some of the rough tracks. Much of the region's attraction comes from the architecture of the villages, largely unspoiled by concrete. There is also more vegetation here than further west, with conifer forests surviving at high altitude. As well as wide flat valleys, there are deep gorges and small rivers which can easily turn to flood after a rainstorm on the mountains. The highest mountain in the region is the long shoulder of the Irghil Mgoun, which reaches 4071 m.

The town of Azilal gives access to both the beautiful, remote high valley of the Aït Bougmez, an area increasingly popular with walkers and the Cascades d'Ouzoud, Morocco's highest waterfall. Other attractions include the natural stone bridge of Imi-n-Ifri near Demnate.

## Demnate & Imi-n-Ifri

*A 10-km detour off the R210, about 2 hrs' drive from Marrakech.*

Demnate was once a picturesque, whitewashed place. These days the crumbling kasbah, once set in the middle of olive groves, is surrounded by unsightly new building. Nearby, Imi-n-Ifri ('the door to the cave'), is a natural rock bridge formed by the partial collapse of a huge cavern. If you don't have transport, there are transit vans which do the short run up from Demnate. Opposite the closed auberge of the same name, a path winds down to the stream bed and a small reservoir where it's possible to swim and camp. Concrete steps, partly gone, take you up to the grotto. Above your head, there are great sheets of calcareous rock, and above that, cawing choughs circling overhead. You may also see the odd Barbary squirrel.

## Cascades d'Ouzoud

*Often offered as an excursion from Marrakech, the waterfalls, about 2½ hrs drive away, make a long day trip. The left turn off the R304, about 20 km before Azilal, is signposted.*

Tumbling 110 m down cliffs east of Azilal and red with clay after heavy rains, the Cascades d'Ouzoud are an impressive sight, and can be seen from above as well as below. The word *ouzoud* comes from the Amazigh *izide*, meaning delicious. After the turn-off the R304, the road heads north through beautiful landscapes where the dominant colours are red earth, dark green thuya and the paler grey green of the olive trees. Arriving in the village of Ouzoud, various local men will emerge waving sticks to help you park. For the cascades, head past the riad, and a few metres of market garden land crossed by rivulets of fast flowing water lead you to the edge of the precipice (watch out for slippery clay). Look out for the traditional water-driven barley mills. There are various paths which will take you down to cafés on the rocks below the falls. It's possible to swim at the base of the falls, but be careful diving in as the pool is shallow.

## Tip...

Altitude sickness can be a problem over 3000 m. If you get into difficulties get down to a lower altitude.

## Vallée des Aït Bougmez

*From Azilal it is a slow 2½-3-hr drive south over the mountains into the Aït Bougmez; from Marrakech allow 4½ hrs.*

The Aït Bougmez is one of the most beautiful valleys of the High Atlas, so far unspoiled by breeze-block building. Electricity arrived in early 2001, and a new sealed road will continue to bring changes. The stone and *pisé* built villages above the fields of the valley bottom are fine examples of housing, perfectly adapted to local environment and needs. One of the most isolated regions of the High Atlas, the Aït Bougmez was until recently annually cut off by snow for part of the winter. Though walking groups are beginning to make a contribution to the local economy, life is still hard.

Tabant, 1850 m up, is the main centre and the wide, flat-bottomed valley provides some excellent walking out from here. You should be able to find a local to walk you up to the dinosaur footsteps near Rbat. Tabant to Agouti is an easy 8-km walk along the valley road. Look out for the granary of Sidi Moussa up on a mound-like hill. There is another, slightly longer route from Tabant to Ifrane along the old main piste to Aït M'hamed.

For longer, more serious treks, head to the Massif du Mgoun, Morocco's second highest mountain massif. It has no soaring peaks but it is the largest area of land above 3000 m in the whole country, and snow remains late into the year in these highlands.

# Sleeping

Accommodation in the mountains varies enormously – it's usually possible to find a bed, but often not much more than that, though a few places now offer very luxurious lodging indeed.

## Western High Atlas

### Asni

#### Kasbah Tamadot €€€€

*T(+44) (0)208-600 0430 (UK), T877-577 8777 (USA) or T0524-368200, kasbahtamadot.com.*

One of Morocco's best-known hotels, Kasbah Tamadot is run by Virgin and calls itself 'Sir Richard Branson's Moroccan Retreat', though chances are you won't bump into him here. Complete with all the creature comforts you can imagine, the cheapest of the 18 rooms is more than 3000dh a night and for your investment you get indoor and outdoor pools, gardens, spa and a hammam as well as some spectacular views. The restaurant uses ingredients from the hotel's own gardens and the library comes equipped with a telescope. Despite all its good points, however, ultimately the Kasbah has a little less character than its two main rivals, Kasbah Toubkal and Kasbah Bab Ourika.

### Ouirgane

#### Chez Momo II €€€

*Coming from Marrakech, 800 m past La Roseraie, up a road on the left; T0524-485704, aubergemomo.com.*

After the original Chez Momo was engulfed in the water of Ouirgane's new reservoir in 2008, Chez Momo II was born, further up the hill, using local craftsmen and materials. Rooms are homely and elegant, with wrought iron beds, bare wooden beams and lamps in alcoves. There's a beautiful horseshoe arch swimming pool out the front of the house, with trees, roses and sun loungers around, and 'trikking', on foot or on mule, is organized.

#### Le Roseraie €€

*PO Box 769, Marrakech 40000, T0524- 439128, laroseraiehotel.com.*

A peaceful hotel set in 25 ha of exceptionally colourful rose gardens, with 42 rooms and suites, two restaurants, a bar next to the pool and two tennis courts. There's also a spa, scheduled to reopen in 2010. The rooms, however, are less spectacular than the gardens, with rather dated peach bathrooms. Horse riding is organized.

#### Auberge Au Sanglier Qui Fume €€

*T0524-485707, ausanglierquifume.com.*

A small country hotel run by a French couple, the 'boar that smokes' has 22 chalet-style rooms, a restaurant serving excellent French country food, a bar, tennis and a pool in the summer. There are mountain bikes and quad bikes for rent, and the management will put you in touch with guides should you wish to do some walking or horse riding. The titular boar, complete with pipe, watches over the bar.

#### La Bergerie €€

*About 2 km before Ouirgane village as you come from Marrakech, turn right at the signpost for Marigha, T0524-485717, labergerie-maroc.com.*

Particularly well set up for families, French-run La Bergerie is spread amongst 5 ha of grounds in a valley away from the village. The restaurant serves a good mix of French and Moroccan food, combining dishes such as kefta and egg tagine with apricots and goats' cheese. There's beer on tap and a good outdoor seating area and they'll even knock up a fondue on request. Rooms come in

La Bergerie.

different varieties, the best of which are the bungalows set in the grounds. These offer a good degree of privacy, as well as a bit more style, with nicely worn old furniture and private gardens with peach, apricot and apple trees.

### Imlil & Aremd

The Bureau des Guides, in the centre of Imlil, can provide information on accommodation in homes: locals, who are used to walkers, are generally keen to provide a floor or mattresses to sleep on.

### Kasbah du Toubkal €€€€

*T0524-485611, kasbahdutoubkal.com.*
Imlil's restored Kasbah, perched spectacularly above the village, played the role of a Tibetan fortress in director Martin Scorsese's film *Kundun*. It is run by the UK-based travel agent Discover Ltd, in conjunction with locals, and is often cited as a good example of eco-tourism. There is a range of accommodation, from three dorms for groups, to five de luxe rooms. The best rooms come with CD players, slippers and even Berber clothes to borrow. The building, once HQ of the local caïd, is worth a visit – for a 20dh contribution to the local development fund, you can have mint tea and walnuts on the roof terrace. A day trip to the Kasbah can also be arranged from

Marrakech for €85, including lunch, a mule ride and a visit to a Berber house.

### Riad Imlil €€

*T0524-485485, T0661-240599 (mob), riadimlil.com.*
Good rooms with tv, room service, Wi-Fi, fridges and air conditioning. *Tadelakt* and stone are both used, though the rooms are a little dark. There's a restaurant with a fire and a small 'salon Berbere'.

### Café du Soleil €

*T0524-485622, cafesoleil44@yahoo.fr.*
Café du Soleil has recently expanded its accommodation options and has simple but adequate singles and doubles which are offered half board. You can hear the stream from the rooms and those in the new wing are quite smart, though not all have private bathrooms.

### Auberge Imi N'Ouassif €

*Chez Mohamed Bouinbaden, T0524-485126, T0662-105126 (mob), iminouassif@wanadoo.ma.*
On the western outskirts of the town, along paths between high stone walls, this is a simple, quiet place that also provides guides.

### Auberge El Aine €

*T0524-485662, T0666-647999 (mob), iframed@hotmail.com.*
On the right as you arrive in the village from Asni, this is a bargain,

for just 40dh per person per night. Rooms are small but cute, with windows opening onto a garden with cherry blossom in spring. It's friendly and bright colours, topsy-turvy stairs and a big tree in the courtyard give the place extra character. Upstairs rooms are best, or there are small apartments with bathroom and kitchen – good for families or small groups.

### Refuge du Club Alpin Français €

*T0524-485122, T0677-307415 (mob).*
Minimal facilities but clean and with a very friendly welcome and good information from Lydia, the French manager. Forty beds in dormitories, open all year round.

### Gite Atlas Aremd €

*Aremd, T0668-882764, atlastreking@yahoo.ca.*
Mustapha Ibdlaid runs this basic gîte in Aremd with 12 rooms and good views across the valley to the mountains. There's the option to sleep on sofas in the salon. Hot showers included.

### Gite Id Mansour €

*Aremd, T0524 485613, T0662-355214 (mob).*
A good gite in Aremd, Id Mansour has hot water and towels and is very clean. Beds are comfortable and new and some rooms have mountain views. Stark but fairly comfortable.

### Ourika Valley & Setti Fatma

**Kasbah Bab Ourika €€€€**
*45 mins from Marrakech off the Setti Fatma road near Dar-Caid-Ouriki, T0524-389797 or T0661-252328 (mob), babourika.com.*
Unfussily elegant, Kasbah Bab Ourika is in an extraordinary location, perched on its own personal hill overlooking the mouth of the Ourika valley, with craggy red mountain rock to one side and Marrakech in the distance behind. Built, set up and run by the owner of Riad Edward (see page 110), the Kasbah is decorated with a similar insouciance – rooms are huge and have an antique, rustic style that makes guests feel immediately at home but are also luxurious, with thick rugs, generous bathrooms, open fires and wonderfully comfortable beds. The pool is spectacular, with views to the mountains, and the food is exquisite, with dishes such as chilled carrot soup and lemongrass beef brochette with stir-fried spinach and turmeric expertly mixing flavours. The environmental and social policies of the place are ground-breaking and guests can take a guided walk through the extraordinarily fertile valley and Berber villages below. The track that needs to be navigated to reach the front door is an eroded adventure, but one that increases the dramatic sense of arrival, and of being in a very special place indeed.

**Kasbah Bab Ourika.**

**Dar Piano €€**
*T0524-484842, T0661-342884 (mobile), darpiano.com.*
Closed Jun-Aug.
On the right of the road from Marrakech, about 10 km south of Setti Fatma, Dar Piano is a cosy, French-run place, with simple, homely rooms, good cooking and roof terrace views.

**La Perle d'Ourika €€**
*T0661-567239, laperledourika@hotmail.com.*
A couple of minutes downstream from Setti Fatma, the Perle has a degree of decoration rare in Setti Fatma, with furry sequined bed covers and painted floors. It's a little over the top, but it is at least an attempt at style. Good shared facilities, 24-hour hot water and a roof terrace with fantastic views up and down the valley. The restaurant is also recommended and has wine.

**Evasion €**
*T0666-640758.*
Near the bottom of the village, on the opposite side from the river, this is a modern place with good rooms, as long as you're not too disturbed by the strange blue blurry glass. There are balconies with views over the valley and good bathrooms. The attached café has a proper coffee machine and a glassed-in room for rainy days.

### Hotel Asgaour €
*T0524-485294,*
*T0666-416419 (mob).*
A friendly place with 20 basic, clean rooms and small but comfy beds. Some rooms have views over the valley and the hotel has a pretty terrace across the other side of the river as well as some chairs and tables outside. Rooms with private shower and toilet are more expensive.

### Azilal €
*T0668-883770.*
Next to Hotel Asgaour, is a bright and cheerful place, lacking in some creature comforts and with small rooms but with hot water and views over the river. For those really on a budget, there's a big room you can sleep in for 30dh per person.

### Oukaïmeden
Oukaïmeden has a small but adequate supply of accommodation. In practice, the resort only gets crowded on snowy weekends, and many visitors from Marrakech prefer to return home to sleep. Out of season, rooms in mountain chalets can be found.

### Hotel Kenzi Louka €€
*T0524-319080.*
Open all year round.
A large, triangular-shaped hotel, with fairly basic but comfortable rooms. Outside pool (generally heated), information and advice on skiing and trekking.

### Chez Juju €€
*T0524-319005, hotelchezjuju.com.*
Open all year (except Ramadan).
Eight clean and well looked after wood-clad rooms with a decent restaurant serving French as well as Moroccan cuisine, and a bar with cold beer. Half board is obligatory.

### Refuge of the Club Alpin Francais
*T0524-319036.*
Open all year.
Dormitory bunks as well as private double rooms. Skiing equipment and mountain bikes etc can be hired and there's a bar and games room.

**Eastern High Atlas**

### Cascades d'Ouzoud
### Riad Cascades d'Ouzoud
*Riad Cascades d'Ouzoud,*
*T0523-459658, ouzoud.com.*
The best accommodation option near the waterfalls, this riad has a combination of whitewashed and rough *pisé*-style walls, nine tastefully decorated rooms and a spacious roof terrace with panoramic views over the surrounding countryside. There are wooden beamed ceilings and some rooms have open fireplaces. The riad also does decent food, both Moroccan and French, using good local ingredients, either on the terrace or in a traditional Moroccan lounge downstairs.

### Aït Bougmez
Options are limited in Tabant but there's a clean gîte d'étape (a sort of rural youth hostel) in nearby Imeghas.

### Hostel Dar Itrane €€€
*T0524-313901, dar-itrane.com.*
The best option in the area is this fine ecolodge, a traditional red adobe building 1800m up near the village of Imeghas. There are 17 en suite rooms, a roof terrace, a hammam and a chef prepares local Berber dishes. The name means 'House of the Stars', and is so called because the remoteness of the place make it perfect for viewing the night sky. Advance reservations are essential and there's a minimum three-night stay.

### Demnate
### Kasbah Timdaf €€€
*BP 151, Demnate 22300,*
*T0523-507178, T0662-607684*
*(mob), kasbah-timdaf.com.*
90 km from Marrakech, this rural retreat is a handsome, traditional Berber construction, built using earth and stones. Surrounded by olive groves and almond trees, there are good walks in the area and breakfast comes with great views over the hills and mountains. The eight rooms are generous and colourful, and many come with their own open fire.

# Eating

# Activities & tours

Almost nowhere in the High Atlas operates just as a restaurant, though there are cafés, and most hotels also serve food.

## Western High Atlas

### Asni
In the centre of the village are a number of stalls and cafés cooking harira soup and tagines. This is the last major place to stock up on basic supplies for a visit to the Toubkal region.

### Ouirgane
The hotels in Ouirgane all have restaurants attached – **La Bergerie** is a good stopover for lunch.

### Imlil and Aremd
Most places offer half board, so the stand-alone eating options are limited, but **Café Soleil** and **Atlas Tichka** offer good lunches. **Les Amis** does good chicken brochettes and genuine coffee;

**Café Grand Atlas** is more of a local place, where you can eat tagine on the roof terrace. **Café Imlil** was the first café in town, and hasn't changed much since. For something smarter, and for the best views, go to the **Kasbah de Toubkal**.

### Tizi-n-Test
For a nearby lunch stop, the cheap **Restaurant La Belle Vue** (boumzough.free.fr) is about 1 km after the pass on the Taroudant side. Cheap rooms are also available, but have a sleeping bag ready – it gets cold 2100 m up.

### Setti Fatma
There's little to choose between the different waterside eateries – wander around and pick one that smells good, or go for a table with a view.

### Oukaïmeden
**Chez Juju** is probably the best option.

### Imlil & Aremd
You can find a guide at the **Bureau des Guides** (T0524-485626, bureau.guides@yahoo.fr, 0700-1900 summer, 0800-1700 winter, daily), in the centre of town. Especially recommended is Brahim Ait Zin (T0667-690903 (mob), trekadventurer@yahoo.fr), who knows the mountains very well and speaks good English. Reckon on about 350dh per day per person and tip generously – about 50dh a day is probably about right.
  Also recommended is local outfit **Hassan Agafay**, T0667-842236 (mob), ishwah.com.

### Setti Fatma
Setti Fatma makes a good base for exploring the Jbel Yagour, a plateau region famed for its numerous prehistoric rock carvings. About 10 km from Setti Fatma is Tachedirt, where there is a Refuge du CAF. To set up a trek, contact the **Bureau des Guides de Montagne**, on your right before the hotels. The place is run by the very capable and English-speaking Abderrahim ('Abdou') Mandili. T0524-291308, T0668-562340 (mob), abdoumandili@yahoo.fr.

Left: Tagine in Setti Fatma.
Opposite page: Boys cling to the back of a truck in Setti Fatma.

# Transport

## Western High Atlas

**Asni, Ouirgane & Settl Fatma**
Buses and taxis leave from Bab
Rob, taxis around 25dh per place.

**Oukaïmeden**
Daily buses from Marrakech in
the winter.

## Eastern High Atlas

Two or three buses daily
between Marrakech and Azilal.
If driving, take the P24 out of
Marrakech heading for Fès.
Azilal is the transport hub
for the regions of the High Atlas
to the south, with a *gare routière*
next to the main mosque. For Aït
Bouqmez, two Landrovers and
two transit vans go on to Tabant.

# Contents

199 Introduction
200 Ouarzazate & Aït Benhaddou
204 Dadès Valley & gorges
208 Draâ Valley & desert
210 Great days out: Draâ driving
212 Listings:
212 Sleeping
217 Eating
217 Shopping
218 Activities & tours
219 Transport

Dadès Gorge.

Gorges & desert

# Introduction

The great valleys south of the High Atlas have some of the finest scenery in Morocco, with some magnificent drives for those with their own transport, ranging from arid mountains to gentle oases, a volcanic massif and some splendid canyons. Most travellers to this area pass through Ouarzazate, where the Tizi-n-Tichka route over the mountains from Marrakech meets the main east-west axis running along the southern edge of the High Atlas. Ouarzazate is the centre of Morocco's film industry, the desert surroundings standing in as various parts of this or other planets. Beyond the fantasy film sets are the real life wonders of the rusty crumbling walls of Aït Benhaddou, the biggest film star of all, a stunning sand castle of a kasbah. To the east, the spectacular, green, winding valleys of Dadès and Todra become narrow gorges before they rise into the High Atlas, their red rocks glowing in the southern sun. To the south, the Draâ Valley winds its way through more spectacular vistas, with palm-filled oases, kasbahs and sand dunes before the river finally dries up in the arid plains of the Sahara. This is camel trekking country, with plenty of outfits around Zagora and M'Hamid offering nights under canvas out in the dunes.

The view north towards the Atlas from Aït Benhaddou.

## What to see in...

**... a weekend**
Long distances and slow mountain roads mean that you'll need at least two or three days for a trip beyond the Atlas. Near Ouarzazate, stop at the stunning crumbling kasbah of **Aït Benhaddou** before continuing on to the oasis town of **Skoura** or one of the gorges, where bright green fields of the valley floor shine against the rust red of the steep rocky surroundings.

**... four days or more**
Make an excursion to the edges of the desert for some camel riding and a night or two in Berber tents in the dunes of **Erg Lehoudi** or **Chigaga** near M'Hamid. If you prefer wheels to humps, there are plenty of good 4WD routes along and near the arid **Draâ Valley**. Isolated **Nekob** offers good accommodation and you could also visit various ksour and kasbahs in the area and the old *zaouia* and potters in nearby **Tamegroute**.

# Ouarzazate & Aït Benhaddou

The very name Ouarzazate (pronounced 'waa-za-zat') evokes a desert fort, and there have been attempts in recent years to brand the town as the Moroccan Hollywood. The reality of Ouarzazate is a little more prosaic. The once isolated French military outpost now has an international airport and a core of luxury hotels alongside its kasbah. Though the garrison remains, the needs of the regional administration and migrant workers have created a large and not especially attractive town. Ouarzazate is a solid, if sleepy, little town with a market on Sunday and Tuesday and a small handicrafts fair in May and the moussem of Sidi Daoud in September. It is best seen as a base for exploring valleys and oases south of the High Atlas, as a transit point for mountain and desert. The region is at its best in early spring when blossom is on the almond trees and snow still covers the summits of the Atlas. Since *Lawrence of Arabia* was filmed at Aït Benhaddou, the region, close to mountains and desert, has been a popular film director's choice. Visitors can visit the film studios outside Ouarzazate, but the bigger attraction is the stunning kasbah of Aït Benhaddou.

### Kasbah Taourirt

0800-1830, 10dh.

Though Ouarzazate has a large modern mosque, the first stone of which was laid by King Mohamed V in 1958, the historic highlight of Ouarzazate is the Kasbah Taourirt, located east of the town centre along Avenue Mohamed V. Constructed largely in the 19th century, the building had its heyday in the 1930s when it housed the Glaoui chief's extended family, servants and followers, as well as a community of tradesmen, artisans and cultivators. Today the kasbah is one of Ouarzazate's poorest areas. The part adjacent to the road, probably quarters for the Glaoui family, has been maintained and can be visited.

### Atlas Studios

*T0524-882166, atlasstudios.com.*
0900-1800, 50dh.

Giant Egyptian sarcophagi mark Ouarzazate's huge main film set, 5 km along the road to Marrakech. Films such as *Hideous Kinky*, *Gladiator*, *Kudrun*, *The Last Temptation of Christ*, *Babel* and *Alexander the Great* were all made here and you can see various bits of set and props on a half-hour guided tour, as long as there's no filming in progress. Nearby, CLA Studios (cla-studios.com) is another large film set, but not usually open to visitors.

### Aït Benhaddou

On a dramatic hillside, the Kasbah of Aït Benhaddou, 30 km from Ouarzazate, is one of the largest complexes of traditional packed-earth buildings in Morocco, hence its place on the UNESCO World Heritage List. The place's fame has spread far and wide and in season coach after coach drives up, pauses for a photograph to be taken and then leaves.

    Aït Benhaddou grew because of its strategic location on the south side of the Atlas, near the convergence of the Draâ and Dadès Valley routes. The village is a must for tourists, both because of its

# A short history

Strategically placed at the confluence of three rivers, Ouarzazate has had a military presence since the Almohad period. In the late 19th century, the kasbah came under control of the Glaoui family, who used it as a power base to develop their control of the South. In 1926, the first airfield was built, and in 1928 a regular French military garrison was installed. Ouarzazate was henceforth the main administrative town for the region. A few buildings from this period straggle along the main street. Around and above them are the large hotels, built mainly in the 1980s.

Kasbah Taourirt.

Aït Benhaddou.

unique architecture and its role in the film industry, with *Lawrence of Arabia*, *Jewel of the Nile* and *Gladiator* filmed here, as well as *Jesus of Nazareth*, for which part of the settlement was rebuilt. Despite all the visitors, the place is an awesome sight, and largely unspoilt.

Visitors are free to cross the river and wander through the kasbah, which is mostly an uninhabited shell these days. Despite money from the film industry and UNESCO to restore it, parts are much in need of repair. From the top, there are great views across the area and the old village also includes a large communal *agàdir*, or store house. Back on the western side of the river, mud-walled hotels and restaurants (see page 212) make good use of the views.

The turn-off for Aït Benhaddou is clearly signed from the N10, 22 km from Ouarzazate. The route follows the valley, with the river on the right, passing through the village of Tissergate. After a further 10 km the kasbah comes into view on the right, set up above the bright green of the irrigated fields.

### Kasbah Tamdakht

*T0678-459008.*
Open for tours daily.

The road continues beyond Aït Benhaddou to the ford at Tamdakht, a splendid site where there is a kasbah inhabited by the Glaoui until the 1950s. A family lives here and are restoring the structure – they're also happy to offer tours of the kasbah. Beyond, with a four wheel drive you could carry on the 40 km or so remaining up to Tourhat, along the Asif Ounila and then west to Telouet (see page 190). The route should not be risked when there is lots of melt water or after late summer thunderstorms. Even the best off-road vehicle can become bogged down in the wet clay.

### Mansour Edabhi Dam

To the east of Ouarzazate, the Mansour Edhabi Dam on the Oued Draâ has created a lake over 20 km long. Birdwatchers come here to see the wintering and migrating wildfowl. Winged visitors include spoonbills and flamingos, when there is sufficient water in the dam. Tracks from the N10 lead down towards the northern shore. The southern shore is more difficult to reach and access to the dam itself is prohibited. The best time to do this trip is spring or autumn.

## Kasbah of Tifoultoute

*T0524-882813, take the road from Ouarzazate west across the causeway and turn north. After about 7 km you will come to Tifoultoute.*
10dh.

The village of Tifoultoute has a splendid kasbah built for the Glaoui family in the early 20th century. It stands alongside the Oued Igissi. Still owned by the family, it has adequate food and magnificent views. Climb up to the roof terrace to see the surrounding countryside and a stork's nest on one of the turrets.

## Oasis of Fint

For those with 4WD or hardy cars, the oasis of Fint is a possible destination, a few kilometres out in the desert west of Ouarzazate, across the Tabount causeway. A beautiful spot, palm trees cluster at the bottom of a valley under bulbous outcrops of red rock.

*Lawrence of Arabia, Jewel of the Nile* **and** *Gladiator* **filmed here, as well as** *Jesus of Nazareth,* **for which part of the settlement was rebuilt. Despite all the visitors, the place is an awesome sight, and largely unspoilt.**

Kasbah Tamdakht.

# Dadès Valley & gorges

The 'Road of the Thousand Kasbahs', as it is marketed, runs between Ouarzazate and Er Rachidia, through arid plains and oases with a backdrop of harsh mountain landscapes, where semi-nomadic Berber shepherds guard their flocks. The modern world has arrived, however: tourist buses and 4WD bring crowds to the growing villages at the start of the spectacular gorges, and the new buildings replacing the crumbling kasbahs use concrete breeze blocks rather than the traditional mud and straw *pisé* walls. Nevertheless, there is plenty to see as well as walking opportunities along this route. Skoura is an oasis town with old kasbahs and El Kalaâ is the centre of Morocco's rose-growing industry. Those with 4WD can try the bumpy mountain tracks leading into the Massif du Mgoun, or the rugged gorge-to-gorge route from Tineghir to Boumalne.

Dadès Gorge.

## Skoura oasis

The large oasis fed by the Oued Idelssan has irrigated gardens with palms, olives and cereals. The Oued Hajag crosses the road on the western side of Skoura. The small settlement here has a white square mosque with a white cupola. You can now bypass the town on the main road. Nevertheless, the palm groves are worth stopping to see. Before the actual village, to the left of the road, is **Kasbah Amerhidl**, the largest of Skoura's kasbahs. The village also includes two kasbahs formerly occupied by the El Glaoui family, Dar Toundout and Dar Lahsoune.

## El Kalaâ des Mgouna & the Vallée des Roses

A ribbon-development place, El Kalaâ des Mgouna, 1¼ hours' drive from Ouarzazate, is the capital of the Moroccan rose-essence industry and centre of the Mgouna tribe. (The name, meaning 'Citadel of the Mgouna' is also spelt Qalat Mgouna.) The former French administrative centre has become a sprawling town with banks, police, small shops for provisions, petrol and a Wednesday market. The blooms in the Vallée des Roses flower in late spring and a rose festival is held in late May/early June with dances and processions under a shower of rose petals to celebrate the harvest. Children at the roadside sell bunches of roses and garlands of rose petals, and there are plenty of shops selling rose water, crème à la rose, rose-scented soap and dried roses.

Fifteen kilometres up the Mgoun Valley is the **Ksar de Bou Thrarar**, at the entrance of the Mgoun Gorges. Less adventurously, there is a dagger-making co-operative on the eastern outskirts of the town. There are trekking options in the Massif Mgoun (see also Vallée des Aït Bougmez, page 189).

## The rose industry

A picturesque local legend runs that pilgrims travelling back from Mecca brought with them 'the Mother of All Flowers', the Damascus rose, initiating the rose industry. It may be, however, that sometime in the 20th century, French perfumers realized that conditions in this out-of-the-way part of southern Morocco would be ideal for the large-scale cultivation of the bushy *rosa centifolia*. Today, there are hundreds of kilometres of rose bush hedges, co-existing with other crops, and two factories, distilling rose essence. The one in a kasbah-like building can be visited. To produce a litre of good quality rose oil requires around five tonnes of petals, you will be told. The locals feel, however, that the price paid by the factories is too low, and prefer to sell dried rose petals on local markets. Pounded up, the petals can be used mixed with henna or other preparations.

## Gorge du Dadès

The R704 leaves the N10 at Boumalne as the Oued Dadès narrows through limestone cliffs, which form the striking Dadès Gorge. The principal destination is the section of the gorge after Aït Oudinar, but the track continues up into the High Atlas, with public transport as far as Msemrir. There are basic tracks from here up into the mountains, and around into the Todra Gorge.

Just beyond Boumalne is **Aït Arbi**, where there are a series of striking *ksar* (Berber villages) above the road. The road continues past areas of unusual rock formations, through Tamnalt and Aït Oudinar, where there is basic accommodation. The valley narrows after Aït Oudinar, creating the most striking area of the gorges, where the cliffs are vivid shades of red. The road continues alongside the *oued* as far as Msemrir, just beyond which it branches. The right-hand branch turns into a difficult track, running east across the pass (2800 m) and continuing to link with the R703 through the Todra Gorge, up into the High Atlas. The gorges and crags offer a good environment for golden and Bonelli's eagles and lammergeiers, and the scree slopes for blue rock thrushes.

## Around the region

### Boumalne du Dadès

At the bottom of the gorge, Boumalne is a small town, with a reasonable selection of hotels, though most people prefer to head on up the Dadès valley and stay there. The town grew from a very basic settlement to its current size mainly in the second half of the 20th century. In the Muslim cemetery there is the domed shrine of Sidi Daoud. He is commemorated in an annual festival, when bread is baked from flour left at the grave, and fed to husbands to ensure their fertility. Wednesday is market day. Approaching from the west, there is usually a gendarmerie checkpoint at the intersection before the bridge, so watch your speed.

From a high point above the town, a barracks and some hotels look out over the harsh and rocky landscape. As the name suggests, there are birds to be seen if you head off south to the **Vallée des Oiseaux** (on the road from Boumalne to Iknioun). Otherwise, there are rewarding short walks up into the gorge. Msemrir, 60 km up the gorge, is a possible destination using local transport.

The track southeast which leaves the N10 road just east of Boumalne gives easy access into the desert. It rises steadily to Tagdilt.

### Gorge du Todra

The Todra Gorge, particularly spectacular in the evening when the rocks are coloured in bands of bright sunlight and dark shadow, is narrower and more winding than the Dadès Gorge. There are campsites and places to stay near the narrowest part of the gorge.

The 14-km route up the gorge is very narrow, and you will have to slow down for kids playing near the road. Also watch out for the tyre-splitting road edge when you move over for a bus thundering towards you. Just north of Tineghir as the road climbs up is the village of Aït Ouaritane. There are many good views and some stopping places on the road. The safest place to stop is generally picketed with camels; the most spectacular has fossil and scarf sellers. Neat strips of crops in the oasis gardens and crumbling kasbah villages spread out below.

Around 9 km from Tineghir are campsites in an idyllic location in a palm grove. About 6 km further on is the most visited section of the gorge, where the high cliffs leave just enough space for the road and river. Rocks, palm groves and river make this a good environment for birds. There is a ford (which should present no problems for ordinary cars) near the top, beyond which you can carry on up to the last two hotels, which squat in bogus kasbah style under a spectacularly overhanging bit of gorge.

### Tineghir

Once a tiny oasis settlement, Tineghir, at the bottom of the Todra Gorge, is now an unexpectedly large place. A modern administrative centre, its population is swelled by technicians and staff working for the local mining company.

The older kasbah settlements are a few kilometres north from the town, overlooking the irrigated plain as one climbs out of the town towards the Gorge du Todra. The contrast of magnificent barren mountains and verdant oases is stark.

For the rushed, there are views from the gorge road – otherwise you might explore on foot. Olive and fruit trees are inter-cropped with cereals and vegetables, herds of sheep and goats put out to pasture in the foothills. As elsewhere in the region, there is much new building along the roads, the old *ksar* partly abandoned to the side. The main population belong to the Aït Atta tribe. Try to visit the Kasbah el Glaoui on the hill above the town. Although officially closed, it is normally possible to get in.

Above: The Atlas from the road near Tineghir. Opposite page: Todra Gorge.

## Tamtatouchte & around

The village of Tamtatouchte, beyond the narrow confines of the Gorge du Todra, is a steady climb of about four hours. A couple of rudimentary establishments provide food and accommodation. A few lorries returning from the souk use this route and may provide you with a lift if necessary. With a four wheel drive, many of the smaller villages to the north can be reached, and with a good driver, connections can be made westward with the Dadès Gorge or northwards to Imilchil.

## Aït Mohamed

The village of Aït Mohamed is southeast of Tineghir and clearly visible from the main road. It stands on the minor road which goes along the river to El Hart-n'Igouramène. A track due south leads into the rugged desert mountains of the Jbel Saghra, aiming for the village of Iknioun which nestles under the central heights. It eventually connects with the desert road from Erfoud to Zagora.

## Great days out

Though rough, the 42 km from Tamtatouchte west to Msemri, rising to 2800 m, is popular. It can be done in five hours. This journey is best undertaken in a good 4WD vehicle with a reliable local driver. Ensure that tyre pressure is higher than normal, as tracks are very stony, and that you have a full petrol tank. Find out about the condition of the piste before departure. This route is best undertaken between May and September. At other times of year, potential flash floods make it dangerous. It is probably best to start at the Todra Gorge so you do the most difficult pass, the 2639 m one after Tamtatouchte, first. At Msemrir, a popular base village for treks, there are a couple of simple places to stay, including the Auberge el Ouarda and the Auberge Agdal.

# Draâ Valley & desert

The road southeast from Ouarzazate to Zagora is spectacular, first winding its way across the Jbel Anaouar mountains, and then down along the Draâ valley, a strip of intense cultivation, a band of vivid colour weaving through the desert, one of the most beautiful oasis valleys in Morocco. Here and there are red-earth coloured kasbahs and villages of flat-roofed houses, their rooftops edged with crenellations. Once, the Draâ was one of the longest rivers in North West Africa. Today, the cultivated areas give way to the desert near M'hamid, south of Zagora as the water seeps away into the parched ground. In this region, the classic sights are the village of Tamegroute, once famed as a centre of Islamic learning, and the dunes of Erg Lehoudi and Chigaga, popular for camel treks.

The Draâ Valley was not always so arid – there are ancient rock carvings of animals in the lower Draâ and the ancient writer Polybius mentions it as a river full of crocodiles. After Zagora, near M'hamid, the Draâ disappears into the sandy Debaïa plain. The river only very rarely runs its full course to the Atlantic coast near Tan Tan, some 750 km away. In years of sufficient rainfall, there is good grazing for the nomads in the Debaïa, and even some cultivation.

## Zagora

Zagora is the main town at the southern end of the Draâ valley, the best place to sleep overnight before heading off into the desert. The town goes back to the 13th century, when it was founded by an Arab tribe. In the 1990s, the town woke up to tourism. The arrival of four wheel drive vehicles and the improvement of the N9 road have allowed an influx of visitors. In the space of a decade, the desert settlement has been transformed out of all recognition. To avoid potential hassle, try to use official guides and make travel arrangements into the desert through your hotel or recommended gencies.

Although there are few architectural traces of the town's life before tourism, the paths through the date palm groves to the various *ksour* can help you imagine a time when the world was slower. Of these walks, one of the more pleasant, despite the potential pestering, is around the **Amazrou date palm oasis** across the river. There is also some accommodation here and a kasbah once famed for

its silverwork. Above Zagora and within walking distance are two hills, from where there is an excellent view over the valley and towards the desert. Nearby are the ruins of an 11th-century Almoravid fortress.

During the *moulid* (the celebration of the birth of the prophet), a major religious festival is held in Zagora – the Moussem of Moulay Abdelkader Jilala. The town's market days are Wednesday and Sunday. The souk is an important place for the exchange of produce and livestock for the surrounding region.

## Nekob

On the R108 to the north of Zagora, Nekob is an out-of-the-way place with some grand kasbahs, a couple of good hotels, and good views towards the Jbel Saghra mountains to the north. A Bureau des Guides serves walkers and there are some prehistoric rock carvings nearby. Turn east off the N9 at Tansikht to reach the town.

Taking the flock home near Zagora.

# Draâ driving

Leaving Zagora, there are two main options if you want to avoid going northwards back over your tracks. The first route, the rough track running northeast from Zagora to Tazzarine, a settlement on the main metalled west to east route to Rissani in the Tafilalet, is for 4WD only and needs careful planning.

In a hire car, the R108 is a better route east which, although it means retracing steps 60 km up the Ouarzazate road as far as Tansikht, takes you across some wonderful arid scenery on metalled road all the way east to Rissani. There is a good stopover at **Nekob** (42 km from the junction), where the restored citadel has been given new life as the Kasbah Baha Baha (see page 216), with a tiny ethnographic museum and lots of information on the region, including prehistoric rock art. After Nekob, **Mellal** is the next settlement before **Tazzarine** (75 km from the junction), a small place with petrol (no unleaded) and basic shops, where the direct north-south track from Zagora joins the road. Tazzarine is a good base for searching out the *gravures rupestres* (prehistoric rock carvings) at Tiouririne or Aït Ouazik.

### Tracks from the N12 to the Dadès road
With a solid 4WD, there are a couple of routes from the N12 across wild country to the N10 Rachidia to Ouarzazate road. Heading east out of Nekob, you will find a sign showing right for Tazzarine and left for **Iknioun**, a settlement lying some 65 km to the north in

the Jbel Saghro. It is best to travel this route with a local as the tracks are confusing. Some of the better ones lead up to mines. After crossing the **Tizi-n-Tazazert-n-Mansour** (2200 m), you will have the option of going north on a rather better track to **Boumalne** (about 42 km), or right to Iknioun and then **Tineghir**, via the **Tizi-n-Tikkit**, a rougher but more beautiful route.

The easiest route up from the N12 to the N10 heads north from **Alnif**, however. Although it is best tackled in a 4WD, it can just about be done in a hire care with high clearance. After the **Tizi-n-Boujou**, the track takes you onto the N10 some 20 km east of Tineghir, 35 km west of Tinejdad.

### West from Zagora to Foum Zguid
This route was off-limits for years due to the risk of Polisario rebel incursions from neighbouring Algeria. It is another difficult journey best attempted in a 4WD with accompanying vehicles. Much of the road (the 6953) is a very poor surface and 124 km in these conditions are not to be undertaken lightly. The thrill of the open spaces, the wide horizons and the faint prospect of sandstorms makes this a memorable journey. The road runs east-west following the line of the **Jbel Bani** to the south. From **Foum Zguid**, further rough tracks take you southwest and west towards **Tata** in the Anti-Atlas.

Always check you have a good spare tyre before setting out on rudimentary pistes into rough country.

## Tamegroute

Tamegroute, 20 km southeast from Zagora, lies on the left bank of the Oued Draâ and is visited mainly because of the *zaouia*, founded in the 17th century and headquarters of the influential Naciri Islamic brotherhood. The outer sanctuary and library are open to public view (closed 1200-1500), the latter containing a number of impressively old *korans* and 12th-century, antelope-hide manuscripts. The village is interesting to explore, a close-knit area of old housing with potters at work producing characteristic green and brown pottery, and a souk, main day Saturday.

Around 8 km south of Tamegroute, the **Tinfou dunes** are a small and popular but nevertheless memorable area of Saharan sand.

## M'Hamid

M'Hamid is popular as a base for camel trips in to the dunes. The most common destinations are the sands of the **Erg Lehoudi**, some 8 km north of M'hamid, and the dunes of **Chigaga**, 55 km out towards the Algerian frontier, a 90-minute drive by 4WD, or a four- or five-day camel trek. There are plenty of outfits (and hustlers) here who will set you up with a trip of any length, from a short camel ride and a single night in a camp under the stars to a week-long camel trek west to Foum-Zguid. Shop around and make sure you know what you're getting.

M'Hamid itself has basic facilities, cafés and accommodation and a Monday souk. If visiting on a Monday, there may be some 'blue men of the desert', but in the main they dress more for tourists than tradition. These days the great camel caravans led across the desert wastes by indigo-swathed warriors are a mirage from the past.

Drâa Valley kasbah.

# Sleeping

### Hotel Berbère Palace €€€€
*T0524-883105, ouarzazate.com/ leberberepalace.*
The clientele includes tourists, business people, film producers and even the odd star at this smooth but impersonal hotel with 235 good rooms off garden patios. There's a pool, a bar, tennis, Moroccan, Italian and international restaurants, a piano bar, and even a hammam.

### Dar Daïf €€€
*Talmasla, next to the Kasbah des Cigognes on the Tabount side of town, T0524-854232, dardaif.ma.*
About 5 km out of town, a traditional restored kasbah with 12 rooms and a pool, well looked after by its French Moroccan owners. Some rooms have private terrace.

### Hotel Riad Salam €€€
*Av Mohamed V, T0524-882206.*
Two converted kasbahs luxuriously equipped, with 14 suites, 63 rooms, TVs in room, restaurant, bar, spectacular pool, sauna, massage, horse-riding and tennis, shops and conference facilities. It is, however, a bit overpriced.

### Hotel Oscar Salam €€€
*T0524-882212, atlastudios.com.*
On the northern outskirts of town, right in the Atlas Corporation Studios, this is a film set hotel, used by film crews and with various slightly surreal bits of film paraphernalia around the place. The 64 rooms have air conditioning and there's a great pool with Egyptian gods to watch over you. However, it's a bit tatty, and service can be poor.

### Hotel La Vallée €€
*Zagora road, T0524-854034, hotellavalleemaroc.com.*
Surrounded by the Tabounte palm grove, this is a good option in large grounds, with 40 cosy rooms. It's used by tour groups for lunch, but is generally quiet in evening and has a restaurant and horseshoe-arch pool.

### Villa Kerdabo €€
*22 Blvd Sidi Bennaceur, near the airport, T0524-887727, villakerdabo.com.*
Five simple rooms around a courtyard pool in a kasbah-style structure.

### Hotel la Gazelle €
*Av Mohamed V, T0524-882151.*
Fifty-one good-value rooms, a bar-restaurant, and a small pool, a little out of town on the Marrakech road.

At peak times of year, try to reserve accommodation in advance. Aït Benhaddou has a number of decent hotels, most offering half board. None are in the actual kasbah itself, but many offer good views of it across the river, and staying here gives you the opportunity to see it late evening and early morning when the tour buses have gone.

### Dar Mouna €€
*T05240-843054, darmouna.com.*
With a pool in an internal garden and views of the kasbah (for which you pay extra), this is a classy place with big beds and a restrained riad style, though the warmth of the welcome may not match the quality of the accommodation.

### Kasbah Ellouze €€
*Tamdaght, T0524-890459, kasbahellouze.com.*
Four kilometres north of Aït Benhaddou, out of sight of the kasbah, Ellouze is a new construction but is built in traditional fashion and overlooks almond orchards. Cosy and warmly lit, with plentiful arches and tiles, it is quiet, and well away from the tourist buses.

### Riad Maktoub €€
*T0524-888694, riadmaktoub.com.*
Though on the 'wrong' side of the road, and therefore a distance from the kasbah, Maktoub is a well-designed place, with *pisé* walls around a garden courtyard.

### Filante €
*T0524-890322.*
Big family rooms and a friendly welcome make the Filante good value. Rooms have solid pine

Countryside around Ouarzazate.

furniture, small bathrooms and traditional bamboo ceilings. There's a Berber tent on the terrace for sheltering you and your mint tea.

### Auberge Sousou €
*T0524-887773.*
It has a musty, semi-abandoned feel and the route to the roof terrace is downright precarious, but the friendly women staff, huge dining room and baths compensate, as does the low price.

Skoura

### Dar Ahlam €€€€
*Palmeraie de Skoura, Ouarzazate, T0524-852239, maisondesreves.com.*
A kasbah-style boutique hotel, Dar Ahlam has a pool and hammocks in beautiful gardens and views to the mountains. Rooms are pristinely done, with smooth pink walls, luxurious fabrics and oversized pottery.

### Kasbah Ait Ben Moro €€€
*3 km west of Skoura, T0524-852116.*
South of the Atlas, there are many hotels built in the kasbah style, but this one is a bona fide 18th-century building, recently restored. It's a beautiful, authentic structure, with plenty of traditional grandeur, though the nature of the place means that the windows in the 24 bedrooms are small and the place has a nicely crooked feel, with decor on the austere side of elegant. On the edge of a palmery, there are good views from the terrace to the Kasbah d'Amerdihil and the food is good too. The manager was born in the kasbah. Horse riding organized.

### Jardins de Skoura €€€
*lesjardinsdeskoura.com.*
With hammocks by the pool, breakfast in the gardens and open fires for cold winter

evenings, this is a popular stopping-off point deep in the palmery from where you might not want to move on. Beautiful *pisé rooms* and *tadelakt* bathrooms.

### Dar Lorkam €€
*T0524-852240, darlorkam.com.*
Over the river in the palmery, an attractive place with six colourful rooms with en suite bathrooms and a pool. Half board.

### Chez Slimani €
*T0524-852272.*
A simple gîte-type place in an old kasbah rather hidden in the palmery about 200 m from the Kasbah d'Amerdihil.

El Kalaâ des Mgouna

### Kasbah Itran €€
*T0524-837103, kasbahitran.com.*
A tiny auberge run by a Spanish Moroccan partnership, perched up on a cliff on the road up into the Massif du Mgoun. Six attractive, homely rooms, three with en suite bathrooms. Great views of Kasbah Mirna to the south and Kasbah du Glaoui to the north. Mountain guide Mohamed Taghada can organize treks.

### Hotel Les Roses de Mgouna €€
*T0524-836336.*
With 102 rooms above the town at 1927 m, this is a relic of the 1970s, with accommodation built

# Listings

around courtyards planted with bamboo and fruit trees. There's a reasonable restaurant, a bar, and a nice pool with views of the Mgoun Massif. It's a sleepy sort of place, apart from the bar, which is much used by locals. Prices are negotiable out of season.

### Gorge du Dadès

Make sure you have enough blankets, as it gets cold here at night. Most places offer half board. The better places are mostly further up the valley, though there are plenty of choices.

### Kasbah de la Vallée €€
*T0524-831717,*
*kasbah-vallee-dades.com.*
Of the 40 rooms, 15 have generous balconies overlooking the silver poplars and fruit trees in the valley and there's air conditioning and heating. When it's warm enough, breakfast can be taken on the terrace. The restaurant has an open fire and live music but big groups mean the atmosphere is less than intimate. Trips are organized up into the mountains or down to the Vallée des Roses. It's also possible to camp cheaply opposite the hotel.

### Timzillite €€
*T0677-264347.*
Up above the much-photographed hairpins at the top of the canyon, Timzillite has views that are hard to better, as

long as you don't suffer from vertigo. Rooms are small but cosy and there's solar power for electricity and water. Building is continuing, and 63 rooms are planned, by which point its size may detract from its appeal. The roadside café is a popular stopping place.

### Atlas Berbere €€
All rooms here have heating and a view, and some have two: over the stream and down the valley. The food is good and there are veggie options, such as ratatouille. The friendly owner will proudly tell you that he is the creator of the fake *pisé* wall effect ubiquitous in the Dadés valley. There's music every evening and a wood fire. It's worth trying to bargain on the price, or you can sleep on the roof terrace for 25dh.

Atlas Berbere.

### Auberge Tissadrine €€
*T0524-831745.*
The hotel faces a side canyon that you can walk up across the other side of the stream. All 14 rooms have en suite bathrooms – the best rooms have a little balcony over the stream; some look onto the road.

### La Gazelle du Dadès €
*T0524-831753.*
The fake *pisé* and the 1980s-style bathrooms don't detract from the friendly welcome here. There's a good big terrace with tables and an accompanying soundtrack of birdsong and the stream to go with your mint tea. Comfortable new mattresses or the option of camping opposite, beside the stream.

**Les 5 Lunes €**
*Ait Oudinar, T0524-830723.*
Belgian-Moroccan run, this traditionally built little place has a different vibe to most of the accommodation in the valley. Flamenco music plays, there are old Berber wooden locks on the doors and the freshly made pancakes for breakfast are excellent. There are only five rooms, a salon with a fire, and a roof terrace with good views over the greenest part of the valley. Thoroughly laid-back.

### Boumalne du Dadès

**Auberge de Soleil Bleu €**
*Up a slightly rough track past Hotel Xaluca, T0524-830163.*
Twelve rooms with bath, a good restaurant and fine views. Camping is permitted and treks are organized into the High Atlas and Jbel Saghro. Popular with walkers and birdwatchers.

**Kasbah Tizzarouine €**
*T0524-830690,*
*T0661-34812 (mob).*
A large hotel complex on the plateau overlooking Boumalne from the south (at the top of the slope, turn right just before a large mural). There are fine views over the Oued Dadès and the mountains to the north. Accommodation includes fairly traditional buildings with modern comforts, tiny underground rooms, cool in summer and cosy in winter, and nomad tents kept cool by the breeze.

### Gorge du Todra

In winter it gets pretty chilly at night, and in late summer the river can swell suddenly after thunderstorms in the mountains, so choose your camping place with care.

**Hotel Amazir €€**
*T0524-895109, lamazir.com.*
A stone building with 15 rooms and a pool, Amazir is in a sunny spot on a bend in the valley and has good, simple rooms with rugs and en suite bathrooms.

**Hotel Yasmina €**
*T0524-895118.*
Near the top of the valley, Yasmina has 50 rooms, all renovated with heaters and air conditioning. There are the obligatory fake *pisé* walls, lots of blankets, very blue bathrooms and candles. It's not the most beautiful hotel but it's comfortable, though it gets almost no sunshine and can be cold. Camping is possible by arrangement, and sleeping on the roof is also a possibility. Hot water is only provided when the generator is working to produce light, so have your shower in the evening and carry a torch. Some tour groups.

### Tineghir

**Hotel Tomboctou €€**
*Av Bir Anzane (take 1st major left coming into Tineghir from west), T0524-834604, hoteltomboctou.com.*
Cool rooms in a restored kasbah with a small pool. There is secure car parking available and the hotel has mountain bikes for rent, plus sketched maps of region. The best option in town.

### Zagora

**Kasbah Asmaa €€**
*T0524-847599,*
*asmaa-zagora.com.*
Two kilometres from the centre of Zagora, Asmaa is just over the bridge to Amazrou on the eastern side of the Oued Draâ. It's an attractive kasbah-style place with restaurant, pool and garden. Best to reserve in high season.

**Villa Zagora €€**
*mavillaausahara.com.*
Seven elegant rooms and a Berber tent in a palmery hotel. Eat locally grown food, freshly cooked, in the garden, on the terrace or in the dining room. Rooms have contemporary touches and there is art, an open fire and good views.

**Kasbah Sirocco €€**
*Amazrou, T0524-846125, kasbahsirocco.com.*
Good views and good rooms in the usual fake kasbah style.

# Listings

There's a nice pool, a licensed restaurant, and desert trips are organized. Go left over the bridge as you come from Zagora; the hotel is 150 m on the left.

### Hotel La Palmeraie €€
*Av Mohamed V, near road junction to south of town and bus station, T0524-847008.*
A friendly and popular place with 56 rooms, a few with air conditioning, a restaurant and a small pool. Compulsory half-board in April and December.

### Auberge Chez Ali €
*Avenue Atlas-Zaouite, T0524-846258, chez-ali.com.*
Simple but colourful and comfortable rooms at a range of prices – pay more for showers, or less to sleep in a Berber tent. Large verdant gardens and good food. A good place to book camel treks. Popular, so book ahead.

Nekob

### Kasbah Baha Baha €€
*Nekob, T0524-839078, kasbahabaha.com.*
East from Zagora in Nekob, Baha Baha is truly remote. A genuine restored kasbah, it has cool, quiet rooms and a pool in a green garden. From the roof terrace there are good views over the village and surrounding countryside. You can also stay in cheaper Berber

tents. A small museum and a library have information about local culture and there are displays of traditional artefacts. Not all rooms have private bathrooms.

### Ksar Jenna €€
*Nekob, ksarjenna.com, T0524-839790, T0671-731976 (mob).*
Just west of Nekob, Ksar Jenna is a relaxed and elegant retreat far from the madding crowd. The building, surrounded by large gardens, uses *zellij* and *tadelakt* to good effect.

Tamegroute

### Jnane Dar €€
*T0524-840622, T0661-348149 (mob).*
A kasbah-style place with comfortable rooms set in vegetable and flower gardens. Nine rooms, five of which are en suite. Camel trips arranged from Ouled-Driss into the Chigaga dunes.

### Kasbah Sahara Sky €€
*T0524-848562, hotel-sahara.com.*
A well-appointed observatory on the roof, as well as some very dark skies, attract astronomers to this comfortable and friendly hotel next to the dunes.

M'Hamid

Many people come to M'Hamid to camp out on the dunes rather than to stay in M'Hamid itself.

Most places will organize a night under the stars as part of a longer stay.

### Dar Azawad €€€
*T0524-848730, darazawad.com.*
As well as attractive, air-conditioned, kasbah-style, *pisé*-walled rooms, Dar Azawad offers 'tents', which actually have beds inside them, as well as walls and a front door.

### Kasbah Azalay €€€
*T0524-848096, azalay.com.*
A kasbah-style hotel, Azalay has 34 good-sized, air-conditioned, en suite rooms and a bar and restaurant. They will pick you up from Ouarzazate or Marrakech airport and offer their own excursions into the desert.

### Hotel Tabarkat €€
*Douar Ksar Bounou BP 35, T0524-848688, tabarkat.com.*
Another newly built, kasbah-style hotel, Tabarkat is run by a Spanish couple and has a beautiful pool and 22 air-conditioned rooms, in the main kasbah as well as in the garden. The restaurant serves buffet food and the hotel organizes quad and camel trips and hot-air balloon flights.

# Eating

Many hotels in the area offer half board as standard, and outside Ouarzazate there are few standalone restaurants.

Ouarzazate

### Chez Dmitri €€
*22 Av Mohamed V,*
*T0524-887346.*
Once the focus of Ouarzazate, as the bar of the Foreign Legion, the restaurant serves excellent Italian and Greek food, with a good lasagne, as well as some Moroccan choices.

### La Kasbah €€
*T0524-882033.*
Opposite the Kasbah Taourirt, a scenic spot with a fixed-price menu where you can eat outside on the terrace.

### La Datte d'Or €€
*Av Moulay Rachid, T0524-887117.*
Alpine-Berber chalet decor, a fixed price menu and attentive and efficient service.

### Le Relais de Saint-Exupéry, aka Le Petit Prince €€
*13 Av de Moulay-Abdallah,*
*Quardier El Qods, T0524-887779.*
For varied French and Moroccan cuisine in a setting dominated by old photos of flight and flying. In the Skoura direction, leaving Ouarzazate on your left just before the Total station.

### Restaurant Chez Hellal €
*6 Rue du Marché.*
A good choice just to the left of the entrance to the market; the terrace is also good for people watching.

# Shopping

Ouarzazate

Sun cream, batteries, writing paper and stamps can be obtained on Av Mohamed V. Almost opposite Chez Dimitri there is a supermarket which sells alcohol (the last place before Tineghir as you head east). On the same side of the street as the supermarket, look out for Abdallah Medkouri's shop selling various local souvenirs, in particular pieces of *hizam*, a sort of carpet belt once worn by women in the region.

Tineghir

There is a Tuesday souk behind the Hotel Todra and small shops on the main square (Place Principale). **Chez Michelle**, T0524-834668, sells alcohol. There's also a supermarket on your right after Zlz petrol as you come in from west. Look out for the green façade.

Tajines cooking in M'Hamid.

# Activities & tours

## Ouarzazate

### Biking
**Rent-a-Bike**
*Av Moulay Rachid near the big hotels, T0524-887117.*
Can provide guides and helmets as well as bikes.

### Karting
**Kart aventure**
*Av Moulay Rachid, between hotels Berbère Palace and Kenzi Belère, T0524-886374.*
Full day's excursion in off-road go-kart.

### Swimming
At major hotels and in particular the **Complexe de Ouarzazate**, next to the campsite. The **Hotel Bélère** pool can be used by non-residents for 50dh.

## El Kalaâ des Mgouna & the Vallée des Roses

### Trekking
El Kelaâ is a good base town for trekking, call in at the Bureau Des Guides de Montagne, 1 km before the town centre on south side of the road, clearly signed (T0524-836311). As elsewhere, the daily rate for a guide is around 200dh per person. The Hotel du Grand Atlas has plenty of contacts with guides. Ambitious walkers in late spring and summer may want to try to climb Irhil Mgoun, at 4068 m one of the highest peaks in the central High Atlas.

## Zagora

### Bikes
Bikes can be hired in Av Hassan II and at the Hotel La Fibule.

### Swimming
Hotel Tinsouline lets non-residents use the pool for a small fee.

## M'Hamid

### Desert trips
Most agencies in the area, and indeed in Marrakech, will organize desert trips.

Southern Moroccan dunes.

# Transport

**Sahara Services**
*T0661-776766,*
*saharaservices.info.*
An agency with a good reputation – their 'sunset tour' is €38 per person, including food and a night's accommodation, or you can do a whole day's trek, getting you deeper into the desert, for €55.

Around six buses daily from Marrakech, six hours; one or two onward to Zagora, four hours; Three daily to Tineghir, four hours.

Travelling by public transport, you come into the *gare routière* on the Marrakech side of Ouarzazate. After a hot bus journey, you may want to take a petit taxi to go into town, a couple of kilometres away. **CTM** buses come into Av Mohamed V.

### Tineghir & Boumalne du Dadès

There are buses and grands taxi to many locations from Tineghir, including Ouarzazate (five hours), and Boumalne du Dadès (one hour). They leave from Place Principale. Grands taxi and vans run from Tineghir to the Gorge. If driving, pass through villages in the region with care, especially in the evenings, watching out for small children, bicycles, mopeds and donkeys.

### Zagora & Draâ Valley

Regular buses and grands taxi connect Ouarzazate, Agdz and Zagora. A car allows you to make photo stops at will, and visit the smaller, less spoilt oases and villages. The most difficult section of this route is between Ouarzazate and Agdz, with a winding climb up to the Tizi-n-Tinifitt.

Once in Zagora, you can visit the oasis on foot. Tamegroute is 20 km from Zagora, and you might be able to get a grands taxi or a lift if you don't have your own transport. There are buses from Zagora to Tamegroute. There is a slow local bus between M'hamid and Zagora, which means that M'hamid, only 88 km further south, is not a day-trip option without your own car. The dunes of Chigaga require 4WD.

There is a comfortable daily CTM bus from M'Hamid to Casablanca via Zagora (two hours), Ouarzazate (seven hours) and Marrakech (12 hours). There are also slower private bus alternatives along the same route. There are grands taxi between Zagora and Ouarzazate.

## Contents

222 Getting there
223 Getting around
226 Directory
228 Language
232 Food & cooking glossary

**Practicalities**

Marrakech street.

# Getting there

## Air

Major European airlines run frequent scheduled flights to Marrakech, with most flights operating from France and Spain. National carrier **Royal Air Maroc** (RAM) (royalairmaroc.com) is reliable. The cheapest flights are usually with budget airlines **EasyJet** (easyjet.com), **Ryanair** (ryanair.com) and **Atlas Blue** (atlas-blue.com), a subsidiary of Royal Air Maroc. There are direct flights from Paris to Essaouira; work on the airport and a new golf course mean that more airlines may fly there soon.

### From the UK and Ireland
**EasyJet** fly daily from London Gatwick to Marrakech. **Ryanair** fly daily from London Luton and Bristol and **Atlas Blue** fly from London Gatwick. Budget airlines aside, options from the UK to Morocco include **Royal Air Maroc**, who fly from Heathrow. Indirect flights to Ouarzazate and Essaouira are also possible.

### From the rest of Europe
RAM fly to Marrakech out of main western European airports. Ouarzazate has flights from Paris-Orly (**Atlas Blue** and **RAM**), Berlin-Tegel (**Hamburg International**) and regional flights from Casablanca. Essaouira has **RAM** flights from Paris-Orly and Casablanca.

### From North America
RAM flies between Casablanca, Montreal and New York. Flight time New York to Casablanca is six hours and 40 minutes. There are short onward flights to Marrakech.

## Airport information

Marrakech's airport, **Aéroport Marrakech Menara** (T0524-447910, onda.oeg.ma), is just 6 km from the city centre. The BMCE and the Banque Populaire have bureaux de change, closed outside office hours, and there are ATMs. There's a reliable 20dh bus every hour from the airport to Jemaa El Fna and the train and bus stations. Otherwise, the quickest way into Marrakech is by petit taxi, from the front of the terminal building. A petit taxi should not set you back more than 60dh (90dh at night), for the run from airport into the centre, though overcharging is common. Euros may be acceptable to taxi drivers. There are also grands taxi on hand if you want to go further afield – agree a price first and be prepared to haggle mercilessly. Most riads will send someone to meet guests at the airport. **Avis**, **Budget**, **Europcar** and **Hertz** all have offices at the airport.

    **Ouarzazate** airport (T0524-882297, onda.org.ma) is 2 km north of the town; taxis meet incoming flights. Bear in mind that flights may be seasonal.

    **Essaouira** airport (Aéroport Mogador, T0524-476704, onda.org.ma) is about 20 km southeast of the town. A bus every two hours shuttles into town and there are also taxis.

## Rail

Morocco's rail network (oncf.ma) is good, and improving, though Marrakech is at the end of the line, so the train is only useful if you're arriving from more northerly cities, such as Casablanca, Fes or Tangier, all of which have direct services. It's possible to travel all the way from London to Marrakech by train and ferry: allow around 48 hours and €200 one way. A good site for advice on routes and tickets is seat61.com/Morocco.htm.

# Getting around

When planning a trip out from Marrakech, remember that the distances are large. Bus journeys are often excruciatingly slow, even over relatively short distances, especially over the High Atlas. Internal flights are an option to the south, though they require careful planning. Public transport is reasonably priced; car hire, on the other hand, can be expensive: although you may be able to get a small car for 1800-2500dh a week, you still have petrol or diesel costs on top of this. In many places, however, a car enables you to reach places which are otherwise inaccessible.

## Air

**Royal Air Maroc** (royailairmaroc.com) runs domestic flights, most routed via Casablanca and requiring waits in the airport. RAM may also operate flights seasonally between Marrakech and Ouarzazate.

## Road

### Car

There are a number of dangerous stretches of road which you may have to deal with. Serious concentration is needed on the four- or five-hour drive on the winding, mountainous N9 from Marrakech to Ouarzazate via the Tizi-n Tichka pass, and fog and icy surfaces are possible in winter. Sudden dips and turns can surprise drivers on routes such as Ouarzazate to Skoura and Agdz to Nekob. In the High Atlas barriers are put across the road on routes over the Tizi-n-Tichka and Tizi-n-Test passes when snow blocks roads.

Road accidents cost the Moroccan state about US$1.2 billion a year, according to official figures. In one week in July 2008, 23 people were killed and 1309 injured, including 87 seriously, in 1001 traffic accidents in the country.

Speeds are limited to 120 kph on the autoroute, 100 kph on main roads, 60 kph on approaches to urban areas and 40 kph in urban areas. Speed restriction signs do not always follow a logical sequence. There are two types of police to be met on the roads: the blue-uniformed urban police and the grey-uniformed gendarmes in rural areas. The latter are generally stationed outside large villages, at busy junctions, or under shady eucalyptus trees near bends with no-overtaking marks.

The wearing of seat belts is compulsory outside the cities, and the gendarmes will be watching to see you're wearing them. It is traditional to slow down for the gendarmes, although as a foreigner driving a hire car you will generally be waved through. They will not, on the whole, ask for 'coffee money' from you. Note, however, that the police are empowered to levy on-the-spot fines.

Red and white curb markings mean no parking. Warning triangles are useful but not compulsory. In the case of an accident, report to nearest gendarmerie or police post to obtain a written report, otherwise the insurance will be invalid.

In addition to well over 10,000 km of surfaced road, Morocco has several thousand kilometres of unsurfaced tracks, generally referred to as pistes. Some of these can be negotiated with care by an ordinary car with high clearance. Most cannot, however, and 4WD vehicles are increasingly popular for exploring the remote corners of Morocco.

In towns, parking is fairly easy. Parking meters rarely function and instead a watchman, identified by blue overalls and a metal badge, will pop up. Give him some spare change, say 10-20dh, when you return to your undamaged vehicle. At night, it is essential to leave your vehicle in a place where there is a night watchman (*le gardien de nuit*). All good hotels and streets with restaurants will have such a figure who will keep an eye out.

## Car hire

All the main hire car companies are represented and there are numerous small companies, varying hugely in reliability. The smallest car available is generally a Fiat. Also available are 4WDs, for around double the price. Toyotas are said to be the best desert 4WD. Always try to have the mobile phone number of an agency representative in case of emergency. Many cars do not as yet use unleaded petrol – if you have one that does, you will find that not all petrol stations have unleaded, especially in the south.

Remember that you are responsible for damage if you take a car unsuited to the piste into areas suitable only for 4WD. Usually, the car will be almost empty when you collect it, and you fill up yourself.

A reasonable rate is 500dh a day. You may well be able to do better, getting something like a small Fiat with unlimited kilometres, but avoid the lesser known firms if possible and make sure there's cover, or at the very least a plan B, if you break down in the middle of nowhere. A driver will cost you around 250dh a day extra.

**Avis**, 137 Av Mohamed V, T0524-433727. **Europcar Inter-Rent**, 63 Blvd Mohamed Zerktouni, T0524-431228, and at the airport. **Euro Rent**, 9 Av al Mansour Ad-Dahbi, T0524-433184. **Hertz**, 154 Av Mohamed V, T0524-434680, airport T0524-447230.

## Bikes & motorbikes

Off-road biking is popular in the Atlas and most agencies will be able to organize trips; road biking through Moroccan traffic has less to recommend it. For motorcyclists, helmets are compulsory and gendarmes will be happy to remind you of the fact. Outside Marrakech, in Essaouira, for example, hiring a bike for the day is a good way of getting to the further beaches. Watch out for stray pedestrians and note that vehicle drivers will not show you much respect.

## Bus

Domestic bus services are plentiful. Price variations are small while the quality of service varies enormously. Broadly speaking, if the train, a Supratours bus or grand taxi run to your destination, don't bother with the small bus companies. For early morning services it's worth getting your ticket in advance. You will generally find that there is a man who helps stow luggage on the roof or in the hold, so have a couple of dirham coins handy for him.

The safest, most reliable and most comfortable service is **Supratours** (run by the train company, oncf.ma), closely followed by **CTM** (Compagnie de transport marocain, ctm.co.ma). In Marrakech both Supratours and CTM have their own departure points in Guèliz, away from the main *gare routière*.

Within Marrakech, buses can be caught from Rue Moulay Ismaïl, just off the Jemaa El Fna, and elsewhere along Av Mohamed V and Av Hassan II. Numbers 1 and 7 are the most useful, running from Jemaa El Fna along Av Mohamed V. Numbers 3 and 8 run from the railway station to the bus station, via Jemaa El Fna, number 10 from Jemaa El Fna to the bus station, number 11 from

Jemaa El Fna to the Majorelle Gardens and number 4 to the Menara gardens. Pay the 3dh ticket price to the driver when you board – you'll need the right change.

### Calèche

Green-painted horse-drawn carriages can be hailed along Av Mohamed V, or from the stands at Jemaa El Fna and Place de la Liberté. There are fixed prices for tours around the ramparts; other routes are up for negotiation, but they are not normally prohibitively expensive, and this is a pleasant way to see the city.

### Taxi

Long distance grands taxi, generally Mercedes 200 saloon cars, run over fixed routes between cities, or within urban areas between centre and outlying suburbs. There is a fixed price for each route and passengers pay for a place, six in a Mercedes. Taxis wait until they are full. You may, however, feel rich enough to pay for two places in order to be comfortable at the front (and be able to wear a seatbelt).

Between towns, grands taxi are quicker than trains or buses, and normally only a little more expensive. Each town has a grand taxi rank, generally, although not always, next to the

main bus station. The drivers cry out the name of their destination, and as you near the taxi station you may be approached by touts eager to help you find a taxi.

In mountain areas the same system applies, although the vehicles are Mercedes transit vans (where there is tarmac) or Landrovers, which have two people next to the driver and 10 in the back.

Petits taxis are used within towns, and are generally Fiat Unos and Palios. Officially they are metered, with an initial minimum fare followed by increments of time and distance. There is a 50% surcharge after 2000. A petit taxi may take up to three passengers. Drivers often pick up other passengers en route if they are going the same way, thus earning a double fee for part of the route. Taxi drivers welcome a tip – many of them are not driving their own vehicles, and make little more than 100dh a day. A short run between old and new town in Marrakech will set you back about 10dh.

Practicalities
# Directory

### Customs & immigration

Visitors may take in, free of duty, 400 g of tobacco, 200 cigarettes or 50 cigars and up to one litre of spirits. Foreign currency may be imported freely up to €4500. Visas are not required for EU, US, Canadian, Australian, Irish or New Zealand citizens but your passport should be valid for at least six months from the date of arrival.

### Disabled travellers

Marrakech makes few concessions for anyone with mobility issues. Only the large ville nouvelle hotels have anything like European standards of accessibility and much of the medina is effectively off limits.

### Emergencies

**Police** T19; **Fire service** T15. Larger towns will have an SOS Médecins (private doctor on-call service).

### Etiquette

Clothes should cover knees, and, in more conservative areas, shoulders too. Generally, Morocco does not have especially strict dress, however, and most women go unveiled. On the beach, normal European beachwear is fine.

### Families

Moroccans generally love children and there should be no problems travelling as a family. Some riads are happier to have kids than others – check in advance. If you hire a car via an international agency, specify the sort of child seats you require. Most local car hire agencies will be unlikely to have children's seats.

### Health

Tap water in major cities is safe to drink, but some may still react to drinking different water. No vaccinations are required. Food preparation hygiene can be a problem: if you're buying street food, go for things that are freshly cooked rather than reheated. Almost all towns have a pharmacy on duty at night, the *pharmacie de garde*. Any riad or hotel should be able to give you the telephone/address of these.

## Insurance

Take out travel insurance before you go and make sure that it covers Morocco. Consider special coverage if you're thinking of skiing or other mountain adventure sports.

## Money

The local currency is the dirham, usually abbreviated to dh or MAD. There are 100 centimes in a dirham, but prices are usually rounded up. The most useful coins come in 1, 2, 5 and 10 dirham denominations. Banknotes come in 20, 50, 100 and 200 denominations. Larger notes are difficult to get change for. The easiest way of getting dirhams are cash machines, which feature in most towns, though take a decent supply of cash if you're heading far off the beaten track.

## Post

Most shops will arrange to send purchases home for you. Stamps are better bought in a tabac than queuing in a post office. Packages should be taken unwrapped if you're sending them from a post office.

## Safety

Unwanted attention may be rife, but Marrakech is actually a very safe city, where it's highly unlikely that any serious crime will happen to you. Watch your valuables on Jemaa El Fna, however, where pickpockets operate. Road safety (see page 223) is another matter entirely.

## Telephone

The Morocco country code is 212. Local numbers have recently changed from nine to 10 digits, and many places have been slow to catch up – if you see a number beginning 024 you will need to change it to 0524. An old nine-digit mobile needs a 6 added after the initial 0. Foreign mobile phones generally work well in Marrakech, which also has a decent 3G signal. Call prices are high however – for making calls within the country it's worth buying a local sim card.

## Time difference

As of 2009 Morocco now operates on Central European Time.

## Tipping

Tip 10% or so in cafés and restaurants and give guides or porters 10-20dh. Tipping taxi drivers isn't necessary. Kids (and many grown ups) will try to get tips from you for telling you where to go – this can occasionally be useful, but it is behaviour that many Moroccans think shouldn't be encouraged. If you're not sure where to go, it may be better to ask in a shop than to accept the pestering of someone on the street.

## Tourist information

Tourist information offices around the region are reliably useless. Hotel and riad owners usually fill this gap and are very well informed and happy to provide advice. In the mountains, look for the local *bureau des guides* to help you out.

## Voltage

Morocco uses 220V and European two-pin plugs.

# Language

## Moroccan Arabic

In and around Marrakech, most locals speak Moroccan Arabic, a dialect of the Arabic spoken elsewhere in North Africa and the Middle East. In the mountains and the south, the Berber Tachelhit language is more common as a first language, though most people will also speak Arabic. French is used widely and is seen as the educated language. It is very useful for getting by, though it's also common to meet people whose French is very rudimentary and a few phrases of Arabic are much appreciated. English is spoken in just about all hotels, riads, cafés and restaurants.

For the English speaker, some of the sounds of Moroccan Arabic are totally alien. There is a strong glottal stop (as in the word 'bottle' when pronounced in Cockney English), generally represented by an apostrophe, and a rasping sound written here as 'kh', rather like the 'ch' of the Scots 'loch' or the Greek 'drachma'. And there is a glottal 'k' sound, which luckily often gets pronounced as the English hard 'g', and a very strongly aspirated 'h' in addition to the weak 'h'. The symbol 'i' is used to represent the English 'ee' sound. The French 'r' sound is generally transcribed as 'gh'.

### Polite requests & saying thank you
excuse me, please  *afek* (for calling attention politely)
please  *min fadhlek*
one minute, please  *billati*
to call the waiter  *esh-sherif or ya ma'alem*
thank you  *teberkallah alik/Allah yekhallik*
thank you  *shukran*

### Saying hello (and goodbye)
Good morning  *sabaH el-khir*
How's things?  *ki yedirki dayir?*
Everything's fine  *el Hamdou lillah* (lit Praise be to God)
Everything's fine  *kull shay la bas*
Congratulations  *mabrouk*
Goodbye  *bisslema*
Goodbye  *Allah ya'wnek*

### Handy adjectives and adverbs
Like French, Moroccan Arabic has adjectives (and nouns) with feminine and masculine forms. To get the masculine form, simply knock off the final 'a'.
good  *mezyena*
happy  *farhana*
beautiful  *jmila, zwina*
new  *jdida*
old  *qdima*
cheap  *rkhissa*
clean  *naqia*
full  *'amra*
in a hurry  *zarbana*
quickly  *dghiya dghiya*
it doesn't matter  *belesh*

### Quantities
a lot  *bezaf*
a little  *shwiya*
half  *nesf*

### Days of the week
Monday  *nhar el itnayn*
Tuesday  *nhar ettlata*
Wednesday  *nhar el arba*
Thursday  *nhar el khemis*
Friday  *nhar el jema'*
Saturday  *nhar essebt*
Sunday  *nhar el had*

### A few expressions of time
today  *el yawm*
yesterday  *el-bareh*
tomorrow  *ghedda*
day after tomorrow  *ba'da ghedda*
day  *nhar*
morning  *sbah*
midday  *letnash*
evening  *ashiya*
tonight/night  *el-lila/lil*
hour  *sa'a*
half an hour  *nes sa'a*

## Numbers

| | |
|---|---|
| one *wahed* | two *zouj* or *tnine* |
| three *tlata* | four *arba'* |
| five *khamsa* | six *setta* |
| seven *saba'* | eight *tmaniya* |
| nine *ts'oud* | ten *ashra* |
| eleven *hedash* | twelve *t'nash* |
| thirteen *t'latash* | fourteen *rb'atash* |
| fifteen *kh'msatash* | sixteen *settash* |
| seventeen *sb'atash* | eighteen *t'mentash* |
| nineteen *ts'atash* | twenty *'ashrine* |

twenty-one *wahed ou 'ashrine*
twenty-two *tnine ou 'ashrine*
twenty-three *tlata ou 'ashrine*
twenty-four *'arba ou 'ashrine*
thirty *tlatine*
forty *'arba'ine*
fifty *khamsine*
sixty *sittine*
seventy *saba'ine*
eighty *temenine*
ninety *t'issine*
one hundred *miya*
two hundred *miyatayn*
three hundred *tlata miya*
thousand *alf*
two thousand *alfayn*
three thousand *tlat alaf*
one hundred thousand *miyat alf*

## Miscellaneous expressions

Watch out! *balak! balak!*
No problem *ma ka'in mushkil*
How much? *bayshhal? aysh-hal ettaman?*
Free (of charge) *fabor*
Look *shouf* (pl *shoufou*)
OK, that's fine *wakha*
Good luck! *fursa sa'ida*

## At the café

tea *ettay*
weak milky coffee *un crème*
half espresso, half milk *nes nes*
a small bottle *gara' sghíra*
a large bottle *gara' kbíra*
a bottle of still mineral water
  *gara' Sidi Ali/Sidi Harazem*
a bottle of fizzy mineral water
  *gara' Oulmes/Bonacqua*
ashtray *dfeya, cendrier*
do you have change?
  *'indak sarf/vous avez de la monnaie?*

## At the restaurant

bill *l'hseb*
fork *foursheta, lamtíqa*
knife *mous, mis*

spoon *mu'allaka*
glass *ka's* (pl *kísan*)
bowl *zellafa*
plate *tobsil*
could you bring us some more bread
  *afak tzídna khubz*

## Food & drink
bananas *mouz*
beef *lham bagri*
butter *zebda*
bread *khobz*
chicken *djaj*
chips *ptata maklya, frites*
egg *bid* (sing *bída*)
fruit *fekiha*
mandarins *tchína*
mutton *lham ghenmí*
milk *hlíb*
olive oil *zít zítoun*
oranges *límoun*
rice *rouz*
tomatoes *ma'tísha*
vegetables *khudra*
water *ma*

## At the hotel
room *el-bít/la chambre*
bed *tliq, farsh*
mattress *talmíta*
shower *douche*
without shower
  *bila douche, sans douche*
key *es sarrout/la clef*
blanket *ghta'/couverture*
sheet *zar/le drap*
corridor *couloir*
noise *sda'*

## At the hotel – a few requests & complaints
Can I see the room, please?
  *Afak, mumkin nshouf el bít*
The water's off *El ma maktou'a*

There's no hot water *El-ma skhoun ma ka'insh*
Excuse me, are there any towels? *Afak ka'in foutet*
Could you bring us some towels?
  *Mumkin tjíbilna foutet*
The washbasin's blocked *El lavabo makhnouk*
The window doesn't close
  *Esh sherajim ma yetsidoush*
Can you change the light bulb?
  *Mumkin tebedil el bawla*
The toilet flush doesn't work
  *La chasse ma tekhdemsh*
There's a lot of noise *Ka'in sda' bezef*
Can I change rooms? *Mumkin nebedil el bít*

## On the road
Where is the bus station?
  *Fayn kayin maHata diyal kíran?*
Where is the CTM bus station?
  *Fayn kayin mHata diyal Saytayem?*
road *tríq*
street *zanqa*
neighbourhood, also street *derb*
bridge *qantra*
straight ahead *níshan*
to the right/left *ila l-yemin/sh-shimal*
turn at the corner *dour fil-qent*
wheel *rwída*

## Public transport
aeroplane *tayyara*
bus *tobís, Hafila*
inter-city bus *kar* (pl *kíran*)
customs *díwana*
express service *sarí', mosta'jal, rapide*
luggage *Hwayaj, bagaj*
porter *Hamal*
ticket *bitaqa*, also *warqa* (lit 'paper')
train *qitar*
How much is the ticket? *Aysh Hal taman diyal warqa?*
I didn't understand *Ma fehimtiksh*
Speak slowly please *Tekellem bishweyya min fedlek*
Could you write that down please?
  *Afak, uktebhu liya*

## French

Do you speak English? *Parlez-vous anglais?*
What is your name? *Comment vous appellez-vous?*
How do you say…? *Comment est-ce qu'on dit…?*
What is this called? *Comment ça s'appelle?*

### Some basic vocabulary and phrases
toilet/bathroom *les toilettes/la salle de bain*
where are the toilets? *où sont les toilettes?*
police/policeman *la police*
hotel *hôtel, auberge*
youth hostel *auberge de jeunesse*
restaurant/fast food *le restaurant/le snack*
post office *les PTT, la poste*
stamps *des timbres poste*
corner grocery *l'épicerie*
market *le marché*
bank *la banque*
ATM machine *GAB guichet automatique*
bureau de change *le bureau de change*
notes *les billets de banque*
coins *les pièces de monnaie*
do you have change?
 *est-ce que vous avez de la monnaie?*
cash *du cash/du liquide*

### Meals
breakfast *petit déjeuner*
lunch *le déjeuner*
dinner *le dîner*
meal *le repas*
without meat *sans viande*
drinkla *boisson*
mineral water *l'eau minérale*
fizzy drink *une boisson gazeuse*
wine *le vin*
beer *la bière*
dessert *le dessert*
without sugar *sans sucre*

### Some useful adjectives
French and Spanish adjectives have masculine and
feminine forms, which correspond to noun genders.
far *loin*
hot *chaud/chaude*
cold *froid/froide*
that's great *c'est super!*
beautiful *beau/belle*

### Travelling around
on the left/right *à gauche/à droite*
straight on *tout droit*
first/second street *la première/deuxième rue*
to walk *marcher*
bus station *la gare routière*
town bus/inter city coach *le bus/le car*
city bus stop *l'arrêt (des buses)*
ticket office *le guichet*
train station (Moroccan railways) *la gare (de l'ONCF)*
train *le train*
airport *l'aéroport*
airplane *l'avion*
first/second class *première/deuxième classe*
ticket (return) *le billet (aller-retour)*
ferry/boat *le ferry/le navire*
a hire car *une voiture de location*

### Accommodation
room *une chambre*
I'd like to see the room *J'aimerais voir la chambre*
with two beds *avec deux petits lits*
with private bathroom *avec salle de bain*
hot/cold water *de l'eau chaude/froide*
there's no hot water *il n'y a pas d'eau*
noisy (there's a lot of noise)
 *bruyant (il y a beaucoup de bruit)*
to make up/clean the room
 *arranger/nettoyer la chambre*
sheets/pillows *des draps/des oreillers*
blankets *des couvertures*
clean/dirty towels *des serviettes propres/sales*
loo paper *le papier hygiénique*

# Food & cooking glossary

## Health

chemist/all night chemist
  *la pharmacie/pharmacie de garde*
doctor *le médecin*
Do you have the number of a doctor?
  *Avez-vous le numéro de téléphone d'un médecin?*
emergency medical services *la SAMU*
stomach *l'estomac*
fever/sweat *la fièvre/la sueur*
diarrohea *la diarrhée*
blood *le sang*
headache *un mal de tête*
condoms *les préservatifs*
contraceptive pill *la pillule*
period/towels *la règle/serviette hygiénique*
contact lenses *les lentilles de contact*

## Numbers

| | |
|---|---|
| one *un* | six *six* |
| two *deux* | seven *sept* |
| three *trois* | eight *huit* |
| four *quatre* | nine *neuf* |
| five *cinq* | ten *dix* |

## Days of the week

| | |
|---|---|
| Monday *lundi* | Tuesday *mardi* |
| Wednesday *mercredi* | Thursday *jeudi* |
| Friday *vendredi* | Saturday *samedi* |
| Sunday *dimanche* | |

## Expressions of time

today *aujourd'hui*
yesterday *hier*
tomorrow *demain*
day *le jour*
morning *le matin*
midday *midi*
evening *le soir*
night/tonight *la nuit/ce soir*
hour *une heure*
in half an hour *dans une demie heure*
later *plus tard*

*Amlou* Runny 'butter' from argan kernels.
*Argan* Tree producing an almond-like nut. The kernel of the nut produces the highly valued argan oil.

*Beghir* Thick pancakes often served for breakfast.
*Bissara* Bean and pea soup, a traditional working man's breakfast.
*Briouet* Filo pastry envelopes, filled with crushed nuts and basted in olive oil, then dipped in honey.
*Brochettes* Kebabs made with tiny pieces of liver, meat and fat.

*Chermoula* Marinade sauce.
*Couscous* Steamed semolina made from durum wheat, heaped with meat and vegetables. Couscous may also be served with nuts, dates, raisins, sugar and milk for dessert. In the countryside, couscous is made from barley.

**F**

*Fliou* Peppermint, also used in tea preparations.

**H**

*Harcha* Thick round unleavened bread, popular for breakfast.
*Harira* Chickpea and mutton soup, especially popular when breaking the fast in Ramadhan.

**K**

*Kaâb el-ghizal* Gazelles' horns. Traditional marzipan-filled pastry.
*Kahoua* Coffee.
*Kefta* Minced meat.
*Khliaâ* Preserved meat (dried, boiled).

**L**

*Likama* Mint.
*Luiza* Verbena herbal tea.

**M**

*Mahchi* (or *mo'ammar*) Stuffed (chicken, vegetables, etc).
*Mechoui* Barbecued meat.
*Mqali* Meat dishes simmered with sauce reduced rapidly on high flame at end.
*Mouhallabiya* Milk pudding.

**N**

*Na'na* Mint, essential for preparing tea, also called 'likama'.

**O**

*Orz bil-bahiya* Paella.

**P**

*Pastila* Elaborate sweet and sour pie made of alternating layers of filo-pastry and egg, pigeon, and crushed almonds.

**Q**

*Qa'ida* Tradition – vital to any meal prepared for guests in a Moroccan home.

**R**

*Ra's el Hanout* (lit. 'master of the shop') Special spice mix.
*Roumi* (lit. 'from Rome') Adjective designating things foreign or modern, especially with regard to food and recipes. Used in opposition to things 'bildi' (qv), indigenous and traditional.

**S**

*Seksou* (Amz) Couscous.

**T**

*Tajine* Moroccan stew traditionally cooked slowly in a clay pot over a fire.
*Tajine barkouk* Sweet and sour prune and mutton stew.

**Z**

*Zitoun* Olives.
*Zit el oud* Olive oil.

# Index

### A

About the region 24-65
accommodation 48
activities 60
Agdal Gardens 100
air travel 222
Aït Arbi 205
Aït Benhaddou 201
Aït Bougmez 189
    sleeping 193
Aït Mohamed 207
Aït Ouaritane 206
Aït Oudinar 205
Alaouites 29
Almohads 28
Almoravids 28
Alnif 210
Amazrou date palm oasis 209
Arabic 228
architecture 34
art 38
Asni 181
    eating 194
    sleeping 190
    transport 195
Atlas Studios 201

### B

Bahia Palace 93
ballooning 60
Beldi 104
bikes 224
birdwatching 60
books 23
Boumalne 210
Boumalne du Dadès 206
bus 224

### C

calèche 225
camel trekking 60
car 224
carpets 58
Cascades d'Ouzoud 189
Chigaga 211
children 226
cinema 57
CLA Studios 201
colonialism 30
Consul's cemetery 153
cooking 61
customs & immigration 226

### D

Dar Bellarj 87
Dar Cherifa 87
Dar El Makhzen Royal Palace 96
Dar Si Said 93
Demnate 189
disabled travellers 226
Draâ Valley 208
drink 54

### E

Earth Café Farm 104
eating 168
El Badi Palace 95
El Kalaâ des Mgouna &
    the Vallée des Roses 205
El Mansour 96
emergencies 226
Erg Lehoudi 211
Essaouira
    activities & tours 173
    eating 168
    map 146

shopping 172
sleeping 160
transport 174
**Essaouira & coast 142-175**
etiquette 226

**F**

fauna 42
film 22
Fint oasis 203
flora 42
fondouks 83
food 52
Foum Zguid 210
French 228

**G**

Galerie Damgaard, Essaouira 151
galleries, Marrakech 100
gay & lesbian 57
Glaoui family 31, 201
golf 61
Gorge du Dadès 205
Gorge du Todra 206
**Gorges & desert 196-219**
Guéliz 99

**H**

haggling 59
hammans 138
health 226
**High Atlas 176-195**
hiking 63
history 26
horse riding 62
hotels 48

**I**

Iknioun 207, 210
Iles Purpuraires 153
Imi-n-Ifri 189
Imlil 183
    activities & tours 194
    eating 194
    sleeping 191
**Introducing the region 6-23**

**J**

Jardin Majorelle 99
Jardins de l'Agdal 100
Jardins de la Mamounia 97
Jbel Bani 210
Jbel Toubkal 184
Jemaa El Fna 74
jewellery 59
Jewish cemetery 95

**K**

Kasbah, Marrakech 96
Kasbah el Glaoui 206
Kasbah Mosque 96
Kasbah of Tifoultoute 203
kasbahs 37
Kasbah Tamdakht 202
Kasbah Taourirt 201
Koutoubia Mosque 79
Ksar de Bou Thrarar 205

**L**

Lalla Fatna 159
Lalla Takerkoust 103
La Mamounia Gardens 97
language 228

La Pause 103
La Plage 153

**M**

Maison Tiskiwin 93
Majorelle garden 99
Mansour Edabhi Dam 202
**Marrakech 66-141**
    accomodation 106
    activities & tours 137
    ATMs 70
    bars 132
    clubs 132
    cultural &
      language centres 133
    eating 122
    entertainment 132
    excursions 102
    hospital 70
    maps 72, 146
    pharmacy 70
    post office 70
    shopping 133
    sights 74
    sleeping 106
    tourist information office 70
    transport 141
Medersa Ben Youssef 84
medina, northern sights 74
medinas 36
medina, southern sights 92
Mellah 94
Mellah, Essaouira 151
Mellal 210
Ménara Gardens 101
Merinids 28
M'Hamid 211
Miaâra Jewish cemetery 95
money 227
Mosquée de la Koutoubia 79

# Index

mosque
  architecture 35
motorbikes 224
mountain biking 62
Moussem of Moulay
  Abdelkader Jilala 209
Msemrir, 207
Musée d'Art Islamique 100
Musée de Marrakech 85
Musée Sidi Mohamed Ibn
  Abdallah, Essaouira 150
Museum of Moroccan
  Arts and Crafts 93
music 57

Nectarome 104
Nekob 209, 210

 (O placement)

Oasiria 104
Oualidia 158
Ouirgane 181
  eating 194
  sleeping 190
  transport 195
Oukaïmeden 186
  eating 194
  sleeping 193
  transport 195
Ourika Valley 186
  sleeping 192

Palais de la Bahia 17, 93
Palais El Badi 95
Palais Royal Dar El Makhzen 96

petits taxis 225
Place des Ferblantiers 95
Place Moulay Hassan,
  Essaouira 149
Plage de Safi 153
Plage Rouge 104
post 227
**Practicalities 220-233**

Qoubba Ba'Adyin 86

rafting 62
rail travel 222
ramparts 88
retreats 50
riads 48
  Marrakech 106
  rental agencies 106
road travel 223

Saadians 29
Saadian Tombs 97
safety 227
Setti Fatma 186
  activities & tours 194
  eating 194
  sleeping 192
  transport 195
shopping 58
Sidi Bel Abbes 87
Sidi Daoud 206
Sidi Kaouki 156
Skala de la Ville, Essaouira 149
Skala du Port, Essaouira 149

skiing 62
Skoura oasis 205
Souk Jedid, Essaouira 151
souks, Marrakech 82
spas 50
surfing 63
Synagogue Lazama 94

Taguenza 157
Tamegroute 211
Tamnalt 205
Tamtatouchte 207
tanneries 88
Tata 210
taxi 225
Tazzarine 210
telephone 227
Telouet 187
time difference 227
Tineghir 206, 210
Tinfou dunes 211
Tin Mal 181
tipping 227
Tizi-n-Boujou 210
Tizi-n-Tazazert-n-Mansour 210
Tizi-n-Test 183
Tizi-n-Tichka 186
Tizi-n-Tikkit 210
Tombeaux Saadiens 14, 97
Toubkal Parc National 183
tourist information 227
tours 60
transport
  getting around 223
  getting there 222
trekking 63, 64

**V**

Vallée des Aït Bougmez 189
Vallée des Oiseaux 206
vegetation 42
ville nouvelle 98
voltage 227

**W**

walking 63
  Toukbal 184
weather 18
wildlife 42

**Y**

yoga 50

**Z**

Zagora 209

# Tread your

## Footprint Lifestyle guides

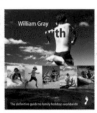

Books to inspire and plan some of the world's most compelling travel experiences. Written by experts and presented to appeal to popular travel themes and pursuits.

**❝❞**

*A great book to have on your shelves when planning your next European escapade*
**Sunday Telegraph**

## Footprint Activity guides

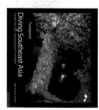

These acclaimed guides have broken new ground, bringing together adventure sports and activities with relevant travel content, stunningly presented to help enthusiasts get the most from their pastimes.

**❝❞**

*This guide is as vital as a mask and fins.*
**David Espinosa, Editor of Scuba Diver Australasia**

# own path

## **Footprint** Travel guides

For travellers seeking out off-the-beaten-track adventures. Rich with places and sights and packed with expertly researched travel information, activities and cultural insight.

**66 99**

*Footprint can be depended on for accurate travel information and for imparting a deep sense of respect for the lands and people they cover*
**World News**

**Available from all good bookshops or online**  footprintbooks.com

# Credits

## Footprint credits

**Project Editor**: Jo Williams
**Picture Editors**: Angus Dawson and Julius Honnor
**Layout and production**: Angus Dawson
**Maps**: Kevin Feeney
**Proofreader**: Tamsin Stirk

**Managing Director**: Andy Riddle
**Commercial Director**: Patrick Dawson
**Publisher**: Alan Murphy
**Publishing managers**:
Felicity Laughton and Jo Williams
**Design and images**:
Rob Lunn and Kassia Gawronski
**Digital Editor**: Alice Jell
**Design**: Mytton Williams
**Marketing**: Liz Harper, Hannah Bonnell
**Sales**: Jeremy Parr
**Advertising**: Renu Sibal
**Finance and administration**: Elizabeth Taylor

## Print

Manufactured in Italy by EuroGrafica
Pulp from sustainable forests

## Footprint Feedback

We try as hard as we can to make each Footprint guide as up to date as possible but, of course, things always change. If you want to let us know about your experiences – good, bad or ugly – then don't delay, go to footprintbooks.com and send in your comments.

Every effort has been made to ensure that the facts in this guidebook are accurate. However, travellers should still obtain advice from consulates, airlines etc about travel and visa requirements before travelling. The authors and publishers cannot accept responsibility for any loss, injury or inconvenience however caused.

## Publishing information

FootprintAfrica
Marrakech, High Atlas & Essaouira
1st edition
© Footprint Handbooks Ltd
December 2009

ISBN 978-1-906098-87-2
CIP DATA: A catalogue record for this book is available from the British Library

® Footprint Handbooks and the Footprint mark are a registered trademark of Footprint Handbooks Ltd

### Published by Footprint
6 Riverside Court
Lower Bristol Road
Bath BA2 3DZ, UK
T +44 (0)1225 469141
F +44 (0)1225 469461
www.footprintbooks.com

### Distributed in North America by
Globe Pequot Press

The colour maps are not intended to have any political significance.